POST-OTTOMAN TOPOLOGIES

Studies in Social Analysis
General Editor: Martin Holbraad
University College London

Focusing on analysis as a meeting ground of the empirical and the conceptual, this series provides a platform for exploring anthropological approaches to social analysis while seeking to open new avenues of communication between anthropology and the humanities, as well as other social sciences.

Volume 8
Post-Ottoman Topologies: The Presence of the Past in the Era of the Nation-State
Edited by Nicolas Argenti

Volume 7
Hierarchy and Value: Comparative Perspectives on Moral Order
Edited by Jason Hickel and Naomi Haynes
Afterword by David Graeber

Volume 6
Animism beyond the Soul: Ontology, Reflexivity, and the Making of Anthropological Knowledge
Edited by Katherine Swancutt and Mireille Mazard

Volume 5
Affective States: Entanglements, Suspensions, Suspicions
Edited by Mateusz Laszczkowski and Madeleine Reeves

Volume 4
Stategraphy: Toward a Relational Anthropology of the State
Edited by Tatjana Thelen, Larissa Vetters, and Keebet von Benda-Beckmann

Volume 3
Straying from the Straight Path: How Senses of Failure Invigorate Lived Religion
Edited by David Kloos and Daan Beekers

Volume 2
Emptiness and Fullness: Ethnographies of Lack and Desire in Contemporary China
Edited by Susanne Bregnbæk and Mikkel Bunkenborg

Volume 1
Being Godless: Ethnographies of Atheism and Non-Religion
Edited by Ruy Llera Blanes and Galina Oustinova-Stjepanovic

POST-OTTOMAN TOPOLOGIES
The Presence of the Past in the Era of the Nation-State

Edited by

Nicolas Argenti

berghahn
NEW YORK • OXFORD
www.berghahnbooks.com

First published in 2019 by

Berghahn Books

www.berghahnbooks.com

© 2019 Berghahn Books

Originally published as a special issue of *Social Analysis*, volume 61, issue 1.

All rights reserved.
Except for the quotation of short passages for the purposes of criticism and review, no part of this book may be reproduced in any form or by any means, electronic or mechanical, including photocopying, recording, or any information storage and retrieval system now known or to be invented, without written permission of the publisher.

Library of Congress Cataloging-in-Publication Data

Names: Argenti, Nicolas, editor.
Title: Post-Ottoman topologies : the presence of the past in the era of the nation-state / edited by Nicolas Argenti.
Description: New York : Berghahn Books, 2019. | Series: Studies in social analysis ; Volume 8 | Includes bibliographical references and index.
Identifiers: LCCN 2019011296 (print) | LCCN 2019011513 (ebook) | ISBN 9781789202410 (ebook) | ISBN 9781789202397 (hardback : alk. paper) | ISBN 9781789202403 (pbk. : alk. paper)
Subjects: LCSH: Nationalism—Balkan Peninsula. | National characteristics, Balkan. | Collective memory—Balkan Peninsula. | Balkan Peninsula History—20th century.
Classification: LCC DR38.2 (ebook) | LCC DR38.2 .P67 2019 (print) | DDC 320.5409496—dc23
LC record available at https://lccn.loc.gov/2019011296

British Library Cataloguing in Publication Data

A catalogue record for this book is available from the British Library.

Dedicated to the memory of Peter Loizos (1937–2012)

Contents

List of Illustrations	ix

Introduction
The Presence of the Past in the Era of the Nation-State   1
    Nicolas Argenti

Chapter 1
Fossilized Futures: Topologies and Topographies of Crisis Experience in Central Greece   28
    Daniel M. Knight

Chapter 2
Prayer as a History: Of Witnesses, Martyrs, and Plural Pasts in Post-war Bosnia-Herzegovina   43
    David Henig

Chapter 3
Surviving Hrant Dink: Carnal Mourning under the Specter of Senselessness   57
    Alice von Bieberstein

Chapter 4
The Material Life of War at the Greek Border   71
    Laurie Kain Hart

Chapter 5
(Re)sounding Histories: On the Temporalities of the Media Event   88
    Penelope Papailias

Chapter 6
Between Dreams and Traces: Memory, Temporality, and the Production of Sainthood in Lesbos   104
    Séverine Rey

Chapter 7
"Eyes Shut, Muted Voices": Narrating and Temporalizing the
Post–Civil War Era through a Monument 117
Dimitra Gefou-Madianou

Chapter 8
Uncanny History: Temporal Topology in the Post-Ottoman World 131
Charles Stewart

Index 145

Illustrations

Figure 2.1	Šehitluci—a burial site for unknown Ottoman soldiers in the Central Bosnian highlands	46
Figure 3.1	Flash mob restaging Hrant Dink's murder in January 2009	58
Figure 3.2	Hrant Dink's grave	66
Figure 4.1	Abandoned settlement, 1994	72
Figure 4.2	Stolac, ruined house and defaced monument, 2003	78
Figure 4.3	Building under reconstruction, Prespa, 2010	81
Figure 4.4	Stolac, river, 2002	83
Figure 5.1	"Criminal for the Greeks, Hero for the Albanians": Article in the Greek newspaper *Eleftherotypia*, 2004	91
Figure 5.2	Cassette cover, "Song for Flamur Pisli" by Ded Gjini (*sic*)	97
Figure 5.3	Ded Gjinaj jotting down lyrics in Baz, Albania, 2002	97
Figure 5.4	A poem for Pisli from his father's personal archive	98
Figure 5.5	Another poem for Pisli from his father's archive	99
Figure 8.1	Laurence Sterne, *The Life and Opinions of Tristram Shandy, Gentleman*	133

INTRODUCTION
The Presence of the Past in the Era of the Nation-State

Nicolas Argenti

> The melancholy of this dying culture was all around us. Great as the desire to Westernise and modernise may have been, the more desperate wish, it seemed, was to be rid of all the bitter memories of the fallen empire: rather as a spurned lover throws away his lost beloved's clothes, possessions and photographs. But as nothing, Western or local, came to fill the void, the great drive to Westernise amounted mostly to the erasure of the past. (Pamuk 2005: 27)

The Ottoman world was plural—religiously, culturally, linguistically, and legally, with members of the *millets* or castes within the empire subject to different regimes of taxation, dress code, legal rights, and obligations—but it was by the same token a unified social and political space in which Christians and Jews as well as Muslims could thrive as traders and professionals and could ascend to the highest levels of political authority and influence. The demise of the Ottoman Empire in the nationalist wars of the early twentieth century gave

Notes for this section begin on page 19.

rise to a multiplicity of autonomous nation-states defined by their ethnicity in a forced movement of peoples the likes of which the world had never seen before. This volume examines how individual and collective memories, affective states, and embodied experience are born from episodes of rapid social transformation, crisis, and political violence in the transition from an ethnically and culturally plural empire to a congeries of nation-states defined by nationalist ideologies predicated on the realization of ethnic and religious homogeneity.

Space without Places, Time without Duration: Temporalities of Culture/Cultures of Temporality

Maria Couroucli (2012: 1–2) has recently referred to the newly nationalized, "monocultural and monochromatic societies" of the Eastern Mediterranean as a "post-Ottoman space" in which religious pluralism gave way in the twentieth century to nationalist cultural homogeneity in the image of Western nation-states.[1] The term 'post-Ottoman' as we use it here is intended to question the nationalist assumptions that are often used to explain the fracturing of the Ottoman Empire and the dissemination of the modernist ideal of the ethnically pure and sovereign nation-state. To adopt a post-Ottoman perspective is to ask what the loss of Ottoman identity as a supra-ethnic affiliation has entailed and how the violent ruptures occasioned by the collapse of the empire live on in contemporary social formations. In doing so, the contributions to this collection question the applicability of dominant models of linear time, revealing that peoples of the post-Ottoman world do not always experience their relationship to the historical transformations they have witnessed in a straightforwardly chronological fashion, as the Time of the State would have it, with the beginning of political time marked (and commemorated annually) by the birth of the sovereign nation in the violent destruction of an inevitably derided original state of ethno-religious and cultural pluralism. This is not to suggest that post-Ottomanism is a form of collective social atavism, nor does it entail an idealization of the Ottoman Empire in terms of a Rousseauesque prelapsarian Eden of uninterrupted equality and peace. Nationalist historiographies have nonetheless focused on the breakers and white caps of historical crises while ignoring the underlying tides of intercommunality that bound plural communities and *millets* together across linguistic and religious divisions for centuries in the empire (Albera and Couroucli 2012; Doumanis 2013; Theodossopoulos 2006).[2] Lest such allegiances be forgotten, it is good to remember that the proto-martyr of the Greek revolution Righas Pheraios (Velestinlis) supported not a unilateral Greek uprising against the Ottoman Empire, but a joint insurrection of "both Christians and Turks, without any distinction of religion," against what he saw as the oppression of all its subjects by the Sublime Porte (cited in Woodhouse 1995: 68).

Nor, a century after the revolution, in the decades following the Greco-Turkish War of 1919–1922 and the forced exchange of populations, did the Anatolian and Pontian Greeks, who lost everything in the splintering of a plural empire into the grouping of an ethnically purified nation, remember their Muslim neighbors with rancor or bitterness but as friends and community members with whom they had shared their day-to-day existence (Hirschon 1998, 2007). With the children and grandchildren of the original victims of the exchange of populations referring to themselves to this day as refugees (*prosfighes*), we must ask whether the unilinear, historiographical time of the nation is not confronted everywhere in the post-Ottoman state by the absence of a collective temporal experience that would afford the distance and with it the safety and reassurance that the ante-national past can be definitively isolated from the present. As Sarah Green (2010: 267) has astutely observed, the transition from an "Ottoman order of things" to a "national order of things" implied a connection with the past as much as a break from it.[3]

The workshop that gave birth to this publication, part of the Balkan Futures series of the British Schools at Athens and Ankara, was entitled "Balkan Topologies," and one may wonder why the title of this collection now uses "Post-Ottoman" instead of "Balkan." Antonis Liakos (2007), Mark Mazower (2000), Maria Todorova (2004, 2009), and Dimitris Tziovas (2003b) have all delineated the associations of the term 'Balkan' with long-standing notions of 'Balkan mentality' and 'Balkan myths', including the myth of the '500-year Turkish yoke'. They point out that these stereotypes all stem from and say more about the Western preoccupation with the militant nationalisms of this region than they do about the peoples and places within it. The Orientalist trope of a 'Balkan mentality' supplants the complex realities of international politics at the fall of the Ottoman Empire with the myth of a purely local, nationalist belligerence that nevertheless is meant to typify and unite a whole region in a putative predisposition to animosity. Rather than dwell on the nationalist rejection of Ottoman cultural heritage, this collection examines not the power but the poverty of nationalistic discourses and historiographies, highlighting the counter-currents with which they are often confronted. It exposes the aporias that a national order of things has hollowed out of bodies of collective memory in the drive to construct temporally and territorially bounded histories, while exploring what lies buried and encrypted in the drive to demonize the Ottoman past. Shunning the myth of Balkan belligerence, the chapters in this volume bear witness to the presence of a loss.

The post-Ottoman nation-state has made of its birth a cause for celebration, but its annual commemorations perpetually return the nation to the moment of its violent origins. The state recalls in public celebration and in formal education moments of official history that its citizens may privately remember with conflicting emotions of sadness, anxiety, guilt, loss, and melancholy as much as with patriotic joy (Bryant 2015; Doumanis 2013; Mills 2006, 2010; Navaro-Yashin 2012; Neyzi 2008). The post-Ottoman condition records the moment when the fanfare of the annual parades and the fireworks has ended, when the minorities marginalized by national discourses quietly remember the violence of the birth of the nation and face the loss of the plural forms of identity that had preceded it. In Michael Herzfeld's (2005: 2) words, the state "converts revolution into conformity, represents ethnic cleansing as national consensus and cultural homogeneity, and recasts the sordid terrors of emergence into a seductive immortality," but this effort is not everywhere and always equally successful. Memory of absence, post-Ottomanism marks the struggle against the absence of memory.

Albeit a geographically and demographically delimited phenomenon, post-Ottomanism also illustrates features of the human condition in late modernity and what we might term 'late nationalism' more generally. Post-Ottomanism reflects a global aspect of the nationalist era in which apparently discarded and long-forgotten political formations and their attendant affective registers seem uncannily to rise again as the integrity and supposed timelessness of national identities are weakened from above by neo-liberal world markets, sovereign debt crises, supra-state organizations, practices of terror and of counter-terror, and the erosion of Enlightenment ideals of human rights and equality, and from below by virulent micro-nationalisms, widespread disenchantment with the unraveling of the nationalist project, and—more promisingly—resurgent awareness of pluralist forms of belonging. The post-Ottoman condition is not an elitist nostalgia for the lost spoils of empire felt by the descendants of those in the metropolis who once enjoyed its fruits (Bissell 2005; Mills 2006, 2010; Stoler 2008).[4] Rather, it represents a critical memory of loss more akin to that identified by Svetlana Boym (2001), born of the contemporary disappointment of those disaffected, marginalized, or unheard by the national project. Its affective dimension takes the form of an unvoiced mourning for what the monolithic nation-state that supplanted the great plural metropolises after the revolution was meant to have been but never became. At the grass roots, in the diasporas, and in the refugee settlements, post-Ottomanism is the genius loci of a regret in part for a lost past, but also for an absent present. In this sense, guarding the memory of a pre-national(ist) *belle époque* (which in some places and times existed and in some cases was constructed post facto) in the face of the ethnicization of the nation and the state-sponsored demonization of difference takes on a critical political dimension in the present.

While evolutionary theories of social development have been left behind by the discipline, anthropology has nonetheless inherited from Enlightenment thinking a teleological model of political formation in which the nation-state is the natural endpoint of a universal process of state formation. Hobbes's state of nature—in which 'man is a wolf to man' (cf. Agamben 1998: 105–107) and the loss of freedom entailed in citizenship was thought necessary for human security—was not to him an abstract notion, but contemporary reality demonstrated by the newly discovered 'savages' of America. Montesquieu—at first implicitly in *Persian Letters* ([1721] 1973) and then explicitly in *The Spirit of the Laws* ([1748] 1989)—was also thinking of particular places when he identified the state of despotism, including the Ottoman Empire. But Montesquieu was not using the Ottoman Empire in a reified manner as the Orientalist Other to a civilized Europe: Montesquieu's Levant was not Hobbes's America. More subtly, Ottoman despotism encoded the potential for the abuse of power by the king of France: far from being distant and exotic, it was near at hand and familiar but hidden and unrecognized. Apparently applied as it is to a range of places and to peoples over an indefinite time-scale, Althusser (1972: 78) derided Montesquieu's despotism as a category that "lacks any social space," on the one hand, and historical duration, on the other: "Space without places, time without duration" (ibid.).[5] But above and beyond his critique, Althusser may have been unknowingly prescient in his intended slight: far from being chimerical, such placeless spaces and recursive temporalities would become all too real in the post-Ottoman world.

Montesquieu ([1748] 1989) and Rousseau (1973) bequeathed to Durkheim ([1892] 1960) (through his mentor, the historian Fustel de Coulanges), Lévi-Strauss (1952), and Sahlins (1972) (via Rousseau's disciple Karl Marx), the idea of state formation as an irreversible linear progression through increasingly hierarchical forms of domination and the notion of contemporary small-scale egalitarian societies as examples of the distant past of the Western world. Michael Herzfeld (1986) has delineated the Greek variant of this theory, which required nineteenth- and early-twentieth-century folklorists to cast the five centuries of Ottoman suzerainty as a state of arrested development and the present as a return to a classical past that simultaneously represented a new state of national efflorescence. But is the nation-state a natural endpoint of political development? Was the Ottoman Empire adequately accounted for as a state of despotism that represented a vestigial throwback to the tumultuous birth of social and political life? The post-Ottoman state is never without a foundational myth of origin referring to Ottoman oppression, corruption, exploitation, weakness, or inefficiency, and it follows Enlightenment thinking in placing the nationalist project at the apex of its civilizing mission. But the collective memory and the lived experience of the post-Ottoman sphere also encompass the wars, the massacres, the displacements, the crises, and the multiple failures of the nation-state. While official national memory is a memory of Ottoman failure and of national glory, post-Ottomanism is not a historical memory of Ottoman grandeur or glory. It does not claim the territory of Ottomanism. Rather, it haunts the lived experience of the failures of nationalist projects: space without places.

The revolutionary Greeks of the eighteenth and nineteenth centuries propagated Montesquieu's and Rousseau's ideas, such as when the Francophile Chiot patriot (and self-exiled expatriate) Adamantios Korais declared in his autobiography that to him "'Turk' and 'wild beast' were synonymous" (Clogg 1992: 3). But this Western European perspective represents an intellectual and a political construct wedded to the war of independence that is not representative of the lived experience of the majority of Greeks under Ottoman rule, many of whom expressed more anxiety regarding the religious incursions of the Catholics in the empire than they did hatred for Muslim overlords.[6] Indeed, Christians did not think of themselves as 'Greek' in the Ottoman Empire. The tradition of Hellenic continuity had yet to be invented, and people moved with relative freedom between religious, national, and ethnic categories (Barkey 2008: 21; Herzfeld 1986; Smyrnelis 2005). Be that as it may, post-Ottomanism refers not to a romantic attachment to a longed-for Ottoman past, but rather to the loss that the violence of the end of the empire entailed for so many.

The loss of home, family, community, and property, accompanied by displacement, dispersal and exile, also entailed the necessity to celebrate all of these injuries as gains for a nascent state to which people now had to find a way of belonging. When the state is relatively strong and enjoying a period of legitimacy, it is possible to accommodate this conflicted identity, but when it is in crisis and losing legitimacy, the foundational sacrifices that had been made are harder to hide and easier to mobilize, and the post-Ottoman condition becomes more acute.

It was by means of the mass forced movement of peoples, of pogroms and massacres, of religious persecution, and of wars and acts of para-statal violence that the states of the post-Ottoman sphere were able to secure ethno-nationalist sovereignty. After the wars, the quotidian structural violence engendered by the shortcomings of the nationalist project resurrects from oblivion the violence that accompanied the formation of the state. In an irony of which the Young Turks may have been only partially conscious, the nationalist ideology that underpinned their revolutionary program was borrowed from Western models originally inspired by ancient Greek ideals of the *oikoumenê*. Originally denoting inhabited land as opposed to desert, the *oikoumenê* gradually came to designate territories inhabited by Greeks and later was restricted to the Christian dominions and people of the Roman and Byzantine empires (Brunet et al. 1992: 166). The *oikoumenê* eventually found a place in Western political ideology as a myth of state according to which a group of people were primordially suited to a landscape that they had inhabited since time immemorial. In this vision, the cradle of nature nurtured the infant of culture as much as culture nurtured nature (J. Berque 1970). The Ottoman Empire is remarkable for having uncoupled the essentialized relationship linking ethno-religiously defined peoples to places in the early modern world.

There is a second meaning to *oikoumenê*, however, whereby Ottoman cosmopolitanism can be described in contradistinction to European nationalism. Igor Kopytoff (1981) and Jean-Pierre Warnier (1985, 2014) reworked the term to describe the complex process by means of which a congeries of culturally distinct peoples nevertheless could form an interdependent social whole in the Grassfields of Cameroon. Sidney Mintz (1996), building on Kopytoff (1981) and Kroeber (1946), used the term in this reconstructed sense to refer to the confluence of peoples in the West Indies as a result of the upheavals of the slave trade.[7] Like the West Indies, the Ottoman Empire was always too plural to be a 'culture area', and yet whatever their cultural background might have been, neighbors from different *millets* in the villages, towns, and cities of the empire were made much more alike than they were different from one another. They were, as Boas's mentor Ratzel put it when he borrowed the concept from its classical context, all part of "a great historic unit" (cited in Mintz 1996: 293)— one in which newcomers (and the living are all newcomers to the landscape created by the dwelling of previous generations) could be enfolded together with the dead in a temporal continuum (Green 2010: 270; Ingold 1993). A sense of shared existence between neighbors of different cultural and religious backgrounds characterized the peace that reigned over Anatolia for so much of the Ottoman Empire's existence. In its quest for a monocultural, monolingual, and ethnically homogeneous state, post-Ottoman nation building has had to obliterate the uneventful memory of this intercommunal landscape of peace, "the homeland of our thoughts" (Merleau-Ponty 1962: 26).

The foundational pogroms and massacres of the Greek War of Independence, the Balkan Wars, and World War I; the Armenian genocide (see Suny et al. 2011; von Bieberstein, this volume); and the mass forced movement of peoples throughout Anatolia, the Balkans, Caucasus, Crimea, East Thrace, and the Mediterranean (Toynbee 1922) became for perpetrators 'things hidden since the foundation of the world' (Girard 1987), while for the nations defining themselves as victims of these events, their commemoration constituted the world. These cataclysmic events thus came to be nurtured in revanchist memories by the nascent states that divided the empire. As a result, while the foundational violence of which it was the object is engraved upon the memory of the post-Ottoman state, and the violence to which it subjected its Others is consigned to a restless oblivion, the state is amnestic about the centuries of peace enjoyed by the peoples of the Ottoman Empire. The storms of official memory—Fernand Braudel's ([1949] 1972: 21) surface disturbances of history—are belied by the routines and habits of silent centuries of intercommunal living (Doumanis 2013: 3). No longer acceptable to official memory, these centuries of peace still form part of the inheritance of the refugees and their descendants. In other cases, it is not lost neighborliness, religious pluralism, and cultural cosmopolitanism that form bodies of counter-memory, but the unconscious pull of unmourned deaths and separations experienced in the pogroms of the past (Bryant 2010; Mills 2006, 2010; Rey 2008). In their immersion beneath official discourse and sanctioned emotion, memories of lost unity or of the desolation born of intercommunal violence take hold at times as nostalgia, but at other times as melancholia (Argenti 2019; Navaro-Yashin 2012).

Not amenable to the progressivist unilinear temporalities of the post-Ottoman state, this melancholic legacy keeps watch over silenced memories of pluralist ideologies that remain alien to the ethno-nationalist project. In his delineation of collective memory, Halbwachs (1992) demonstrates that memories not shared cannot be memories at all, but represent a ghost species of individual human experience doomed to pass into oblivion. The melancholia of post-Ottomanism may not be constituted by memories of specific historical events, but that is not to say that it is not a form of collective memory, or that the Ottoman past is no longer an active social force. Where the historicist paradigm sees the empirical past, post-Ottomanism attests to the enduring presence of what was lost, questioning monolithic models of chronological time.

In a work devoted to the melancholy provoked by his native city of Istanbul, Orhan Pamuk (2005) moves from observations of a personal nature, regarding the losses and sorrows suffered in his childhood and by his family, to the sense of end-of-empire loss that the city's crumbling Ottoman architecture embodies and exudes. In this movement from a purely private to a public melancholia, Pamuk identifies the collective aspect of *hüzün*, the Turkish term for melancholy: "Now we begin to understand *hüzün* as, not the melancholy of a solitary person, but the black mood shared by millions of people together. What I am trying to explain is the *hüzün* of an entire city, of Istanbul" (ibid.: 83). The *hüzün* of Istanbul, Pamuk tells us, is akin to the *tristesse* of South America in Lévi-Strauss's *Triste Tropiques*. As he puts it: "*Tristesse* is not a pain that affects a solitary individual; *hüzün* and *tristesse* both suggest a communal feeling, an atmosphere and a culture shared by millions" (ibid.: 90). In the end, the only protection from *hüzün* available to Istanbulites is to forget about the past, so that "[h]istory becomes a word with no meaning" (ibid.: 92). Just as Halbwachs's memory is collective, so is Pamuk's forgetting a joint project of the city's multitudes. The appeal to oblivion for protection against the pain of memory, however, can only be a Pyrrhic victory. Routing chronology at the cost of a headlong dash into chronicity, it fells the chronological dimension of time only to be haunted by the eternal return of its stunted shadow: the chronic.

In an article on the memories of Istanbul shared by the erstwhile activists of the left who lived through the repression of the 1980 coup d'état known as 12 Eylül (12 September), Christopher Houston (2015) similarly moves from the individual to the collective, tracing the means by which the recently inaugurated Museum of Shame allows for the agglomeration of a myriad of personal traumas to be collectively elicited and reified in a collection of objects that provide a locus for the silenced memories of a stillborn socialist incarnation of the city. In the Museum of Shame, revolutionary Istanbul lives 'only in memory', but in a form of collective memory that has been projected onto the fabric of the city in which it persists up to the present. In its new memorial incarnation, a collective disillusionment—not only with a defeated and discredited communism, but also with the nationalist Kemalism that provided the raison d'être of the state—is made part of the affective present/presence of the city.

Post-Ottoman time marks the limit of models of temporality founded upon the premise of linear chronology. In testifying to an experience of the affective half-life of political violence (remembered not as glory of the state or as culpability of the opponent, but simply as loss) as well as of uneventful coexistence, it challenges the central operative principle of Western historicity: that the past is distant and ever-receding. Because the majority of studies of collective memory in recent years have been studies of political violence, social scientists—influenced by literary theorists—have turned to science and sought to highlight the particular forms of suffering engendered by war with reference to the psychological category of trauma and the psychiatric symptomatology of post-traumatic stress disorder.[8]

Leaving aside the problem of universalization and the consequent erasure of context and history implicit in the trauma discourse (Argenti 2007, 2016; Argenti and Schramm 2010; Broch-Due 2016; Fassin and Rechtman 2009; Hacking 1995; Lewis 2013; Leys 2000; Young 1995), the key point for our current discussion is that trauma is said to break the linearity of psychic time, introducing to it a circularity or short circuit that is the root of the morbidity of the syndrome. The role of the therapist is to interrupt this circularity and to re-establish the linear continuity of psychic time, making of the past a past and of the present an unambiguously monolithic, synchronous moment not haunted by any ghosts. The cure for trauma rests upon the assumption that time is linear and that the perception of time in any other form is a pathological delusion. The collectivization of this model in the notion of 'cultures of trauma' similarly implies a dysfunction at the social level: the idea of a wounded society composed of a mass of indistinguishable victims and perpetrators all equally scarred by the violent moment from which they cannot distance themselves (Fassin and Rechtman 2009).

The assumption that the resurgence of the past in the present represents a pathology deploys universally a culturally specific view of temporality as laminar and unidirectional. The life-worlds explored in this volume challenge and problematize the premise of a linear flow of time that ineluctably distances and insulates individuals from an ever-receding past. Each of the chapters implicitly questions the memory paradigm, moving anthropological research from a focus on memory as traced along a hypostasized single-stranded temporal continuum to exploring chronological models that radically question Western post-Enlightenment assumptions regarding the nature of time itself (*pace* Bloch 2012: 213). Where the past plays the role of an implacable social presence, we can conceive of it not only as remembered but also as immanent. The immanence of the past in the present necessitates a shift from models of memory to a recognition of the presence of the past in everyday life. The post-Ottoman condition is not the memory of the past but its presence: time without duration.

Memory studies have revealed the social dynamics of memorial processes and facilitated the analysis of conflicts over the meaning of the past in terms other than those of an empiricist debate over historical veracity. Studies confined to social memory cannot, however, fully realize the theoretical implications of this departure, which lie in the destabilization of dominant Enlightenment models of time. The field of memory studies thus always contained within it the cause of its own supervention, the archaeology of collective experience it undertook destabilizing the ground upon which it was founded. Rather than redefining what we mean by social or collective memory in order to secure the survival of the paradigm, this volume moves from the ground exposed by memory studies into new territory in which debate can begin over the nature of social time itself, that is, the temporalities of culture. Temporality in the post-Ottoman world marks the site of a battleground disputed by multiple factions in an unresolved conflict, the outcome of which has yet to be determined. It is largely because of the ongoing and urgent relevance of the past to the present in the nation-states of the Balkans, Turkey, and Greece that past, present, and future become mutually juxtaposed and intertwined, particularly following episodes of crisis and political violence. It is to the resulting multi-temporalities of the post-Ottoman world that this volume is devoted.

Ottoman Half-Lives

If post-Ottomanism does not involve nostalgia for a lost empire, neither does it imply that Ottomanism has been definitively left behind, forgotten, or superseded. Beneath official discourse, Ottoman social formations retain a presence in the grassroots culture and collective consciousness of the nation-states that have replaced the empire. The religious and linguistic minorities and the abandoned villages, places of worship, and cemeteries of the post-Ottoman sphere, as well as the displaced people who recall their ties to these places, attest to the stubborn afterlife of the Ottoman Empire and gain strength in the ethos of uncertainty and exclusion that has made so many post-Ottoman states hostile to their minorities. Post-Ottomanism shares an *air de famille* with postmodernity and with post-colonialism to the extent that it bears witness to the waning of belief in the modernist certainties of the nation-state project, marking out the ground in which awareness of alternative pasts and possible futures become matters of popular interest and engagement.[9] This is not to say that post-Ottomanism signals the definitive abandonment of Ottoman identity in the manner that postmodernism and post-colonialism signal a break with modernity or with empire, or that post-Ottomanism implies an unalloyed regressive nostalgia for or continuity with the Ottoman Empire. Post-Ottomanism is neither revolutionary nor reactionary.

Given that post-Ottomanism does not take the form of a memory of Ottoman identity, what is it? What forms does the presence of the Ottoman past take? What are the implications of the post-Ottoman condition for our analytical models of time and historicity, on the one hand, and of collective memory, on the other? In a sense, experiencing Ottoman identity became possible only after the empire had collapsed, making the status of its erstwhile members problematic and open to question—like Mary Douglas's dirt, everyone was suddenly matter out of place. In the sense that Ottoman identity would come to be known after the end of empire, it was to be known only in its futurity. Forever dependent upon what its erstwhile subjects would later become, Ottoman identity today has no stable core; instead, it operates as a deictic term (Durham 2004), or, as Dimitrios Theodossopoulos (2006) has said of the concept of 'Turk' in Greece, as a hollow category pointing to the future in its endless demiurgic generation of new meanings. In his essay "Ottoman Half-Lives," Peter Loizos (1999) has shown that for a plethora of groups in the Mediterranean, Ottoman identity emerged as a result of the population movements occasioned by the collapse of the empire. The massacres, forced displacements, and resulting minority status of the displaced groups of refugees created a vivid sense of identity and difference based upon past experience. One of the case studies that Loizos uses is that of Renée Hirschon on the Asia Minor refugees who settled near the port of Athens after the forced exchange of populations. While recognizing that her informants remembered their Muslim neighbors as people with whom they were on good terms, Hirschon (1998) underlines the role played by the violence of displacement in establishing a tissue of collective memories that would bind this impoverished community together for the next three generations.[10] Dimitris Tziovas (2009: 5) echoes this insight when he identifies a Greek crisis of identity sparked by exile and resulting in a shift from identity through common belonging in locality and space to common belonging in memory and liminality.

To be post-Ottoman in the twentieth century was thus not only to be burdened by the melancholia of forbidden memories of peaceful co-existence, but also to have been victims of political violence, and it was in part through the experience of persecution, displacement, and exile that people became aware of themselves as minorities in the new nation-states emerging from the ruins of the empire. Equally conscious of two conflicting and irreconcilable memories of their origins—of a 'cultural intimacy' (Herzfeld 1997) with Ottoman Turks, on the one hand, and of the Turks' alleged inhumanity, on the other—the past of the refugees and of Greeks more generally became *disemic*, composed of uncomfortably grafted branches whose strange fruit would always be an ambivalent scion of Western, Hellenic identity and of Eastern, Romeic (Byzantine, then Ottoman) memory. While the former was publicly lauded, the latter was intimately encrypted (Herzfeld 1987, [1997] 2005; cf. Said [1984] 2001).

Examining this phenomenon in Greek literature of the nineteenth and twentieth centuries, Iraklis Millas (2006) refers to the 'simultaneity' through which Turks and the period of Ottoman rule could be depicted by those who had lived in Anatolia before the exchange of populations at once as a time of despotic oppression and as one of fondly remembered cohabitation or of lost happiness. The Turkish characters in these novels are accordingly either dehumanized stereotypes or equals 'who could be like the Self'—helpful and kind to the Greek characters (ibid.: 53–54, 57). Following the collapse of the Great Idea and the loss of Asia Minor in the Greco-Turkish war, the writers who became known as the generation of the 1930s would develop the dialogical tension between a parochial Greek identity—expressed in a neo-folkloric genre of writing—and a lost cosmopolitanism, identifying, in contrast to the diasporic identity of the nineteenth century, on the one hand, and the putative homogeneity of the nation, on the other, a new sense of exilic "non-existence" (Polycandrioti 2005: 123; see also Pateridou 2006; Tziovas 2003a; Vitti 1987). Temporalities of exile similar to these have been described by Homi Bhabha ([1994] 2006: 213, 226) as post-colonial counter-narratives that question the essentialist identities of modern nationalism. As described by Benedict Anderson ([1983] 2016: 22–36), the effect of the modern realist novel was to create imagined homogeneous communities in emerging nation-states. Where Anderson had stressed the discursive power of the novel to create the 'homogeneous empty time' of the nation (a concept he borrowed from Benjamin [1950], who in turn had taken it from Bergson [(1896) 1939: 232]), however, Bhabha ([1994] 2006: 227) emphasizes the simultaneous emergence of "a more instantaneous [rather than synchronous] and subaltern voice of the people, minority discourses that speak betwixt and between times and places."

In the social sciences as in literature, the cauldron of national identities that the sudden collapse of the Ottoman Empire produced has resulted in one of the greatest regional concentrations of studies of collective memory and critical historiography. Reflecting the juxtaposition of past and present at both the popular and the national levels in the twentieth century, Laurie Hart's (1992) work on Christianity, time, and memory in the Eastern Peloponese, Nadia Seremetakis's (1991, 1994) writing on the memorialization of the dead in Inner Mani, and David Sutton's (1998) inquiry into history and memory in Kalymnos all demonstrate the means by which religion, nationalist politics, and memory have been wedded in the ethnography of Greece. In his work on Crete, Michael Herzfeld (1985) describes the manner in which contemporary masculine identity is justified with reference to Ottoman domination and the banditry, theft, and illegality that thrived in the socio-political environments that replaced Ottoman occupation. Herzfeld (1991) also examines the contradictions between bureaucratic models of 'monumental time'—the time of the nation-state—and 'social time', representing a popular 'counter-archaeology', while Daniel Knight (2012a, 2012b, 2015) explores the temporal juxtapositions between the present crisis in Greece and the Ottoman past.

Rey (2008) delineates the ways in which a visionary movement among Asia Minor refugees in Lesbos came to play the role of surrogate memories of repressed, unremembered suffering to which the dreamers' refugee parents were subjected in the cataclysm of the exodus from Anatolia. Apparitions of the *oikoumenê*, such memories are not condemnatory of an essentialized Turkish barbarian. In a similar fashion, processes of collective dreaming among members of a millenarian Orthodox cult on the Aegean island of Naxos, as Stewart (2012) describes, implicitly questioned the legitimacy of the emergent Greek nation-state, and the recent sovereign debt crisis is experienced in Chios—through visionary experience, dream premonition, symbolic warfare, and commemorative and religious practice—in juxtaposition with past epochs and events that have befallen the island (Argenti 2019). Time, according to the vernacular authors of the 'mythistory' (Mali 2003; Stewart 2012), which these authors uncover, is recursive, tidal, and turbulent.

Leyla Neyzi (2002, 2008) has studied the 'forgetting' of Greek origins among Turks of Sabbatean heritage from Salonika and conflicting discourses of the past in Smyrna after what the Greeks call 'the Catastrophe' and Turks 'the Liberation'.[11] A similar appropriation of history to nationalist ends is noted in Anastasia Karakasidou's (1997) analysis of the 'anti-historicity' of Macedonian neo-Hellenist origin myths. Like Rey, Karakasidou (ibid.: 32, 36) recounts the atemporality of local origin myths in the Macedonian town of her study, which often juxtaposed the prehistoric with the ancient Greek, the Byzantine, and the Ottoman periods, blending myth, legends, and history in the construction of a 'national time'.[12] In the same region, Loring Danforth and Riki Van Boeschoten (2012: 35–36) describe the movement of children out of Greek Macedonia during the Greek Civil War as another population displacement that was experienced by the ethnic groups involved as a continuation of the conflicts of the Ottoman era.[13] In Cyprus, Yael Navaro-Yashin (2012: 152) has recently delineated the resurgence of Ottoman categories in new, unwelcome guises in the phenomenon of *ganimet*, an Ottoman term for war booty that became overlaid with connotations of loot or plunder after the 1974 partition of the country. The unspoken sense of unease that Turkish Cypriot settlers in Northern Cyprus feel on a daily basis leads Navaro-Yashin to look to their material world and physical surroundings as the source of a political sentiment that is incorporated more than it is verbalized.

Everywhere in the nation-states of the Balkans and the Greek peninsula, the proliferation of references to the Ottoman past and to post-Ottoman state formation points to tears, scars, hauntings, and occluded, doubled, or contested epochs that remain alive today in the social fabric of collective life and in the ideologies of state. Even when these memories or returns do not explicitly reference the Ottoman Empire—for example, when they seem restricted to a narrower, nationalist time frame or to a deeper, classical or prehistoric one (see Knight, this volume)—it is still the case that the collapse of chronological time itself can be located in the demise of the Ottoman Empire and the following sequence of events which that upheaval set in motion for so many people. It is in this temporal collapse that we can speak of post-Ottoman identities or temporalities. Like other forms of post-colonialism, the post-Ottoman condition need therefore not refer exclusively to the Ottoman period or to the Ottoman Empire, but more broadly to the sequelae of nation building and nationalisms, to sub- and supra-national identities, and to the loss of a sense of being anchored in linear time that ensues from the multiple catastrophes of state formation: the forced population movements, the massacres, the wars, and the polarization to the violent extremes of the political spectrum that Bruce Kapferer ([1988] 2011) has chronicled for Sri Lanka and Australia.

But where Kapferer reveals the means by which the distant mythical past can fall prey to the nationalist manipulations of radical politicians and clergy, this volume records the half-lives of melancholia for lost co-existence emergent in collective affects that bear witness to mass violence not for the purpose of creating new monolithic identities, but of tending the absent memories of lost worlds.[14] Where, as Ernest Renan (1947–1961) had emphasized, national narratives and temporalities are based on forgetting, memory can reintroduce the lost polyvocality muted by the production of a homogeneous national subjectivity. And yet where does Blanchot's (1995: 42) entreaty with reference to the Shoah to watch over 'absent meaning' fade into irredentist or xenophobic nationalism? Like the complexity of time, the indeterminacy of affect allows a community to conceal the sword of revanchism beneath the cloak of victimhood.[15] So it was that the memory of the fall of Constantinople in 1453 kept open a wound that would become infected with the tragedy-in-waiting of the irredentist Great Idea, the Greco-Turkish War of 1919–1922 and the final demise of that ill-fated project in the Great Fire of Smyrna in September 1922 (Herzfeld 1986). Smyrna—city of infidels (*giaour Izmir*) to the Kemalist insurgents who reduced the wooden metropolis to ashes, seat of a violated Hellenic civilization to the invading Greek army—had in fact been a wellspring of social effervescence and tolerance to its heterogeneous population. Like Alexandria, Constantinople, and Beirut, it had ranked among the great cosmopolitan centers of the world (Kirli 2005; Mansel 2010; Neyzi 2008).

The Immanence of the Past: Post-Ottoman Topologies and the Paradox of Co-existence

Hirsch and Stewart's (2005) and Stewart's (2012, this volume) theory of historicity makes explicit what the ethnographic evidence adumbrates: that the unilinear model of historical time is a modern Western construct that is not applicable in much of Western culture, let alone in non-Western contexts.[16] In making a distinction between modernist or objectivist Western models of chronological time, on the one hand, and non-linear, social, or subjective formations of time, on the other, it is important to point out that the contributions to this volume do not draw a Manichaean or neo-evolutionary opposition between Rankean Western history and post-Ottoman memory. While the centrality of Pierre Nora's contribution to the field of collective memory is not to be disputed, the point of this project is not to rehearse Nora's (1992) dichotomy between societies with (written, authoritative, empirical) history and those with (subjective, mythical, pre-Enlightenment) memory.[17] Herzfeld's (1991) description of 'monumental time' underlines that Enlightenment historical chronology can be appropriated as a discourse of state and used in a politics of distinction that has little to do with scientific advancement and rather more to do with the imposition of power. The point, then, is not to revive the Geertzian opposition between societies beholden to cyclical time versus those graced with linear time (Geertz 1966, 1973; cf. Bloch 1977; Howe 1981) or to repeat Leach's (1961) dichotomy between a modern, Western grasp of linear chronology and a primitive belief in 'alternating time', nor to promote the Lévi-Straussian distinction between 'hot' and 'cold' societies (Charbonnier 1969; Lévi-Strauss 1952, 1969; cf. Gell 1992: 23–29). The chapters in this collection move beyond these dichotomies, recognizing that people the world over live with multiple registers of time: linear and cyclical, modernist and anachronistic, empiricist and subjective/affective, collective and individual, deep and diurnal.

The intention of this volume is thus not to explore which societies exist in linear time and which in 'ethnic' or 'cultural' time; rather, the goal is to uncover the social and political conditions that interrupt, complexify, or problematize the unitary or laminar flow of time *in any society*. The focus is not on time per se, but on the effects on memory and the experience of time that exposure to such violence begets. The post-Ottoman condition—the effects on temporality brought about by large-scale violence, political transformation, and the forced movement of peoples—refers to the looping effects that flow from different sources against the current of the national narrative. These looping effects and turbulences are part of society and culture in late modernity. They trace the global dynamic of post-Ottomanism in the states that emerged from the Ottoman Empire but can also be viewed as a latent force to which all states are susceptible.

Violence and crisis potentially affect the peoples residing in or having been banished from any nation-state constructed from the violent reduction of once pluralist and cosmopolitan societies into putatively homogeneous groups that have been given a sense of common purpose through the invention of a manifest destiny. The prime exemplar of post-Ottoman society outside the Balkans is the irremediably melancholy sight of the swaths of Europe that lost their Jewish populations in World War II. The twentieth century is forever marked in our memory by its desiccation and splintering of human identities within ever narrower and stricter ethnic, religious, or racial boundaries and the insistence that these were worthy causes for mass exile and industrial murder. But the post-Ottoman condition exists not simply in the half-lives of fascist nationalism and the untold violence wrought on once plural communities; it also bears witness to the enduring presence of the time before the Fall (re)constructed after the Exodus. Joëlle Bahloul's (1992) description of her family's exile from Algeria due to their Jewish heritage is therefore a tale of post-Ottomanism—a tragic inversion of the exodus following the Spanish Reconquista in contemporary Sephardi Jewish memory described by Lévy and Olazabal (2015). So too is the plight of the Greeks of Alexandria under Nasser, of the Greek-speaking Christians and Muslims in Crete and Cyprus (Herzfeld [1997] 2005: 118; Loizos 1988), of the Indians of Uganda under Idi Amin, of the Tamils of Sri Lanka under state Buddhism (Tambiah 1992), of the Muslims of India at the time of partition, and of the Rohingya Muslims of western Burma in the boat crisis now unfolding in the Indian Ocean. In all of these cases, the loss of a plural space—for both the rejected minority and the remaining majority—is replaced with alienation from an essentialized one.

The melancholic but insistent immanence of plural pasts in a monocultural present calls for a new framework that will replace the unilinear chronology still implicit in memory studies with multiple and complex chronologies of transformation and flux, of Brownian motion and of chaos. The transition from memory to multi-temporalities would mirror the transition from Euclidian geometry to topology in the study of shape and surface. Just as the shift to topology in the sciences allowed for the study of space not as fixed but in movement and distortion, so too new socio-cultural models of time might allow us to account more fully for cultural models and experiences of the nonlinear flow of time, its doubling back and enfolding in eddies and whirlpools, and its apparent differential rates of flow as some critical events become ever-present while others fade away from public consciousness.[18]

In geometric terminology, some shapes are homeomorphic: they are not in outward appearance identical or even similar, but can nevertheless distort into perfect juxtapositions of each other without the need for any incisions or additions. Moreover, there are qualities of certain masses that do not depend upon their shape and of certain sets that do not depend upon the sizes of their parts. Such masses or sets can transform topologically without affecting the qualities inherent in them. In this manner, topological geometry, or the study of *topos* (space/place), asks not what is peculiar to a given shape, but what are the potentialities of a given mass or set in all of its possible distortions. Just as topology examines the qualities of space in all of its dimensions and in flux and transformation, this volume analyzes the post-Ottoman condition not only as *topos*, but also as *chronos*, accounting for the effects on time and history, as well as on space and place, of the transformations and continuities that space-time undergoes in the social or national body. We have all experienced, at both a personal and a collective level, how some critical events, such as the birth of Christ (year zero) and of the First French Republic (*an zéro*), become ever-present, all-enveloping, or sempiternal, remaining close and everywhere, while others fade away from public consciousness, becoming distant and placeless.

This collection outlines the homeomorphism of events in time, highlighting the transformations and juxtapositions that collective memory fashions out of chronologically distant events. It delineates a topology of time-space instead of space alone: a chrono-topology or chronotope.[19] In Bakhtin's (1981) analysis, the chronotope is applied to the form of time typical of a literary genre, where time and place intersect as dimensions of one another. Exploring ancient Greek literature, Bakhtin was interested in the literary conjunction of people to place (as expressed in the classical model of the *oikoumenê*). However, in post-Ottoman topologies, it is time rather than place that plays the leading role in the conceptual pairing, with place for many of the contributions to this volume having become problematic through its loss, absence, or destruction. Forever placeless, the post-Ottoman subject lives in time and is at home only through the folds, reversals, and recursivities that culture affords to chronology. The multiple potential of space in geometry exemplifies the transformations of time in post-Ottoman culture and society.

In his work on the anthropology of time, Alfred Gell (1992) distinguishes between 'objective' (B-series) and 'subjective' (A-series) time. In his argument, B-series time (static, untensed, quantitative) is not accessible to human perception and can only be grasped through A-series time—the qualitative experience of chronology and tenses (ibid.: 150; cf. Hodges 2008; Mellor 1981). Arguing that only 'objective' time—imperceptible to all, by Gell's own admission—should be afforded reality status, Gell (1992: 318) does not consider Bergson's philosophy of time, which places more importance on human experience. In counterpoint to Gell, Bergson ([1896] 1939) had viewed B-series time as an intellectual construct with no lived reality. Supposedly empirical, B-series time is in fact a mathematical abstraction.

The time we live, Bergson ([1896] 1939: 232; my trans.) insisted, cannot be "that impersonal and homogeneous duration, the same for all things and all people, which would flow onward, indifferent and void, external to all that endures."[20] Such a time, if it did exist, would be true but trivial, devoid as it is of human content. "In reality," Bergson concludes, "there is no one rhythm of duration" (ibid.). Bergson's argument is empiricist but also phenomenological. The fullness of all time lies beyond the senses just as the atomic dimension of nature, which was being discovered during Bergson's lifetime, is also invisible to us. Different forms of perception—were they *per impossibile* to exist—would be able to discern multiple temporalities co-existing.

Deleuze (1966) retraced Bergson's admonition that the past returns to us as a means of acting in the present, and that the past in its undivided entirety has not ceased to be, but *is*. The present, by contrast, is not but, at every instant, *was*. In this sense, the present is past and the past present. For Deleuze, the past and the present are not successive moments but two elements that co-exist: "Bergsonian duration is, in the end, … defined less by succession than by co-existence" (ibid.: 56; my trans.). Thus, Deleuze sees a first paradox as the "contemporaneity of the past with the present it *has been*" (1968: 111; orig. italics; my trans.). The second paradox is that of co-existence: "If each past is contemporaneous with the present it has been, *all* the past co-exists with the new present in relation to which it is now past" (ibid.). Deleuze's reworking of Bergson's theory of *durée* offers a radical philosophical underpinning for the popular persistence of achronological, non-linear models of time and memory.[21]

In this collection, we do not pronounce on what the ontological nature of time might be, but ask how time is experienced in human sociality, cosmology, and practice. The collective sense of the fullness of time has only relatively recently disappeared from Western culture, occluded by the dominant discourse of Western historicism and its unilinear chronology. Despite the imperial dominion of the dominant model of unilinear time across the globe, the peoples of the nation-states of what was once the Ottoman Empire live with plural temporal registers. Born of collective suffering, post-Ottoman time is the time of collective consciousness. It is social time, and, like Bergsonian *durée*, it does not flow evenly or irreversibly. Bergson's and Deleuze's models of temporality describe time generically. In this volume, we examine how the experience of *durée* is affected by rapid social change, political violence, and crisis. It is not *all* past time that remains present, but certain specific episodes of the past that appear to return or to become immanent in culture and experience.

Michel Serres's (1990) focus in an interview with Bruno Latour on the temporal effects of political violence underscores this point. Reflecting on his childhood in German-occupied France, Serres describes himself as still hungry with the famine that he survived as a child, and he depicts time as chaotic, non-laminar, and polychronic precisely because of the violence of history. While not all of Serres's childhood appears present to him, the atrocities committed by the Axis and Allied forces come to seem, in their temporal dislocation, as at once futuristic and archaic. Such memories—together with others from the war and its aftermath that he did not witness directly but by which he was equally wounded in his youth—live on in his experience today because of their atrocity, and they return to him at key moments in history that seem to replay past events in their brutality.[22] For Serres, it is the indelible stain of evil and suffering that causes the wrinkles, tears, scars, and deformations in time that call for a topological analysis of human temporalities.

The chapters in this volume explore the topological dimensions of time not *sui generis* or ontologically, but in relation to specific case studies of human experience and suffering. Whether this be the collective anxiety triggered by the Greek sovereign debt crisis (Knight), the 'uncanny' returns caused by the Great Depression or the civil war (Stewart), or the longer-term effects on Asia Minor refugees of political violence and displacement (Rey), anthropology needs to do justice to the social reality of temporal collapse and looping that violence, exile, crisis, mourning, and precariousness engender. Even when the past seems safely dead and buried, as the civil war appears to be in the Greek village that Gefou-Madianou describes, it can burst through the surface of everyday calm to revive communal conflicts. Alternatively, the past can remain present and open to interpretation in the aporias of media broadcasting (Papailias). Regimes of denial and amnesia may likewise be brushed aside by contemporary events, as in Turkey (von Bieberstein). War remembered at first hand has an enduring existence in the daily lives of survivors in Bosnia-Herzegovina, but, through prayer, it also excavates collective memories of past wars from the Ottoman period (Henig). What is life in the aftermath of conflict if not a deracination? Uprooted from one's home by the threat of imminent violence, one returns to a place—if one returns—that no longer exists. The returned refugee remains off-balance, one foot in the past in a land that is both 'here' and 'nowhere'. Hart examines this predicament in her comparison of a border zone in northwest Greek Macedonia with Bosnia. In both cases, the return in the aftermath of violence begets an indeterminacy in space and time that bespeaks the fractured social ties of people displaced by war: space without places, time without duration.

Acknowledgments

This collection—dedicated to the memory of Peter Loizos—emerges from a workshop held at the British School at Athens on 19–21 May 2013 in which Peter had been planning to participate. The event was funded by the Economic and Social Research Council (ESRC) as part of a two-year fellowship, "Remembering Absence: Catastrophe, Displacement and Identity among Chiots and the Chiot Diaspora," for which Peter had acted as my mentor. I thank the ESRC and the British School at Athens—Catherine Morgan in particular—for making the workshop and the resulting volume possible. I additionally thank Charles Stewart for co-organizing the workshop with me; Penelope Papailias, Eleana Yalouri, and Eftihia Voutira for their invaluable input as discussants at the event.

Nicolas Argenti is a Senior Lecturer in Anthropology at Brunel University. He has focused his research on Cameroon since the early 1990s and on Greece since 2010. He is the author of *The Intestines of the State: Youth, Violence, and Belated Histories in the Cameroon Grassfields* (2007), *Remembering Absence: The Sense of Life in Island Greece* (2019), and co-editor (with Katharina Schramm) of *Remembering Violence: Anthropological Perspectives on Intergenerational Transmission* (2010).

Notes

1. See also Philip Mansel (2010) on the great Ottoman trading cities and Humphrey and Skvirskaja (2013) on post-cosmopolitan cities. For a critique of modern visions of past intercommunal harmony in Istanbul, see Amy Mills (2006, 2010).
2. And few have studied the class-based manner in which the elite and the bourgeoisie often had more to gain from independence than did the peasantry and the working class, as Pieter Judson (2016) has in his examination of the contemporaneous end of the neighboring Habsburg Empire and the human cost of its reconfiguration along nationalist lines.
3. On the time of the nation in relation to the temporality of exile, see Homi Bhabha (1994: 199–209). As Green (2010: 267) says of the exchange of populations between Greece and Turkey: "Something remained of that earlier logic of border-ness: the decision about who was to be moved from Turkey to Greece and vice versa was based on the key Ottoman distinction of religious affiliation, which had in the past been used to organize people into *millets*—the administrative, legal and tax groupings of the Ottoman regime. The national difference between contemporary Greece and Turkey thus became integrally related to the difference between Orthodox Christian and Muslim. An extended relation between earlier and later forms of border-ness was thus embedded within the apparent complete break between past and present." On the ongoing shared use of religious sites by Muslims and Christians to which Green refers in her article, see also Albera and Couroucli (2012).
4. Michael Herzfeld's (2005: 147–182) theory of structural nostalgia has provided an analytical model through which to understand this form of affect, not only in individual, psychological terms, but as a collective social and political phenomenon. In his critical analysis, structural nostalgia is deployed by the post-revolutionary nation-state as a discourse of self-legitimation, positing an original perfection and purity from which the nation is fallen. Where Herzfeld deconstructs the nationalist rhetoric of religious and national purity inherent in structural nostalgia (ibid.: 174–177), this collection seeks to shed light on its alter-ego—the melancholic memory of the pre-national past, the time-before-time that structural nostalgia would elide.
5. For a critique of the Ottoman Empire as a despotic system, see Barkey (2008).
6. After the fall of Constantinople, the priests and hierarchy of the Byzantine Empire debated whether the Muslim forces had been sent by God to protect the Orthodox Christians from the worse scourge of the Catholic armies threatening the empire from the West. Another Greek historian, Makraios, had earlier identified not the Turks but the Catholics as "cruel and bloodthirsty wolves of the west" (cited in Ware 1964: 79). The eighteenth-century Chiot Orthodox theologian Eustratios Argenti likewise aimed all of his polemical writing at the papacy and not at Islam (ibid.).
7. The social geographer Augustin Berque (1996, 2009), son of Jacques Berque, resurrects the term to refer to humanity in relation to its lived space in a phenomenological exploration of Heideggerian dwelling.
8. For more detailed studies in this field, see Alexander (2012), Ashplant et al. (2000), Cohen (2001), Connerton (1989, 2011), Das et al. (2000, 2001), Erickson (1991), Eyerman (2001), Felman and Laub (1992), Forty and Küchler (1999), Kleinman et al. (1997), LaCapra (2001), Laub (1991), Lyotard (1990), Olick and Robbins (1998), Olivier (2008), Passerini (2005), Radstone (2000), Ricoeur (2000: 95), Robben and Suárez-Orozco (2000), Sluka (2000), and Van Boeschoten (2003).
9. See, for example, John Comaroff (2002) and Jean and John Comaroff's (2006) edited volume, the contributions to which locate the emergence of the phenomenon of the post-colony in the failure of democratization of emergent post-colonial states.

10. Eftihia Voutira (2003) and Vasso Stelaku (2003) note the centrality of memory and commemoration in Greek refugee ethno-genesis and Eastern Christianity, respectively.
11. Cf. Kirli (2005) on Turkish amnesia regarding the 1922 burning of Smyrna.
12. Sutton (1998: 123–145) also notes the conflations of time in Kalymnos, in particular, the deep time of biblical stories with revolutionary/nationalist ideologies through the union of church and state. Cf. Herzfeld's (1991) and Papailias's (2005) studies of the protracted and polarized political struggle over history in Greece.
13. Seen by outsiders as a clash between communist and right-wing Greek factions, the conflict was experienced in northern Greece as a complex struggle involving Macedonians with Slav origins and others with ethnic Greek national identities. Nominally on the same side of the conflict, they were nonetheless locked in opposition to one another. In this way, the factions involved in the Greek Civil War of the 1940s had their origins in the collapse of the Ottoman Empire 30 years before. The Ottoman Empire also cast a shadow over the civil war as refugee children taken by communists over the border into Yugoslavia were referred to as victims of a new *paidomazoma*, the Ottoman practice of collecting Christian children for conversion and conscription as janissaries in the sultan's forces. See Hart (2012) and Karakasidou (1997).
14. Allen Feldman's (1991) analysis of political terror in Northern Ireland likewise demonstrates that chronological narratives of violence are replaced with intertwined, relational narratives. Jennifer Cole (2001) similarly speaks of 'layered memories' in her study of the colonial legacy in Madagascar. Marita Sturken's (1997) work on the 'tangled memories' of the Vietnam War in the United States argues that memories of war are not reducible to one authoritative version of events.
15. Derrida (1986: 56) makes this point in his exploration of the shibboleth in Paul Celan's work.
16. Hirsch and Stewart (2005: 264) argue that the claims to disinterested objectivity of history as a science arose as recently as the nineteenth century in a work of Leopold von Ranke (1824). Despite gaining ascendancy in popular culture, however, Rankean empiricism was critiqued by Heidegger ([1927] 2010), whose entire opus *Being and Time* can be seen as a rejection of Ranke's position. In it, Heidegger quotes Yorck's 1894 letter to Dilthey dismissing Ranke as "a great ocularist, for whom things that have vanished can never become *realities*" (ibid.: 380).
17. For critiques of Nora, see Argenti and Schramm (2010) and Sturken (1997).
18. Our use of topology in this volume therefore differs from that set out by Artemis Leontis (1995) in her *Topographies of Hellenism*, in which she names topology the study of topography, and explicitly distances the term from its mathematical applications while emphasizing its geographical rather than temporal dimensions.
19. On the Asia Minor Catastrophe as a chronotope, see Liakos (2007: 214).
20. Walter Benjamin (1950: chap. 17; my trans.) picks up on this aphorism in his final work, "Über den Begriff der Geschichte" (On the Concept of History), where "historicism … has no theoretical armature … it mobilizes a mass of facts in order to fill up a homogeneous and empty time."
21. For a masterly overview of theories of time in anthropology, see Matt Hodges (2008).
22. Daniel Knight (2012a) has recently noted the 'cultural proximity' of World War II in today's crisis-ridden plains of central Greece.

References

Agamben, Giorgio. 1998. *Homo Sacer: Sovereign Power and Bare Life*. Trans. Daniel Heller-Roazen. Stanford, CA: Stanford University Press.
Albera, Dionigi, and Maria Couroucli, eds. 2012. *Sharing Sacred Spaces in the Mediterranean: Christians, Muslims, and Jews at Shrines and Sanctuaries*. Bloomington: Indiana University Press.
Alexander, Jeffry C. 2012. *Trauma: A Social Theory*. Cambridge: Polity Press.
Althusser, Louis. 1972. *Politics and History: Montesquieu, Rousseau, Marx*. Trans. Ben Brewster. London: Verso.
Anderson, Benedict. (1983) 2016. *Imagined Communities: Reflections on the Origin and Spread of Nationalism*. London: Verso.
Angé, Olivia, and David Berliner, eds. 2015. *Anthropology and Nostalgia*. New York: Berghahn Books.
Argenti, Nicolas. 2007. *The Intestines of the State: Youth, Violence, and Belated Histories in the Cameroon Grassfields*. Chicago: Chicago University Press.
Argenti, Nicolas. 2016. "Laughter without Borders: Embodied Memory and Pan-Humanism in a Post-Traumatic Age." In Broch-Due and Bertelsen 2016, 241–268.
Argenti, Nicolas. 2019. *Remembering Absence: The Sense of Life in Island Greece*. Bloomington: Indiana University Press.
Argenti, Nicolas, and Katharina Schramm. 2010. "Introduction." In *Remembering Violence: Anthropological Perspectives on Intergenerational Transmission*, ed. Nicolas Argenti and Katharina Schramm, 1–39. New York: Berghahn Books.
Ashplant, T. G., Graham Dawson, and Michael Roper. 2000. "The Politics of War Memory and Commemoration: Contexts, Structures and Dynamics." In *The Politics of War Memory and Commemoration*, ed. T. G. Ashplant, Graham Dawson, and Michael Roper, 3–86. London: Routledge.
Bahloul, Joëlle. 1992. *La maison de mémoire: Ethnologie d'une demeure judéo-arabe en Algérie (1937–1961)*. Paris: Métailié.
Bakhtin, Mikhail. 1981. *The Dialogic Imagination: Four Essays*. Trans. Caryl Emerson and Michael Holquist. Austin: University of Texas Press.
Barkey, Karen. 2008. *Empire of Difference: The Ottomans in Comparative Perspective*. Cambridge: Cambridge University Press.
Benjamin, Walter. 1950. "Über den Begriff der Geschichte." *Neue Rundschau* 61 (3).
Bergson, Henri. (1896) 1939. *Matière et mémoire*. Paris: Presses Universitaires de France.
Berque, Augustin. 1996. *Être humains sur la terre: Principes d'éthique de l'écoumène*. Paris: Gallimard.
Berque, Augustin. 2009. *Ecoumène: Introduction à l'étude des milieux humains*. Paris: Belin.
Berque, Jacques. 1970. *L'Orient second*. Paris: Gallimard.
Bhabha, Homi. (1994) 2006. *The Location of Culture*. London: Routledge.
Bissell, William C. 2005. "Engaging Colonial Nostalgia." *Cultural Anthropology* 20 (2): 215–248.
Blanchot, Maurice. 1995. *The Writing of the Disaster*. Trans. Ann Smock. Lincoln: University of Nebraska Press.
Bloch, Maurice. 1977. "The Past and Present in the Present." *Man* (n.s.) 12 (2): 278–292.
Bloch, Maurice. 2012. *Anthropology and the Cognitive Challenge*. Cambridge: Cambridge University Press.
Boym, Svetlana. 2001. *The Future of Nostalgia*. New York: Basic Books.

Braudel, Fernand. (1949) 1972. *The Mediterranean and the Mediterranean World in the Age of Philip II*. Trans. Siân Reynolds. London: HarperCollins.

Broch-Due, Vigdis. 2016. "Trauma, Violence, Memory: Reflections on the Bodily, the Self, the Sign, and the Social." In Broch-Due and Bertelsen 2016, 23–58.

Broch-Due, Vigdis, and Bjørn E. Bertelsen, eds. 2016. *Violent Reverberations: Global Modalities of Trauma*. New York: Palgrave Macmillan.

Brunet, Roger, Robert Ferras, and Hervé Théry. 1992. *Les mots de la géographie*. Paris: La Documentation Française.

Bryant, Rebecca. 2010. *The Past in Pieces: Belonging in the New Cyprus*. Philadelphia: University of Pennsylvania Press.

Bryant, Rebecca. 2015. "Nostalgia and the Discovery of Loss: Essentializing the Turkish Cypriot past." In Angé and Berliner 2015, 155–177.

Charbonnier, Georges. 1969. *Conversations with Claude Lévi-Strauss*. Trans. John Weightman and Doreen Weightman. London: Jonathan Cape.

Clogg, Richard. 1992. *A Concise History of Greece*. Cambridge: Cambridge University Press.

Cohen, Stanley. 2001. *States of Denial: Knowing about Atrocities and Suffering*. Cambridge: Polity Press.

Cole, Jennifer. 2001. *Forget Colonialism? Sacrifice and the Art of Memory in Madagascar*. Berkeley: University of California Press.

Comaroff, Jean, and John Comaroff, eds. 2006. *Law and Disorder in the Postcolony*. Chicago: University of Chicago Press.

Comaroff, John. 2002. "Governmentality, Materiality, Legality, Modernity: On the Colonial State in Africa." In *African Modernities: Entangled Meanings in Current Debate*, ed. Jan-Georg Deutsch, Peter Probst, and Heike Schmidt, 107–134. Oxford: James Currey.

Connerton, Paul. 1989. *How Societies Remember*. Cambridge: Cambridge University Press.

Connerton, Paul. 2011. *The Spirit of Mourning: History, Memory and the Body*. Cambridge: Cambridge University Press.

Couroucli, Maria. 2012. "Introduction: Sharing Sacred Places—a Mediterranean Tradition." In Albera and Couroucli 2012, 1–9.

Danforth, Loring M., and Riki Van Boeschoten. 2012. *Children of the Greek Civil War: Refugees and the Politics of Memory*. Chicago: University of Chicago Press.

Das, Veena, Arthur Kleinman, Mamphela Ramphele, and Pamela Reynolds, eds. 2000. *Violence and Subjectivity*. Berkeley: University of California Press.

Das, Veena, Arthur Kleinman, Margaret Lock, Mamphela Ramphele, and Pamela Reynolds, eds. 2001. *Remaking a World: Violence, Social Suffering and Recovery*. Berkeley: University of California Press.

Deleuze, Gilles. 1966. *Le bergsonisme*. Paris: Presses Universitaires de France.

Deleuze, Gilles. 1968. *Différence et répétition*. Paris: Presses Universitaires de France.

Derrida, Jacques. 1986. *Schibboleth: Pour Paul Celan*. Paris: Galilée.

Doumanis, Nicholas. 2013. *Before the Nation: Muslim-Christian Coexistence and Its Destruction in Late-Ottoman Anatolia*. Oxford: Oxford University Press.

Durham, Deborah. 2004. "Disappearing Youth: Youth as a Social Shifter in Botswana." *American Ethnologist* 31(4): 589–605.

Durkheim, Emile. (1892) 1960. *Montesquieu and Rousseau: Forerunners of Sociology*. Trans. Ralph Manheim. Ann Arbor: University of Michigan.

Erikson, Kai. 1991. "Notes on Trauma and Community." *American Imago* 48 (4): 455–472.

Eyerman, Ron. 2001. *Cultural Trauma: Slavery and the Formation of African American Identity*. Cambridge: Cambridge University Press.

Fassin, Didier, and Richard Rechtman. 2009. *The Empire of Trauma: An Inquiry Into the Condition of Victimhood*. Trans. Rachel Gomme. Princeton, NJ: Princeton University Press.
Feldman, Allen. 1991. *Formations of Violence: The Narrative of the Body and Political Terror in Northern Ireland*. Chicago: University of Chicago Press.
Felman, Shoshana, and Dori Laub. 1992. *Testimony: Crises of Witnessing in Literature, Psychoanalysis, and History*. London: Routledge.
Forty, Adrian, and Susanne Küchler, eds. 1999. *The Art of Forgetting*. Oxford: Berg.
Geertz, Clifford. 1966. *Person, Time, and Conduct in Bali: An Essay in Cultural Analysis*. Southeast Asia Studies, Cultural Report Series No. 14. New Haven, CT: Yale University Press.
Geertz, Clifford. 1973. *The Interpretation of Cultures: Selected Essays*. New York: Basic Books.
Gell, Alfred. 1992. *The Anthropology of Time: Cultural Constructions of Temporal Maps and Images*. Oxford: Berg.
Girard, René. 1987. *Things Hidden Since the Foundation of the World*. Trans. Stephen Bann and Michael Metteer. London: Athlone Press.
Green, Sarah. 2010. "Performing Border in the Aegean: On Relocating Political, Economic and Social Relations." *Journal of Cultural Economy* 3 (2): 261–278.
Hacking, Ian. 1995. *Rewriting the Soul: Multiple Personality and the Sciences of Memory*. Princeton, NJ: Princeton University Press.
Halbwachs, Maurice. 1992. *On Collective Memory*. Ed. and trans. Lewis A. Coser. Chicago: University of Chicago Press. Originally published in French in 1941 and 1952.
Hart, Laurie. 1992. *Time, Religion and Religious Experience in Rural Greece*. Lanham, MD: Rowman & Littlefield.
Hart, Laurie. 2012. "Pictures at a Transboundary Basilica." Center for Hellenic Studies, Harvard University. http://chs.harvard.edu/CHS/article/display/4791 (accessed 1 June 2016).
Heidegger, Martin. (1927) 2010. *Being and Time*. Trans. Joan Stambaugh. Albany: State University of New York.
Herzfeld, Michael. 1985. *The Poetics of Manhood: Contest and Identity in a Cretan Mountain Village*. Princeton, NJ: Princeton University Press.
Herzfeld, Michael. 1986. *Ours Once More: Folklore, Ideology, and the Making of Modern Greece*. New York: Pella.
Herzfeld, Michael. 1987. *Anthropology Through the Looking-Glass: Critical Ethnography in the Margins of Europe*. Cambridge: Cambridge University Press.
Herzfeld, Michael. 1991. *A Place in History: Social and Monumental Time in a Cretan Town*. Princeton, NJ: Princeton University Press.
Herzfeld, Michael. (1997) 2005. *Cultural Intimacy: Social Poetics in the Nation-State*. New York: Routledge.
Hirsch, Eric, and Charles Stewart. 2005. "Introduction: Ethnographies of Historicity." *History and Anthropology* 16 (3): 261–274.
Hirschon, Renée. 1998. *Heirs of the Greek Catastrophe: The Social Life of Asia Minor Refugees in Piraeus*. New York: Berghahn Books.
Hirschon, Renée, ed. 2003. *Crossing the Aegean: An Appraisal of the 1923 Compulsory Population Exchange Between Greece and Turkey*. New York: Berghahn Books.
Hirschon, Renée. 2007. "Knowledge of Diversity: Towards a More Differentiated Set of 'Greek' Perceptions of 'Turks.'" In *When Greeks Think about Turks: The View from Anthropology*, ed. Dimitris Theodossopoulos, 61–78. London: Routledge.
Hodges, Matt. 2008. "Rethinking Time's Arrow: Bergson, Deleuze and the Anthropology of Time." *Anthropological Theory* 8 (4): 399–429.

Houston, Christopher. 2015. "Politicizing Place Perception: A Phenomenology of Urban Activism in Istanbul." *Journal of the Royal Anthropological Institute* 21 (4): 720–738.

Howe, Leopold E. A. 1981. "The Social Determination of Knowledge: Maurice Bloch and Balinese Time." *Man* (n.s.) 16 (2): 220–234.

Humphrey, Caroline, and Vera Skvirskaja, eds. 2013. *Post-Cosmopolitan Cities: Explorations of Urban Coexistence*. New York: Berghahn Books.

Ingold, Tim. 1993. "The Temporality of the Landscape." *World Archaeology* 25 (2): 152–174.

Judson, Pieter. 2016. *The Habsburg Empire: A New History*. Cambridge, MA: Harvard University Press.

Kapferer, Bruce. (1988) 2011. *Legends of People, Myths of State: Violence, Intolerance, and Political Culture in Sri Lanka and Australia*. Rev. ed. New York: Berghahn Books.

Karakasidou, Anastasia. 1997. *Fields of Wheat, Hills of Blood: Passages to Nationhood in Greek Macedonia, 1870–1990*. Chicago: University of Chicago Press.

Kirli, Biray Koluoglu. 2005. "Forgetting the Smyrna Fire." *History Workshop Journal* 60 (1): 25–44.

Kleinman, Arthur, Veena Das, and Margaret Lock, eds. 1997. *Social Suffering*. Berkeley: University of California Press.

Knight, Daniel M. 2012a. "Cultural Proximity: Crisis, Time and Social Memory in Central Greece." *History and Anthropology* 23 (3): 349–374.

Knight, Daniel M. 2012b. "Turn of the Screw: Narratives of History and Economy in the Greek Crisis." *Journal of Mediterranean Studies* 21 (1): 53–76.

Knight, Daniel M. 2015. *History, Time, and Economic Crisis in Central Greece*. New York: Palgrave Macmillan.

Kopytoff, Igor. 1981. "Aghem Ethnogenesis and the Grassfields Ecumene." In *Contributions de la recherche ethnologique à l'histoire des civilisations du Cameroun*, vol. 2, ed. Claude Tardits, 371–381. Paris: CNRS.

Kroeber, A. L. 1946. "The Ancient *Oikoumenê* as an Historic Culture Aggregate." *Journal of the Royal Anthropological Institute of Great Britain and Ireland* 75 (1–2): 9–20.

LaCapra, Dominick. 2001. *Writing History, Writing Trauma*. Baltimore: Johns Hopkins University Press.

Laub, Dori. 1991. "Truth and Testimony: The Process and the Struggle." *American Imago* 48 (1): 75–91.

Leach, Edmund. 1961. *Rethinking Anthropology*. London: Athlone Press.

Leontis, Artemis. 1995. *Topographies of Hellenism: Mapping the Homeland*. Ithaca, NY: Cornell University Press.

Lévi-Strauss, Claude. 1952. *Race et histoire*. Paris: UNESCO.

Lévi-Strauss, Claude. 1969. *The Elementary Structures of Kinship*. Boston: Beacon Press.

Lévy, Joseph J., and Inaki Olazabal. 2015. "The Key from (to) Sefarad: Nostalgia for a Lost Country." In Angé and Berliner 2015, 139–154.

Lewis, Sara E. 2013. "Trauma and the Making of Flexible Minds in the Tibetan Exile Community." *Ethos* 41 (3): 313–336.

Leys, Ruth. 2000. *Trauma: A Genealogy*. Chicago: University of Chicago Press.

Liakos, Antonis. 2007. "Historical Time and National Space in Modern Greece." In *Regions in Central and Eastern Europe: Past and Present*, ed. Hayashi Tadayuki and Hiroshi Fukuda, 205–227. Sapporo: Slavic Research Center.

Loizos, Peter. 1988. "Intercommunal Killing in Cyprus." *Man* (n.s.) 23 (4): 639–653.

Loizos, Peter. 1999. "Ottoman Half-Lives: Long-Term Perspectives on Particular Forced Migrations." *Journal of Refugee Studies* 12 (3): 237–263.
Lyotard, Jean-François. 1990. *Heidegger and "the Jews."* Trans. Andreas Michel and Mark S. Roberts. Minneapolis: University of Minnesota Press.
Mali, Joseph. 2003. *Mythistory: The Making of a Modern Historiography*. Chicago: University of Chicago Press.
Mansel, Philip. 2010. *Levant: Splendour and Catastrophe on the Mediterranean*. London: John Murray.
Mazower, Mark. 2000. *The Balkans: A Short History*. New York: Modern Library.
Mellor, D. H. 1981. *Real Time*. Cambridge: Cambridge University Press.
Merleau-Ponty, Maurice. 1962. *The Phenomenology of Perception*. Trans. Colin Smith. London: Routledge & Kegan Paul.
Millas, Iraklis. 2006. "*Tourkokratia*: History and the Image of Turks in Greek Literature." *South European Society and Politics* 11 (1): 47–60.
Mills, Amy. 2006. "Boundaries of the Nation in the Space of the Urban: Landscape and Social Memory in Istanbul." *Cultural Geographies* 13 (3): 367–394.
Mills, Amy. 2010. *Streets of Memory: Landscape, Tolerance, and National Identity in Istanbul*. Athens: University of Georgia Press.
Mintz, Sidney W. 1996. "Enduring Substances, Trying Theories: The Caribbean Region as *Oikoumenê*." *Journal of the Royal Anthropological Institute* 2 (2): 289–311.
Montesquieu, Charles-Louis de Secondat. (1721) 1973. *Persian Letters*. Trans. and ed. C. J. Betts. Harmondsworth: Penguin Books.
Montesquieu, Charles-Louis de Secondat. (1748) 1989. *The Spirit of the Laws*. Trans. and ed. Anne M. Cohler, Basia C. Miller, and Harold S. Stone. Cambridge: Cambridge University Press.
Navaro-Yashin, Yael. 2012. *The Make-Believe Space: Affective Geography in a Postwar Polity*. Durham, NC: Duke University Press.
Neyzi, Leyla. 2002. "Remembering to Forget: Sabbateanism, National Identity, and Subjectivity in Turkey." *Comparative Studies in Society and History* 44 (1): 137–158.
Neyzi, Leyla. 2008. "Remembering Smyrna/Izmir: Shared History, Shared Trauma." *History & Memory* 20 (2): 106–127.
Nora, Pierre. 1992. "General Introduction: Between Memory and History." In *Realms of Memory: Rethinking the French Past*, vol. 1, ed. Lawrence D. Kritzman; trans. Arthur Goldhammer, 1–21. New York: Columbia University Press.
Olick, Jeffrey K., and Joyce Robbins. 1998. "Social Memory Studies: From 'Collective Memory' to the Historical Sociology of Mnemonic Practices." *Annual Review of Sociology* 24: 105–140.
Olivier, Laurent. 2008. *Le sombre abîme du temps: Mémoire et archéologie*. Paris: Seuil.
Pamuk, Orhan. 2005. *Istanbul: Memories and the City*. Trans. Maureen Freely. London: Faber & Faber.
Papailias, Penelope. 2005. *Genres of Recollection: Archival Poetics and Modern Greece*. New York: Palgrave Macmillan.
Passerini, Luisa. 2005. "Memories between Silence and Oblivion." In *Memory, History, Nation: Contested Pasts*, ed. Katharine Hodgkin and Susannah Radstone, 238–254. New Brunswick, NJ: Transaction.
Pateridou, Georgia. 2006. "The Playful Mode of Writing in Psycharis's *Το Ταζίδι μου* (1888)." *Byzantine and Modern Greek Studies* 30 (2): 167–183.
Polycandrioti, Ourania. 2005. "Literary Quests in the Aegean (1840–1940): Identity and Cosmopolitanism." *History and Anthropology* 16 (1): 113–127.
Radstone, Susannah. 2000. "Screening Trauma: *Forrest Gump*, Film and Memory." In *Memory and Methodology*, ed. Susannah Radstone, 79–110. Oxford: Berg.

Ranke, Leopold von. 1824. *History of the Latin and Teutonic Nations, 1494–1514.* London: George Bell & Sons.
Renan, Ernest. 1947–1961. "Qu'est-ce qu'une nation?" In *Oeuvres Complètes*, vol. 1: 887–906. Paris: Calmand-Lévy.
Rey, Séverine. 2008. *Des saints nés des rêves: Fabrication de la sainteté et commémoration des néomartyrs à Lesvos (Grèce).* Lausanne: Antipodes.
Ricoeur, Paul. 2000. *La mémoire, l'histoire, l'oubli.* Paris: Seuil.
Robben, Antonius C. G. M., and Marcelo M. Suárez-Orozco, eds. 2000. *Cultures under Siege: Collective Violence and Trauma.* Cambridge: Cambridge University Press.
Rousseau, Jean-Jacques. 1973. *The Social Contract and The Discourses.* Trans. G. D. H. Cole. London: Everyman.
Sahlins, Marshall. 1972. *Stone Age Economics.* London: Tavistock.
Said, Edward. (1984) 2001. "Reflections on Exile." In *Reflections on Exile*, 173–186. London: Granta Books. First published in *Granta 13: After the Revolution*.
Seremetakis, C. Nadia. 1991. *The Last Word: Women, Death, and Divination in Inner Mani.* Chicago: University of Chicago Press.
Seremetakis, C. Nadia, ed. 1994. *The Senses Still: Perception and Memory as Material Culture in Modernity.* Chicago: University of Chicago Press.
Serres, Michel, with Bruno Latour. 1995. *Conversations on Science, Culture, and Time.* Trans. Roxanne Lapidus. Ann Arbor: University of Michigan Press.
Sluka, Jeffrey A., ed. 2000. *Death Squad: The Anthropology of State Terror.* Philadelphia: University of Pennsylvania Press.
Smyrnelis, Marie-Carmen. 2005. *Une société hors de soi: Identités et relations sociales à Smyrne aux XVIIIe et XIXe siècles.* Paris: Peeters.
Stelaku, Vasso. 2003. "Space, Place and Identity: Memory and Religion in Two Cappadocian Greek Settlements." In Hirschon 2003, 179–192.
Stewart, Charles. 2012. *Dreaming and Historical Consciousness in Island Greece.* Cambridge, MA: Harvard University Press.
Stoler, Ann L. 2008. "Imperial Debris: Reflections on Ruins and Ruination." *Cultural Anthropology* 23 (2): 191–219.
Sturken, Marita. 1997. *Tangled Memories: The Vietnam War, the AIDS Epidemic, and the Politics of Remembering.* Berkeley: University of California Press.
Suny, Ronald Grigor, Fatma Müge Göçek, and Norman M. Naimark, eds. 2011. *A Question of Genocide: Armenians and Turks at the End of the Ottoman Empire.* Oxford: Oxford University Press.
Sutton, David E. 1998. *Memories Cast in Stone: The Relevance of the Past in Everyday Life.* Oxford: Berg.
Tambiah, Stanley J. 1992. *Buddhism Betrayed? Religion, Politics, and Violence in Sri Lanka.* Chicago: University of Chicago Press.
Theodossopoulos, Dimitrios. 2006. "Introduction: The 'Turks' in the Imagination of the Greeks." *South European Society and Politics* 11 (1): 1–32.
Todorova, Maria, ed. 2004. *Balkan Identities: Nation and Memory.* New York: New York University Press.
Todorova, Maria. 2009. *Imagining the Balkans.* Oxford: Oxford University Press.
Toynbee, Arnold. 1922. *The Western Question in Greece and Turkey: A Study in the Contact of Civilisations.* London: Constable.
Tziovas, Dimitris. 2003a. *Cosmopolites kai aposinagogoi: Meletes gia tin elliniki pezografia* [The cosmopolitans and the remote: Studies of Greek prose literature (1830–1930]. Athens: Metaihmio.
Tziovas, Dimitris, ed. 2003b. *Greece and the Balkans: Identities, Perceptions and Cultural Encounters since the Enlightenment.* Aldershot: Ashgate.

Tziovas, Dimitris. 2009. "Introduction." In *Greek Diaspora and Migration since 1700: Society, Politics, and Culture*, ed. Dimitris Tziovas, 1–14. Aldershot: Ashgate.

Van Boeschoten, Riki. 2003. "The Trauma of War Rape: A Comparative View on the Bosnian Conflict and the Greek Civil War." *History and Anthropology* 14 (1): 41–54.

Vitti, M. 1987. *I genia tou trianta: Ideologia kai morfi* [The generation of the 1930s: Ideology and form]. Athens: Ermis.

Voutira, Eftihia. 2003. "When Greeks Meet Other Greeks: Settlement Policy Issues in the Contemporary Greek Context." In Hirschon 2003, 145–159.

Ware, Timothy [Bishop Kallistos]. 1964. *Eustratios Argenti: A Study of the Greek Church under Turkish Rule*. Oxford: Clarendon Press.

Warnier, Jean-Pierre. 1985. *Echanges, développement et hiérarchies dans le Bamenda pré-colonial (Cameroun)*. Wiesbaden: Franz Steiner Verlag.

Warnier, Jean-Pierre. 2014. "L'institution monétaire de la royauté en Afrique Centrale." *Études Rurales* 193: 107–144.

Woodhouse, Christopher M. 1995. *Rhigas Velestinlis: The Proto-Martyr of the Greek Revolution*. Limni: Denise Harvey.

Young, Allan. 1995. *The Harmony of Illusions: Inventing Post-Traumatic Stress Disorder*. Princeton, NJ: Princeton University Press.

Chapter 1

FOSSILIZED FUTURES
Topologies and Topographies of Crisis Experience in Central Greece

Daniel M. Knight

One hundred forty to 200 million years ago, the Plain of Thessaly in central Greece was an ancient sea stretching from the Kalampaka pass, where today stands the geological wonder of Meteora, to the Aegean Sea beyond Larisa. If one knows where to look, numerous types of Mesozoic (Cretaceous, Jurassic, Triassic) fossils can still be found on mountainsides in relative abundance. On New Year's Day for the past five years, three generations of a family from Trikala have gone fossil hunting in the Hasia Mountains above Kalampaka. During their adventures, they discuss history, time, and the current economic turmoil.

After a hearty New Year's lunch, Eleni, aged 69, her son Vassilis and daughter Eugenia, both in their early forties, Stella, Vassilis's seven-year-old daughter, and myself pile into their small Nissan Micra to make the 40-minute journey into the mountains. The car struggles up the winding roads, its boot laden with hammers, chisels, pickaxes, machetes, and a crowbar, essential tools for any fossil hunter. The usual route includes at least three stops for Eugenia and

References for this chapter begin on page 40.

Stella, the most eager fossil hunters, to violently throw up, as pork and potatoes rarely complement motion sickness. This is particularly ironic as 1 January is Eugenia's 'birthday', according to her official papers, although she was actually born on 29 December—perhaps our first example of intriguing notions of time (cf. Hirschon 2014).

Over the course of two to three hours, the family and the anthropologist scour the mountainside for fossils with varying degrees of success. While standing upon the folded topographical strata of ancient rock, where flora and fauna that perished over 140 million years ago finally meet the crisp light of twenty-first-century Greece, their conversation turns to the history of the region, the present socio-economic crisis, and what the future holds. 'Historical' accounts are manifold (see Knight 2015a; Papailias 2005). Some take the form of personal experience, such as when Eleni's family was forced to migrate to Trikala from a village in Greek Macedonia in 1947. Eleni also discusses the junta of 1967–1974 and being relocated to the island of Chios due to her perceived Communist links based on the political tendencies of her village of origin. Other accounts are mediated through intergenerational familial oral history, such as how Papou Vassilis survived the Balkan Wars of 1912 and 1913 and fought on the Albanian border during World War II. However, Eleni believes that given the conditions of social suffering and material poverty associated with the current economic crisis, the most poignant memories are of the Great Famine of 1941–1943 and the Ottoman and Axis occupations. These events have acquired nationalized narratives whereby direct experience is not necessary in order for people to embody moments of the past (Knight 2012a, 2012b, 2015a). Indeed, the Great Famine, which was responsible for over 300,000 deaths in Athens alone, had relatively little impact on western Thessaly, where people continued with subsistence agriculture and employed dense networks of resource sharing (Knight 2012a, 2015a; cf. Theodossopoulos 1997: 264). Yet these historical moments are still embodied in the present 'as if' they were experienced first-hand (cf. Serres 1995a: 57–59; Zerubavel 2003: 3).

I ask Eleni why certain moments of the past gain special significance during the current crisis. Holding up a large fossil to the sky, she says that time and memories are like a fossil bed. Some layers are seen, some hidden. The layers do not see the light in any particular (implying chronological) order. Certain layers in the folded rock are exposed, while others are destined to remain in darkness until a major event, such as the next earthquake (or, may I suggest, crisis), shakes them to the surface. Indeed, Eleni suggests that it may not even require an extravagant earth-moving event but perhaps just a rain shower to wash away a covering of mud or to provoke a landslide. After being twisted, tangled, and condensed under great heat and pressure, preserved moments of the past are brought to the fore by critical events (cf. Das 1995; Knight and Stewart 2017). But in some cases only part of the fossil is unearthed, part of the moment, part of the memory, leaving one to speculate what an untainted version might look like. Eleni says that we search for some memories akin to how we search for fossils, while others are forced to the surface by "earthquakes" or "torrents" that "shake up" time (cf. Pipyrou 2010; Serres 1995a). Perhaps we must think about topographies of time in addition to topologies.

When we return home, the fossils are cleaned and placed in a shoebox labeled with the date and location where they were found. They are put in chronological order in a bathroom cupboard on top of other labeled boxes containing the previous years' findings. The labels read "01/01/2009," "01/01/2010," "01/01/2011," and so on. Fossils that were embedded in folded, twisted layers are now boxed with their 'contemporaries' and linearly catalogued. Chronological stratification is not dead.

Topologies of Crisis Experience

When discussing economic crisis in central Greece, narrators jump from recounting oppression during the Ottoman era to the World War II occupation and the stock market crash at the turn of the twenty-first century. People articulate their relationship to the past, present, and future through objects and landscapes that transport them on multiple temporal trajectories (see also Bryant 2014). This chapter takes liberties with the topologies theme to follow informants as they 'bounce around' through the past, sewing together moments that help them make sense of their current social situation.

In contexts of severe crisis, moments of the past that appear distant in linear time are brought to the fore as people attempt to explain experiences of increasing poverty and suffering. Distant moments of the past are 'relived' in the present as actors invoke personal, intergenerational, and nationalized histories in order to render present conditions bearable or overcomable and to construct possible futures in the midst of chronic turmoil (Knight 2012a: 357; 2015a).

Taking inspiration from Michel Serres's (1995a) work on fluctuating and folded time, I propose that people in crisis-stricken central Greece experience time in a topological and topographical manner, rather than in a geometric, linear fashion as is generally the perception in Western late-capitalist societies. Time is fluctuating, folded, with currents and counter-currents (Serres 1995a: 58) that create a 'scrambled' experience of the past in the present. Furthermore, there are significant localized nuances in how people understand past events.

How specific moments of the past are experienced during the current crisis should be approached as more than simply a recollection of historical events. In Trikala, the crisis is understood as an assemblage of multiple 'rebirths' of past situations (Serres 1995a: 21, 42). Moments are relived, re-embodied. The past acts as a warning of what might be just around the corner, inciting fear and insecurity. But some moments also offer hope that current events are overcomable. It is not necessary for past events to have been experienced first-hand as accounts are transmitted from generation to generation or acquire official nationalized narratives (Knight 2012a: 354–355; 2015a; 2015c; Serres 1995b: 2). Contemporary crisis experience is thus the assemblage of different moments of social turmoil comprising multiple national and familial narratives and rhetorics of the past that provide the 'background noise' to everyday life (cf. Serres 1995b: 71–72).

Serres (1995a) theorizes time not merely as a 'passing', but as an extraordinarily complex mixture of disordered stopping points, ruptures, and gaps. He offers a theory of percolating and fluctuating time that dances like "flames in a brazier" (ibid.: 58): "Time doesn't flow; it percolates. This means precisely that it passes and doesn't pass ... one flux passes through, while another does not" (ibid.; see also Knight 2015a). The current crisis is the filter that provokes some moments of the past to resurface as people try to make sense of a rapidly changing social scene. Some segments of time get caught in the filtration process and remain contemporary, while others are forgotten or lie dormant, like the fossils, to be brought to the surface by the next critical event. Much like Eleni in the opening vignette, Serres (1995a: 58–61) invokes the natural environment to explain his experience of time, comparing it to fluctuations in the weather or to a river flowing beneath a bridge that has unforeseen countercurrents running under the surface in the opposite direction with hidden turbulences that remain out of sight to the casual observer. Describing how the past is preserved in order to elucidate later circumstances, Serres explains how a glacier may preserve a man's body, frozen for 50 years, that looks as young as when he had died, while his children (other memories) have grown old (ibid.: 61). Akin to how my informants discuss the Greek crisis, Serres's ponderings on topological time are rich in topographical metaphor.

As will be demonstrated through ethnographic vignettes collected in central Greece since the outbreak of economic crisis in 2009, the temporal proximity of specific moments of the past may vary from family to family, town to town, valley to valley. The past is experienced in a seemingly disordered, untidy manner, and it is the responsibility of the anthropologist to embrace this messy topology, awash with apparent paradoxes, and decipher the reasons behind locally meaningful historicities (Hirsch and Stewart 2005; Knight and Stewart 2017). This way, a polychromic mosaic of crisis experience can be constructed that does justice to local understandings of critical events. This is especially important when global economic and political bodies, the international media, and even academics continuously seek to make clear cuts in tangled flows of history and culture when discussing social and economic crises (Knight 2013a: 157; 2013b).

In following my informants' adventures through time, in this chapter I identify objects and landscapes as two nodes around which people orient themselves (see also Bryant 2014). When discussing fossils, attention turns to the landscape and recent programs advocating futuristic renewable energy developments on agricultural land. Further discussions on the occupation of the land lead to winding narratives of civil war conflict that vary between inhabitants of the plains and the mountains. Through representative ethnographic vignettes, I argue that topologies are deeply entwined with topographies since diverse moments of the past are experienced as temporally proximate in the context of economic crisis.

Tangible Histories

In western Thessaly, many people believe their future—the future that has been promised for the last 30 years—is over; it is already past. Present and future trajectories are overwhelmingly understood in terms of the past as collective memory is employed to lend meaning to unusual and sometimes inexplicable events. People rhetorically pose these questions: "Who are we?" "What have we become?" "Where are we now … *when* are we now?" In situations of upheaval and uncertainty, people critique historical events in an attempt to situate themselves within a trajectory (Bryant 2014; Kirtsoglou 2010: 2). Moments of the past are discussed and embodied on a daily basis, directly informing perceptions of the future, including shifting notions of modernity and progress (Knight 2014a: 21; 2015b). In some cases, the future is inseparable from the past, whether in terms of land ownership, hunger, or energy practice.

Local perceptions of time are often mediated through objects. Recent examples from the literature on southern Europe demonstrate how objects as diverse as items of food (Knight 2014a; Sutton 2001, 2011, 2014), religious icons (Stewart 2003, 2012), abandoned homes (Bryant 2014; Navaro-Yashin 2012), second-hand clothes (Pipyrou 2014), war debris (Henig 2012: 23), solar panels (Knight 2012b, 2015b), buried treasure (Stewart 2003, 2012), and dowry chests (Bryant 2014) possess the possibility to bend time. As Rebecca Bryant (2014: 683) following Serres has recently argued, objects have their own temporalities, containing different senses of rhythm, speed, and trajectory of time. The things in our lives have their own 'life span', inhabiting a time of their own that usually outlasts ours (ibid.: 682). In this case they can become "unopened time capsules" (Stewart 2003: 487), possessing a temporal dynamism capable of exploding, imploding, twisting, or braiding the past (Bryant 2014: 684). Objects thus mediate history and memory because of the ways in which they aid us in reorienting the relationship of past, present, and future.

Material objects are part of a wider array of "affective images and symbols" (Stewart 2012: 2) around which multifaceted "indigenous historicization" is centered (ibid.: 190), triggering intense historical consciousness that relates to events such as war and famine and to notions of modernity and belonging. This is not a linear perspective of historical continuity, but more a folded, contoured appreciation of historical moments that trigger a critique of the current social situation.

Returning to the opening anecdote, I thought that Eleni's family members were unique in their fossil hunting adventures. However, upon further inquiry, it became evident that many people from the Trikala/Kalampaka area venture into the mountains in search of 'Triassic treasure'. Another avid fossil hunter, Kostas, aged 35, tells me that it brings him "closer to history." Holding a tangible piece of the past in his hand reminds him that his existence and the present-day problems of Greece are insignificant—that the "world will continue to turn whether it is Mr. Samaras, Mr. Venizelos, or Papa Smurf" who eventually destroys the Greek state. The fact that the fossil beds upon which he stands cover a chronological range of 60 million years of inhospitable, unrelenting forces of nature automatically shifts his perspective on five years of Greek economic turmoil. Kostas seems to take some form of comfort from this.

On the day I accompany him into the mountains, Kostas pauses as we come to a high crest. Looking toward the vast Plain of Thessaly stretching toward Trikala and Larisa beyond, he asks me: "What do you see?" Before I have chance to respond, he answers his own question: "Occupation." Once the property of the Ottoman era and later the Greek *tsiflikades* (landlords of great estates), the Plain of Thessaly was divided into private property during the agrarian reforms of the early 1900s. Today, people in western Thessaly temporally condense the period of the *tsiflikades* with the Axis occupation of the 1940s, producing a combined narrative of occupation that they compare to the current suppression experienced in Troika-occupied Greece (with 'Troika' referring to the European Commission, the European Central Bank, and the International Monetary Fund). Notions of neo-colonialism are exacerbated by recent programs advocating land diversification toward renewable energy that openly promotes foreign technology (Argenti and Knight 2015; Knight and Bell 2013). As I stand on the ridge with Kostas, 500 meters below us, glimmering in the winter sun, 10 photovoltaic parks stand on prime agricultural land. Since the solar program was introduced in 2006, there has been a dramatic rise in the number of farmers installing photovoltaics, curtailed only recently by the announcement that the initiative has been frozen for the foreseeable future. The panels are often manufactured in Germany, and German investors have shown significant interest in recent plans to privatize the Greek energy sector as part of the Troika reforms. The energy produced by the panels is rarely consumed by the local community; instead, it is fed into the national grid to contribute to energy needs in urban centers. Local people have recently resorted to 'archaic' methods to heat their homes, burning whatever they can get their hands on to keep warm at night. Kostas repeats something that I have heard regularly over the last four years: "These are the new *tsiflikades*, the new occupying forces. The Germans have returned to take our land. The same rocks upon which we are standing are no longer Greek." Overlooking Kostas's implication that these 'rocks' had always been Greek, and in another twist to the story, due to a failing business Kostas himself has taken a 'second job'—installing both photovoltaic panels and ventilation systems for open fires.

Energizing Objects

A prominent way that people in western Thessaly discuss temporality refers to how the economic crisis has given birth to paradoxical energy practice. From home installations to developments on agricultural land and large solar parks producing energy for international export, photovoltaics has been heralded by the Greek government and the European Union as the future for year-round energy self-sufficiency for local people and as a means to repay the national debt (Argenti and Knight 2015; Knight 2012b: 66–67; 2013b; Knight and Bell 2013: 4). Despite the significant uptake in the solar program, the winters of 2012–2015 witnessed a return en masse to wood-burning open fires (*tzakia*) and stoves (*ksilosompes*), last popular during the 1960s and 1970s.

Two seemingly contrasting energy sources—high-tech photovoltaic panels and open wood-burning fires—have become highly visible material symbols of the economic crisis. Photovoltaics are associated with clean-green energy, futuristic sustainability, ground-breaking technology, ultra-modernity, and international political energy consensus. For local people, open fires conjure images of pre-modern unsustainability, pollution, poverty, and a return to 'village life' and peasantry status. Both are symptomatic of how people negotiate the Troika-enforced fiscal austerity measures, arousing notions of neo-colonialism and occupation (cf. Argenti and Knight 2015; Pipyrou 2014). Furthermore, both solar panels and *tzakia* have raised questions of future environmental impact and food sustainability. Because people can no longer afford high petrol prices to fuel their home central heating systems, thick smog now engulfs Greek towns on a nightly basis as people burn whatever they can, including old varnished furniture, shoes and clothes, and unsuitable firewood. Open fires have turned into a national health hazard, resulting in repeated government appeals for people to revert to petrol heating (see Knight 2014a).

Here I wish to offer some brief representative accounts of how people discuss history and temporality around objects of energy paraphernalia. Giota, aged 68, from Kalampaka, states:

> I remember the days back in the village when everyone had open fires. Now people are just burning anything, and it is so dangerous. People are choking on the thick air—my daughter has asthma and has recently experienced serious problems breathing … Back when I was a child we all used to have wood-burning fires, the whole village, but we knew what to burn and there wasn't the same feeling of desperation. It was normal then. But we thought this time had passed, we are Europeans now. We are all modern now. *Tzakia* are symbols of the past and of our poverty, unless you are a very rich person from Athens who thinks it is fashionable. I saw a report on television that compares what is happening in Athens with the smog from *tzakia* and *sompes* to the Industrial Revolution in England when London transport was stopped for two days as people could only see two meters through the smoke … We feel as though we have been forced back in time to another era of Greece, an era before the dictatorship [1967–1974] when Greece was cut off from the world. We are now supposedly in 'Europe' but actually we are back living in the past. Europe does not care about the impact of austerity on local people who may be starving or freezing to death. And the elites in our government for some reason continue to support them. Something is wrong. Like we say, "There is no smoke without fire."

Michalis, a 55-year-old farmer living near Karditsa, provides comment on the photovoltaic initiative:

> I am proud that I have the ability to change my lifestyle with the future in mind. It is not what I would have expected to do 10 years ago, and I would not have chosen to install photovoltaic panels on my home and land. But they *are* symbols of the future rather than symbols of destitution. I want to help my family and my nation in this moment of crisis. I am too old to pick up my gun and start a revolution. My father fought during World War II against occupation, but this time the intelligent thing is a little collaboration. I know what I am doing may seem manipulative, like colluding with the enemy, but nowadays putting food on the table for my family is more important. I cannot let them starve. While everybody else argues about who is to blame for this terrible crisis, I have put all my assets into creating some form of future for my family. We were not defeated by Ottoman

or German occupation, war, or military dictatorship. Photovoltaic panels are a sign of my defiance. I *will* overcome the economic crisis.

Michalis's narrative resonates with established patterns of 'defending the family' identified by John Campbell (1964), who distinguishes between the responsibilities of adolescents (*pallikaria*) and married men. A *pallikari* must assertively exhibit attitudes of manliness; he must be "prepared to die, if necessary, for the honour of his family or his country" (ibid.: 279). As such, the *pallikari* is the ideal of manhood. However, after marriage a man must exhibit characteristics of cleverness (*eksipnada*) and cunning (*poniria*), demonstrating a quickness of mind and a degree of foresight in protecting his family (ibid.: 280–282). Today, these attributes are still legitimate and praiseworthy where the family is the object of protection, even if this means foregoing conscience and pride. Michalis has shown considerable foresight by investing in photovoltaics, despite historically embedded reservations about 'collaboration'.

Giorgos, a 48-year-old farmer from Trikala, relates another perspective on the historicity involved in photovoltaic diversification:

> I hope that the photovoltaic program may help stop us returning to the situation of the 1960s and 1970s when we were so poor. But by embracing photovoltaics, people are signing over their lives to external forces. They tell me that I should let foreign companies put huge photovoltaic panels on my land—the land that my great-grandfather worked when it was part of a *tsifliki*, that he fought for against the landlords (*tsiflikades*), that my father fought for under German occupation, and that I want my son to work one day. Now, instead of producing cereal, it has 36 polycrystalline silicon-based German-manufactured solar panels, producing an estimated 150 kilowatt-hours of power. Just think of where we were 30 to 40 years ago and where we are now. We cannot write all that off immediately, but must adapt our style of living for the current situation … We have survived much worse in the past, but it is possible that these events will happen again. At this moment a combination of European-backed energy technology [photovoltaics] and 'old' ways of coping with crisis [saving money through wood burners] is the best way of dealing with a desperate situation.

In discussing the 'power relations of power', Michalis and Giorgos condense culturally proximate historical moments that may be distant in terms of linear time in order to explain present-day experiences. As the narrators move seamlessly between historical moments, the Ottoman and later Greek *tsiflikades* and the Axis occupation are condensed into one singularly meaningful moment to simultaneously provide a critique of the current situation and pass comment on possible future trajectories. Objects of energy practice provide connectivity to the past, present, and future and symbolize both fear and hope. Both photovoltaics and open fires represent complex assemblages of temporality: one seemingly looks to the past, while the other is markedly futuristic. This has led people to reflect on their place in modern Europe and question whether they belong to the West through materiality (see Herzfeld 1987; Knight 2014a).

Fossils, the sun, wood, and land are all employed to help people locate themselves in time and place. They are 'affective objects' inextricably linked to the landscape (Navaro-Yashin 2009). Diverse forms of materiality inform temporal assemblage and provide added dimensions to a historically situated "embroilment of subjects with objects" (ibid.: 8).

Topographies of Time: Different Pasts, Same Crisis

My theoretical muse, Michel Serres, and my informants employ the landscape to explicate their experiences of time and history. The landscape plays a prominent role in how local people discuss the past, and thus I suggest thinking about historical consciousness in terms of topography as well as topology. Topography (the surface shape and features of the earth) and topology (primarily the mathematical theory of connectedness and distortion) (see Serres 1995a: 60) are closely related and prove fruitful tools to successfully translate local life experiences. Here, topography refers to the study and depiction of physical features in the landscape, while topology is used to describe the relationships between objects. The past is entwined with the physical features of the landscape—mountains, valleys, caves, fossils, forests, the sun, mineral mines—which act as "indexes of the eventful past" (Stewart 2012: 196). Topography and the closely linked discipline of cartography can thus assist people in developing patterns to organize the past (Rosenberg and Grafton 2010; Zerubavel 2003: 110).

The relationship between the past, time, and the physical landscape has been explored in the ethnography of Greece and Cyprus in terms of icons (Stewart 2008, 2012), cartography (Stewart 1991), human remains (Danforth 1982; Sant Cassia 2005; Seremetakis 1991), buried artifacts (Bryant 2012; Hamilakis and Yalouri 1996), and displacement (Hirschon 1989; Navaro-Yashin 2009, 2012). In the present case, people's relations with the material landscape—from harnessing the power of the sun and burning wood to searching for fossils—reveal localized historicities (Stewart 2012: 21) and unlock "the affects generated by space and the non-human environment" (Navaro-Yashin 2009: 4).

During a two-hour drive into the Pindos Mountains, the topography of the past changes. It is particularly striking how, just a short distance away, people experience the current economic crisis through the embodiment of different moments of the past. On the plains of western Thessaly during this economic turmoil, the two most prominent narratives of past crises pertain to the Great Famine and conflated stories of Ottoman and German occupation. Yet in accounts of the "heavy historical load" (Thanassis Valtinos, cited in Papailias 2005: 139) of the 1940s crises, one aspect is always absent: the civil war.

The Greek Civil War (1946–1949) is not a salient part of collective memory in western Thessaly, and although aspects of history directly pertaining to the event are narrated, such as internal migrations or living conditions in makeshift housing, the conflict itself is absent from everyday discourse on the current economic crisis. The event is still considered collectively sinful, and radical differences are played down and denied through collective silence.

From 1974 onward, any remnants of internal blame for the civil war, brothers against brothers, were supposedly assigned to the pages of history, as a collective rhetoric against the external Other was adopted, denying any "internal divisions and ambiguities" (Marantzidis and Antoniou 2004: 225). Nonetheless, at the local level, the attempt to normalize historical relations had limited impact in western Thessaly. Selective remembering and forgetting are directly related to concepts of collectivization, unity, and division (Das 1995: 128–129), and as such the Great Famine is a collectivizing keystone event while the civil war is a divisive one.

However, the civil war is the key to unlocking contemporary crisis experience in other parts of mainland Greece where it regularly punctuates discourse on the present-day economic turmoil. In the Grevena region, my second field site in Greece, which is situated 1,200 meters into the Pindos Mountains of Western Macedonia, perceptions of history in the village of Kalimera are quite different. People respond to histories that move them (Stewart 2012: 8), and, as has been detailed by scholars such as Keith Brown (2003) and Jane Cowan (2000), historical consciousness in the Macedonian region can vary from one valley to the next. In Kalimera, the ambiguities and paradoxes of civil war regularly penetrate public discourse, and people articulate their experiences of the current economic crisis through an event that is silenced just two hours farther south. As we walk the mountainsides picking mushrooms (see Knight 2014b), Haido tells me:

> I can't remember a time like this since the civil war … that time tore the village apart. We have never recovered properly. My husband fought for the Communist resistance and disappeared in 1947. I was 22 years old. I have waited for him ever since. My brother, Dimitris, joined the nationalists and was kidnapped by the Communist side and his body was never discovered. But we know he was kidnapped and last seen north of the Albanian border. My brother-in-law was murdered outside the church as he was suspected of being a government sympathizer … When the Italians invaded and occupied the village in 1940, it was okay, they didn't do any harm. We actually had to look after them as they were starving and freezing to death. But the civil war is what haunts the mind … Nowadays when you hear of the violence in Athens and see pictures of people homeless and starving on the streets, and then listen to the extremist political views of Golden Dawn, you have to think that we are returning to this time [of the civil war].

The poignancy of the event transcends generations of residents in Kalimera. Panagiotis, aged 27, relives the events his grandfather witnessed:

> Today I feel I am living the stories of my grandfather. They feel closer than ever, more painful than ever. He lived here during the civil war. In the evenings the Communist soldiers would come down from those caves over there [he points in the direction of an adjacent hillside] and demand food from people in the village. If you could not provide it, they would take something else. My uncle was taken from his bed at the age of 12. The majority of the villagers just wanted to get on with a normal life, but this is never reported in history. Every landmark in these mountains has a tale to tell. You can feel the history. I am terrified that our

nation is heading once again toward those dark times. People cannot take any more austerity or they will snap. Those times are close—I feel it in my bones. In fact, I think it is already happening.

Panagiotis's claims of tangible history through the landscape are supported by other villagers who maintain that they can, "touch the history through a single walk in the mountains and the forests, or a single visit to remote chapels … you can feel the wars, you can see the people" (Knight 2014b: 187). Their accounts of the civil war are passionate and authoritative and transgress the 70 years of spatial and temporal transformation. Panagiotis understands the warning signs of further crisis and interprets them in terms of reliving his grandfather's experiences of the civil war. The warning, according to Nadia Seremetakis (1991: 48), "is a knowledge of future events and processes that are manifested in the present through a conventional system of signs." Warnings intertwine "the natural and the social world, life and death" (ibid.). Panagiotis feels that the event—the civil war—is already happening. It is part of the contemporary crisis experience, part of the assemblage, and has penetrated both past and future histories.

Fernand Braudel (1949) recognizes how collective histories are tangled up in the relationship between sea, plain, and mountains. Following this line, Peregrine Horden (2005) argues that social and economic inconsistencies can be the remnants of extreme topographical fragmentation. Horden attributes this fragmentation to the "tectonics of the region" (ibid.: 29) that influence 'micro-ecologies' of society, economics, and history. Micro-ecologies are embedded in localized perceptions of landscape as much as in physical topographical particularity. Although this may sound deterministic at first, what Horden suggests is that people's affective interactions with the landscape inform unpredictable, fluid, and mutable socio-historical creations (cf. Braudel 1949). Here we have topology and topography working hand in hand, which helps to explain the differences in proximate affective history displayed in western Thessaly and in Kalimera.

The significance of specific moments of the past employed to explain national crisis differs according to locale. This gives another meaning to the notion of keeping "memory 'in place'" (Papailias 2005: 1). However, in a Braudelian sense, the "topography of spatial and temporal irregularities" (Dimova 2013: 210) is also systemically interrelated since crisis experience is constructed around "biology, archaeology, linguistics, and history" (Navaro-Yashin 2009: 13, referencing Deleuze and Guattari). The moments of the past assembled to explain the economic crisis experience in the two locales are at once "so different yet so alike" (Braudel 1976: 1239; see also Horden and Purcell 2006: 724). They are interconnected in a topological and topographical manner.

(In)conclusive remarks

With topologies as the topic of this collection, I have taken the liberty to 'bounce around' through history without much order or, some may say, coherence. But this is exactly what my informants do. Temporal leaps occur as people move from the early-nineteenth-century Ottoman era to Troika-austerity Greece, collapsing the *tsiflikades* with the Axis occupation and condensing nationalized accounts with personal experience. Past, present, and future are embraced within a single moment. This is often something that cannot be captured by solely discussing collective memory, because it is a messy reliving of multiple moments of the past. Accounts are mediated by objects or landmarks that symbolize and facilitate temporal trajectories.

Charles Stewart (2012: 202) mentions that fossils stimulate historical imagination as they represent both something old, since they were created 200 million years ago, and something new, since they have only recently been discovered. Moments of the past are also 'recently rediscovered' in the wake of the current economic crisis. Photovoltaic panels not only represent Ottoman and Axis occupation, but also provide hope via their high-tech futurity. *Tzakia* symbolize pre-modern village life but also new employment opportunities for entrepreneurial mechanics.

It is equally important to accommodate the local and regional nuances of crisis experience. The Athens-centric perspective prominent in the international mass media represents the next stage of reproducing a homogeneous national history of a critical event—in this case, the economic crisis experience. However, as the present chapter demonstrates, understandings of both past and present crises differ greatly between landscapes just 40 minutes or two hours apart. These seemingly competing local discourses of crisis experience must be embraced. Heterogeneous historical moments sourced from many temporal points are fused together to form an assemblage of contemporaneity (Deleuze 1991: 38). The heterogeneous nature of multiple moments makes for an uncertain and unforeseeable future not necessarily bound to the present or to any singular historical era (Hodges 2007). Owing to the sudden and unexpected change enforced in the form of fiscal crisis, for people in western Thessaly futures once promised as a birthright in the European neoliberal world have been thrown into disarray (cf. Knight 2014a, 2015c; Price 2012). Experiences of the present crisis are fusions of instances of organic and inorganic matter—an "active synthesis," a temporal "scrambling" (Stewart 2012: 191). In linear time, distant events are "brought into close proximity, into a singularly meaningful moment where past and future are superimposed" (Knight 2014a: 5; see also Hirsch and Stewart 2005: 261; Knight 2012a: 350; Serres 1995a: 57–59; Stewart 2012: 193).

In the face of Western concepts of living for the future rather than the past, understanding local perceptions of time as topological and/or topographical enriches the study of crisis experience. Thirty years of prosperity in these Greek communities has been abruptly ruptured, thrusting people into a state of confusion. The past offers direction for both the present crisis experience and for people's future life trajectory. Photovoltaic panels, *tzakia*, and fossils are characteristic of different understandings of trajectory and shape the rhythm and orientation of temporalities.

Acknowledgments

I would like to express thanks to participants in the British School at Athens conference "Balkan Topologies," workshops at the University of Oxford and Durham University, the 2014 American Anthropological Association annual meeting in Washington, DC, and the 2015 American Ethnological Society spring conference in San Diego for comments on sections of this chapter.

Daniel M. Knight is a Lecturer in Social Anthropology and Leverhulme Fellow at the University of St Andrews and a Visiting Fellow at the Hellenic Observatory, London School of Economics and Political Science. He has published on crisis, time, temporality, historicity, neo-liberalism, neo-colonialism, and renewable energy initiatives. He is the author of *History, Time, and Economic Crisis in Central Greece* (2015), co-editor (with Charles Stewart) of *Ethnographies of Austerity: Temporality, Crisis and Affect in Southern Europe* (2017), and associate editor of the journal *History and Anthropology*.

References

Argenti, Nicolas, and Daniel M. Knight. 2015. "Sun, Wind, and the Rebirth of Extractive Economies: Renewable Energy Investment and Metanarratives of Crisis in Greece." *Journal of the Royal Anthropological Institute* 21 (4): 781–802.
Braudel, Fernand. 1949. *The Mediterranean and the Mediterranean World in the Age of Philip II*. Vol. 1. Trans. Siân Reynolds. Berkeley: University of California Press.
Braudel, Fernand. 1976. *The Mediterranean and the Mediterranean World in the Age of Philip II*. Vol. 2. Trans. Siân Reynolds. Berkeley: University of California Press.
Brown, Keith. 2003. *The Past in Question: Modern Macedonia and the Uncertainties of Nation*. Princeton, NJ: Princeton University Press.
Bryant, Rebecca. 2012. "The Fractures of a Struggle: Remembering and Forgetting Erenköy." In *Cyprus and the Politics of Memory: History, Community and Conflict*, ed. Rebecca Bryant and Yiannis Papadakis, 168–194. London: I.B. Tauris.
Bryant, Rebecca. 2014. "History's Remainders: On Time and Objects after Conflict in Cyprus." *American Ethnologist* 41 (4): 681–697.
Campbell, J. K. 1964. *Honour, Family and Patronage: A Study of Institutions and Moral Values in a Greek Mountain Community*. Oxford: Oxford University Press.
Cowan, Jane K., ed. 2000. *Macedonia: The Politics of Identity and Difference*. London: Pluto Press.
Danforth, Loring. 1982. *The Death Rituals of Rural Greece*. Princeton, NJ: Princeton University Press.
Das, Veena. 1995. *Critical Events: An Anthropological Perspective on Contemporary India*. Delhi: Oxford University Press.
Deleuze, Gilles. 1991. *Bergsonism*. Trans. Hugh Tomlinson and Barbara Habberjam. New York: Zone Books.
Dimova, Rozita. 2013. "Topography of Spatial and Temporal Ruptures: (Im)materialities of (Post)socialism in a Northern Town in Macedonia." In *Macedonia: The Political,*

Social, Economic and Cultural Foundations of a Balkan State, ed. Victor C. de Munck and Ljupcho Risteski, 210–231. London: I.B. Tauris.
Hamilakis, Yannis, and Eleana Yalouri. 1996. "Antiquities as Symbolic Capital in Modern Greek Society." *Antiquity* 70 (267): 117–129.
Henig, David. 2012. "Iron in the Soil: Living with Military Waste in Bosnia-Herzegovina." *Anthropology Today* 28 (1): 21–23.
Herzfeld, Michael. 1987. *Anthropology Through the Looking-Glass: Critical Ethnography in the Margins of Europe*. Cambridge: Cambridge University Press.
Hirsch, Eric, and Charles Stewart. 2005. "Introduction: Ethnographies of Historicity." *History and Anthropology* 16 (3): 261–274.
Hirschon, Renée. 1989. *Heirs of the Greek Catastrophe: The Social Life of Asia Minor Refugees in Piraeus*. New York: Berghahn Books.
Hirschon, Renée. 2014. "Cultural Mismatches: Greek Concepts of Time, Personal Identity, and Authority in the Context of Europe." In *Europe in Modern Greek History*, ed. Kevin Featherstone, 153–170. London: Hurst.
Hodges, Matt. 2007. *The Ethnography of Time: Living with History in Modern Rural France*. Lampeter: Edwin Mellen Press.
Horden, Peregrine. 2005. "Mediterranean Excuses: Historical Writing on the Mediterranean since Braudel." *History and Anthropology* 16 (1): 25–30.
Horden, Peregrine, and Nicholas Purcell. 2006. "The Mediterranean and 'the New Thalassology.'" *American Historical Review* 111 (3): 722–740.
Kirtsoglou, Elisabeth. 2010. "Introduction: Rhetoric and the Workings of Power—the Social Contract in Crisis." *Social Analysis* 54 (1): 1–14.
Knight, Daniel M. 2012a. "Cultural Proximity: Crisis, Time and Social Memory in Central Greece." *History and Anthropology* 23 (3): 349–374.
Knight, Daniel M. 2012b. "Turn of the Screw: Narratives of History and Economy in the Greek Crisis." *Journal of Mediterranean Studies* 21 (1): 53–76.
Knight, Daniel M. 2013a. "The Greek Economic Crisis as Trope." *Focaal: Journal of Global and Historical Anthropology* 65: 147–159.
Knight, Daniel M. 2013b. "Your Money or Your Life: Misunderstandings of Greek Austerity." *Anthropology News* 54 (6): 11–12.
Knight, Daniel M. 2014a. "A Critical Perspective on Economy, Modernity and Temporality in Contemporary Greece through the Prism of Energy Practice." GreeSE Paper No. 81, Hellenic Observatory Papers on Greece and Southeast Europe, London School of Economics and Political Science.
Knight, Daniel M. 2014b. "Mushrooms, Knowledge Exchange and Polytemporality in Kalloni, Greek Macedonia." *Food, Culture & Society* 17 (2): 183–201.
Knight, Daniel M. 2015a. *History, Time, and Economic Crisis in Central Greece*. New York: Palgrave Macmillan.
Knight, Daniel M. 2015b. "Opportunism and Diversification: Entrepreneurship and Livelihood Strategies in Uncertain Times." *Ethnos: Journal of Anthropology* 80 (1): 117–144.
Knight, Daniel M. 2015c. "Wit and Greece's Economic Crisis: Ironic Slogans, Food, and Antiausterity Sentiments." *American Ethnologist* 42 (2): 230–246.
Knight, Daniel M., and Sandra Bell. 2013. "Pandora's Box: Photovoltaic Energy and Economic Crisis in Greece." *American Institute of Physics Journal of Renewable and Sustainable Energy* 5 (3): 1–16.
Knight, Daniel M., and Charles Stewart, eds. 2017. *Ethnographies of Austerity: Temporality, Crisis and Affect in Southern Europe*. London: Routledge. Originally published in 2016 as a special issue of *History and Anthropology* 27 (1).

Marantzidis, Nikos, and Giorgos Antoniou. 2004. "The Axis Occupation and Civil War: Changing Trends in Greek Historiography, 1941–2002." *Journal of Peace Research* 41 (2): 223–231.

Navaro-Yashin, Yael. 2009. "Affective Spaces, Melancholic Objects: Ruination and the Production of Anthropological Knowledge." *Journal of the Royal Anthropological Institute* 15 (1): 1–18.

Navaro-Yashin, Yael. 2012. *The Make-Believe Space: Affective Geography in a Postwar Polity*. Durham, NC: Duke University Press.

Papailias, Penelope. 2005. *Genres of Recollection: Archival Poetics and Modern Greece*. New York: Palgrave Macmillan.

Pipyrou, Stavroula. 2010. "Urbanities: Grecanici Migration to the City of Reggio Calabria, South Italy." *History and Anthropology* 21 (1): 19–36.

Pipyrou, Stavroula. 2014. "Cutting *Bella Figura*: Irony, Crisis, and Secondhand Clothes in South Italy." *American Ethnologist* 41 (3): 532–546.

Rosenberg, Daniel, and Anthony Grafton. 2010. *Cartographies of Time: A History of the Timeline*. New York: Princeton Architectural Press.

Sant Cassia, Paul. 2005. *Bodies of Evidence: Burial, Memory and the Recovery of Missing Persons in Cyprus*. New York: Berghahn Books.

Seremetakis, C. Nadia. 1991. *The Last Word: Women, Death, and Divination in Inner Mani*. Chicago: University of Chicago Press.

Serres, Michel, with Bruno Latour. 1995a. *Conversations on Science, Culture, and Time*. Trans. Roxanne Lapidus. Ann Arbor: University of Michigan Press.

Serres, Michel. 1995b. *Genesis*. Trans. Geneviève James and James Nielson. Ann Arbor: University of Michigan Press.

Stewart, Charles. 1991. *Demons and the Devil: Moral Imagination in Modern Greek Culture*. Princeton, NJ: Princeton University Press.

Stewart, Charles. 2003. "Dreams of Treasure: Temporality, Historicization and the Unconscious." *Anthropological Theory* 3 (4): 481–500.

Stewart, Charles. 2008. "Dreaming of Buried Icons in the Kingdom of Greece." In *Networks of Power in Modern Greece: Essays in Honour of John Campbell*, ed. Mark Mazower, 89–108. London: Hurst.

Stewart, Charles. 2012. *Dreaming and Historical Consciousness in Island Greece*. Cambridge, MA: Harvard University Press.

Sutton, David. 2001. *Remembrance of Repasts: An Anthropology of Food and Memory*. Oxford: Berg.

Sutton, David. 2011. "Memory as a Sense: A Gustemological Approach." *Food, Culture & Society* 14 (4): 468–475.

Sutton, David. 2014. *Secrets from the Greek Kitchen: Cooking, Skill, and Everyday Life on an Aegean Island*. Berkeley: University of California Press.

Theodossopoulos, Dimitrios. 1997. "Turtles, Farmers and 'Ecologists': The Cultural Reason behind a Community's Resistance to Environmental Conservation." *Journal of Mediterranean Studies* 7 (2): 250–267.

Zerubavel, Eviatar. 2003. *Time Maps: Collective Memory and the Social Shape of the Past*. Chicago: University of Chicago Press.

Chapter 2

PRAYER AS A HISTORY
Of Witnesses, Martyrs, and Plural Pasts in Post-war Bosnia-Herzegovina

David Henig

"And at the end, one more prayer for Ottoman martyrs and for Bosniak martyrs," said the imam to the assembly of male Muslims who had gathered for one of the annual outdoor rain prayer feasts in the Central Bosnian highlands in the summer of 2009. "You are witnessing," the imam continued, "by your prayers, by your presence here at this place, the history and continuity of Bosniaks in this region. You are witnessing and confirming our tradition, which has been sustained despite all the attempts to silence us."

The very place of the outdoor prayers (*dovište*), which the imam intertwined with a grand national narrative of the Bosnian War, suffering, and survival in his speech, is nestled in the verdant foothills of the Zvijezda highlands, a historically significant Muslim area in Central Bosnia. The prayer site itself has

Notes for this chapter begin on page 55.

an enormous old lime tree instead of a mihrab in its center, facing in the direction of Mecca, and a cluster of old graves of unknown Ottoman soldiers to the rear, recognized in the vernacular as *šehitluci*—a burial site for Muslim martyrs. These graves are venerated by individual Muslims living in the vicinity or farther afield who pray for the souls of the dead and access divine blessing (*berićet*). For village Muslims, praying for the souls of the dead is a moment of remembrance as well as an act of vital exchange: translated into the language of prayer economy, it is an act that earns good deeds. The person receives in return good fortune and blessings for the living. Thus, there is a perpetual exchange of blessings and prayers on the sacred sites that maintains vital relations between the past and the present (Henig n.d.). In turn, the recent war events have also been absorbed into the prayer economy of vital exchange and have become part of the local histories.

Prayer as a History

This chapter, as an exercise in the ethnography of history (Hirsch and Stewart 2005; Lambek 2002), specifically focuses on how Bosnian Muslims, living in the historical imperial frontiers of the Ottoman and the Austro-Hungarian empires, make and experience history. An ethnography of history is understood here as "the variety of modes in which people learn about and represent the past" (C. Stewart 2012: 7), which goes beyond linearized accounts of historical imagination and consciousness. One such attempt has been offered by Charles Stewart, based on his fieldwork in Naxos, Greece. For Naxos islanders, as Stewart persuasively demonstrates, this involves an enduring and widespread dream faculty as a mode of islanders' engagement with the past. In his recent book, Stewart (ibid.) portrays the Naxos's dreamscape as an assemblage of the affective sensibilities, materialities, practices, and moral-cum-temporal orientations that bundle Naxos islanders' historical consciousness together.

In Central Bosnia, I argue here, the mode of historical consciousness, whereby village Muslims engage with the past, can be attended to through the very act of prayer, as the introductory vignette illustrates. Although the act of prayer is important for Muslims' individual eschatology (Henkel 2005), it is also oriented toward the 'plural pasts' as a cultural model of engagement with the dead and with past events or places. Anthropologists have recognized that prayer is a mode of action with the capacity and efficacy to 'invoke' or 'engage with' a multiplicity of agencies, relations, and exchanges (Fortes 1987: 22–36; Mauss [1909] 2003). In his writing on prayer, Marcel Mauss ([1909] 2003: 22) suggests that prayer is a mode of action that "is often as rich in ideas and images as a religious narrative." We can modify Mauss's argument and conceive of prayer in similar terms as a historical narrative. Therefore, the act of prayer has the capacity to become, topologically speaking, a mode of action that maintains the "insistent immanence of plural pasts" in the present (Argenti, introduction).

The act of prayer as a mode of engagement with the plural pasts reanimates a widely held perspective on issues of post-Ottoman histories, memories, and temporalities, which are predominantly discussed as being in a fatal embrace with nationalism. Rather unsurprisingly, the prayers remembering Ottoman and Bosniak martyrs have also become an indispensable part of highly nationalized political life in post-war Bosnia-Herzegovina. However, praying for a good afterlife for the souls (*duše*) of the martyrs also continues to be apprehended by Bosnian Muslims as part of the individual ethical conduct of being a good Muslim. Put differently, these moments of remembrance are neither solely politically charged performances of Bosniak ethno-national identity nor instances of the nationalistic grand narratives that gained significant prominence in the Bosnian political life during and after the end of the 1990s war. Such narratives often dominate scholarship on post-war Bosnia-Herzegovina, but they can be found in other war-torn, post-conflict polities when it comes to questions about the ways in which people and polities produce knowledge about their violent pasts (cf. Argenti and Schramm 2010). This perspective, labeled as the 'politics of memory' (Hacking 1996), reduces the rich texture of historical experiences into one dimension—that of a public political teleological discourse on collective identity and memory. However, as Nicolas Argenti argues in the introduction to this collection, the great majority of memory literature ignores the immanence of plural pasts in the present. As Argenti puts it, the social fact "is not the memory of the past but its presence" in multiple instantiations. How can we, then, attend ethnographically to such multi-temporalities in the lived human experience?

In this chapter I take the route of an ethnography of history to explore the nexus of memory politics with grassroots affective sensibilities, materialities, and practices as modalities of engagement with the past. This nexus constitutes and reconstitutes what I describe here heuristically as 'vernacular histories' in which grand (nationalized) historical narratives, local historical consciousness, and personal memories intersect. The nexus of these divergent moral-cum-temporal orientations and modalities of engagement with the plural pasts in the present is embedded in narratives and conversations as much as it is inscribed into the landscape and trees, buildings and ruins, and people's bodies (Henig 2012). Seen in this light, the highly nationalized public discourse is just one fold in the multi-layered *topoi* of the past as it is lived and experienced in the present. Specifically, I focus on two local idioms of historical consciousness—witness (*šahit*) and martyr (*šehit*)—that emerge from the very act of prayer in particular sites of vernacular history. I trace how these idioms have become used more widely as a mode of engagement with more recent violent critical events, thus pluralizing the experiences of the pasts in the present.[1] I argue that tracing vernacular idioms, instantiated in specific moments of human situation, enables us to pinpoint how human actions interact with specific materials and places and in the realms of morality and politics to become specific modes of moral-cum-temporal orientations toward the plural pasts in the present. It is this tension and negotiation between hegemonic and grand historical narratives, on the one hand, and grassroots historical consciousness, on the other, that I want to address in this chapter.

Framing: 'The War' as a Critical Event

In her writing on the intersections of larger historical circumstances and everyday life, Veena Das (1995) coined the term 'critical events'. Critical events, such as the Partition of India and Pakistan in 1947 or the Bosnian War in the 1990s, create a frame of reference for stories of individual lives as well as those of communities and nations. The concept of critical events provides a useful frame to explore how "the memory of such events is folded into ongoing relationships" (Das 2007: 8), and thus how history, framed in critical events, is lived and shapes the present in a multiplicity of ways.

The emergence of prayers for Ottoman and Bosniak martyrs in post-war times illustrates the play of critical events in the historical consciousness of Bosnian Muslims and in the nationalistic cosmology. The Ottoman past in the *topos* of historical consciousness is not always articulated so clearly in the public discourses in post-war Bosnia-Herzegovina. Yet it intersects during the events of collective prayers, such as the prayers for rain, or through personal interactions in search of fortune and blessing with the burial sites for Ottoman martyrs (*šehitluci*), scattered across the landscape. On the other hand, World War II and especially the recent Bosnian War in the 1990s are vividly articulated during these gatherings and framed as 'the war' (*rat*).

FIGURE 2.1 *Šehitluci*—a burial site for unknown Ottoman soldiers in the Central Bosnian highlands

Photograph © David Henig

However, there is a disjuncture between critical events as lived frameworks of reference of past-present relationships and as sites of engagement with the past and their appropriation by nationalist grand narratives and cosmologies (cf. Kapferer 1988).[2] This tension is not uniquely Bosnian (see other chapters in this collection). In a similar vein, Michael Herzfeld (1991) describes the disjuncture between monumental and social time. Monumental time is the frame of the nation-state based on bureaucratic measures of history—generic, reductive, and supreme (ibid.: 10). Social time, however, is manifold, affective, and embodied; it is the time frame of everyday experience (ibid.). Herzfeld documents how the nation-state recasts the past in terms of a monolithic, chronological, and thus teleological—nationalized—present and creates 'traditional monuments' or 'gatherings' that often do not conform with everyday experiences (ibid.), that is, with social time and vernacular histories.

Similarly, for Muslims in post-war Bosnia-Herzegovina, it is the most recent war, epitomized by the Srebrenica massacre, the destruction of the bridge in Mostar, and the Sarajevo siege, that forms the basis for the bureaucratization and monumentalization of the past (cf. Hayden 2007; Wagner 2008), including the cult of martyrdom of Bosniaks killed during the conflict (Bougarel 2007). This process of monumentalization of the past in the present attempts to appropriate narratives of suffering and loss into the grand national narratives and cosmologies. However, the Bosniak politics of memory is not a unanimous process. These attempts to monumentalize critical events of the violent past— of martyrdom, for example—resonate as much as provoke anxieties among Bosnian Muslims, who witnessed the violence and suffering during the war and have participated in the monumentalized critical events. The two local idioms of historical consciousness—that of witness (šahit) and of martyr (šehit), which emerge during acts of prayer and also in the public discourses—thus capture the intricate relationship between monumentalized and lived critical events that co-create vernacular histories in Muslim Bosnia.

Beyond Discoursology

During my fieldwork on vernacular Muslim cosmologies in Central Bosnia, which began in 2008, I could hardly avoid encountering the recent painful memories and atrocities of the 1990s war. 'The war' constitutes a significant frame of reference for talking about and reflecting on the past in the present and on the present.[3] However, as argued above, it would be too easy to see such referential frameworks solely as highly nationalized public reflections and performances on past events. Rather, the past is always immanently present in the present in multiple forms.

Indeed, in the municipalities and villages, commemorative monuments have been erected since the end of the war, reminding everyone about the atrocities of the conflict. In every village cemetery there are a number of martyr graves. Since the end of the war, countless anniversaries and commemorative events have been launched, organized, and institutionalized by municipalities, cantons, and the official Muslim body, the Islamic Community (Islamska Zajednica). Critical events have entered the textbooks, television programs, and radio shows to be reinvoked regularly. In sum, the Bosnian War has been incorporated into Bosniak national cosmologies as *the* critical event and has become a constitutive part of memory politics.[4] The war has thus become a monumental mode of temporalization of the past in the present.

Much has been written about how the critical events of the war have been embedded in national discourses on Bosniak collective identity and memory. What is somewhat lacking in these accounts is a more nuanced analysis of the nexus whereby nationalized critical events and vernacular histories cocreate historical consciousness—specifically, how these critical events have been embedded in the cultural models and modes of engagement with the plural past in the present through such modes as prayers, holy site visitations (*zijaret*), and caring for the sacred landscape as a way of making history.

To overcome the discoursology of the monumentalized past, I therefore suggest tracing connections and entanglements among multiple forms of engagement with the past—such as the politics of memory, nationalistic discourses, and individual piety—rather than apprehending these as clearly separated, in order to understand vernacular history in-the-making. The emergence of the cult of martyrdom and the shifting referential frameworks of the local idioms *šehit* (martyr) and *šahit* (witness) are particularly significant for understanding Bosnian Muslims' engagements with the plural pasts in the present. In what follows, I shall discuss two examples of this process: the annual commemorative gathering of the Srebrenica massacre and the less well-known—but for Muslims living in the Central Bosnian highlands equally important—annual gathering of prayer for martyrs in Solun in the nearby Olovo municipality.

Of Martyrs

The Srebrenica massacre, during which over 8,000 male Bosniaks were killed in 1995, has become an iconic trope of the violent dissolution of Yugoslavia. It has become a critical event that shapes historical consciousness for a great number of individuals and families as well as the grand Bosniak national narratives, collective imagination, and monumentalization of the past. Srebrenica as a place indexes in the Bosniak political cosmology an *axis mundi* of the post-war Bosniak nation, where death, loss, and rebirth come together. When thinking of Srebrenica as a past-present frame of reference, it is important to distinguish between the massacre as such, its individual memorialization, and the subsequent collective monumentalization.

In her lucid ethnography of the identification of the Srebrenica missing persons, Sarah Wagner (2008) explores in great detail the aftermath of the massacre. In particular, she analyzes the complex entanglement of science, national politics, and religious imagination in the processes of identification of the missing persons. Wagner describes the opaqueness of the interval of absence during which a person is missing—meaning neither dead nor alive—and is thus for the time being suspended from history. The process of identification of dead bodies, then, is a form of retemporalization, bringing the identified persons back to history and reframing them in a new political cosmology as Bosniak martyrs.[5] More importantly, Wagner (ibid.: 185ff.) chronicles the Srebrenica memorial service as it developed during the early 2000s, culminating in 2005 on the tenth anniversary of the massacre, and its overall institutionalization and monumentalization. She documents how and why Srebrenica became the most important and most media-covered commemorative event in post-war Bosnia-Herzegovina.

I am sympathetic with Wagner's analysis, but I would like to move it a step further. Specifically, I am concerned with the relationship between the Srebrenica massacre as a critical event and its cult of martyrs and how these intersect with moral-cum-temporal knowledge about the past in the present outside of the immediate Srebrenica context in the Central Bosnian highlands. I ask what the memories of the massacre and its monumentalization do to moral-cum-temporal orientations outside the memorial site or to individuals who did not necessarily lose anyone in the massacre and yet have also been encompassed in the grand national narratives of Srebrenica suffering, as Bosnian Muslims and as witnesses of the war.

According to Wagner (2008: 213), the annual commemorative gathering in Srebrenica is not a Muslim pilgrimage, although an inevitable part of the gathering is a collective daily prayer (*namaz*), followed by a *dženaza* (Muslim funeral) for newly identified bodies. However, I suggest that we should not be so quick to distinguish between the commemoration and the act of prayer. Despite the ongoing monumentalization of the Srebrenica massacre, the commemorative service, and the burial of newly identified bodies, the gathering is now leaning toward being a pilgrimage for many Bosnian Muslims. Let us look more closely at the choreography of the commemorative event. In 2009, when he was about to start prayers after his speech, Grand Mufti Mustafa Cerić explained that the prayer would effectively join two of the five daily prayers (mid-day and afternoon prayers) because people in the audience were pilgrims, and this is what a journeying Muslim normally does. Moreover, he kept addressing the audience as 'pilgrims' (*putnici*) throughout the gathering. Furthermore, the date of the event, 11 July, has been introduced into *Takvim*, the official Muslim religious calendar, which is issued by the Bosnian Islamic Community and used daily by pious Muslims to decipher exact prayer times and also to follow important dates of feasts and pilgrimages. Thus, the attendees at the annual gathering are not just relatives of the newly identified martyrs. For many Bosnian Muslims, attending the Srebrenica annual gathering is a patriotic performance as much as a pious act in the individual ethical conduct of being a good Muslim. Hence, participation in the Srebrenica gathering has become a way for an increasing number of Bosnian Muslims, who did not necessarily lose anyone in the massacre, to relate to this critical event of the past in the present through visiting, pilgrimage, commemoration, and prayers for the deceased martyrs.

During my fieldwork in the Central Bosnian highlands, the memorial service on 11 July was widely and vigorously discussed by many village Muslims over coffee and neighborhood visits, as well as during Friday sermons (*džuma*) in the mosques. The local branches of the Islamic Community organized bus trips on that date, usually free of charge. Recurring themes in daily conversations focused on "who has already been there" or the desire to attend "at least once in my life."[6] Asking my interlocutors whether going to Srebrenica was a pious or patriotic act would not make much sense. "Why do you feel so strongly that you should go there?" I asked my friends Mujo, Ika, and Nijas and other villagers. The straightforward reply was "I want to pray there for the souls of the martyrs and thus witness what happened." And the local way to engage with the past in the present is to venerate the site and pray.

However, this is not the only way that villagers commemorate and relate to critical past events in the present. Let me invoke Das's argument again. Critical events create a frame of reference for the stories and memories of individual lives and help to make sense of the shattered world in their aftermath. Indeed, the Srebrenica events were the focus of attention for many days before and after the memorial date. For example, in 2009 I briefly visited the capital Sarajevo before the date of the Srebrenica massacre. On the way back to the villages, I traveled on a bus with a few known faces from the municipality. Listening to news and gossip without even asking about the upcoming Srebrenica commemorative events, I was told that "nothing happened. It's been raining all the time and will last until Sunday, after the funeral in Srebrenica is over. It's always been like that because the sky is crying as well." When I eventually arrived at the village where I was staying, I was given almost the same explanation: "The sky is crying, the rain is Allah's tears."

It was not just the weather that resonated and invoked the events of the past in the present. On the commemorative day during my fieldwork, the village was silent. People stayed in their homes, watching live broadcasts from Srebrenica and other documentaries and programs on television, and the sawmills did not run. While viewing programs about Srebrenica and discussing them, villagers invoked their own recollections and memories of the critical time. At one moment, as we were sitting round a table, one of the women in the room, Ika, burst into tears as she told us her seemingly idiosyncratic story:

> I was living in a place nearby Kladanj. Many refugees from Srebrenica passed through the village at the time. It was quite common for the buses to stop there, and we brought water and bread for refugees. Sometimes we took them into the house, to let them have a shower, rest a little bit, eat something. My sister once brought four girls [as she says this, Ika is breathlessly crying]. They were traumatized and in shock, they were stressfully holding each other's hands. So when my sister offered them a shower, they couldn't because the girls were still holding each other's hand—that's how frightened they were, they simply couldn't. It was so painful for me, I took them to our bedroom, opened the wardrobe, and told them "feel free to take any item of clothing," to make them feel more relaxed. They didn't take anything, just a little bit of food.

For Ika, the Srebrenica massacre intersects with the memory of this traumatic moment of witnessing something she could not, and still cannot, fully comprehend. Rather than partaking in a monumentalized commemorative service as a means to remember the past in the present, for many villagers the mode of invoking this critical event is an affective and experiential one, such as witnessing rain as Allah's tears. Ika's remembrance of trembling bodies, four pairs of hands stressfully holding each other, and gestures of hospitality to reassure the refugees remains unheard and haunts her to this day.

In a similar vein, Charles Stewart (2012) and Yael Navaro-Yashin (2012) have shown that there is not necessarily any causality or linearity in linking the past and the present in the production of historical consciousness. What brings the moral-cum-temporal orientations together is often a matter of affect, emerging in the singularity of situations. Affect is inherent to gestures and the intensity of emotions and feelings. By taking these singular situations seriously while looking at people's engagement with the past to make history, we might overcome the main obstacles to the ethnography of history in terms of a Western model of historicism—that is, linearity, causality, chronology, and monumentalization. Hence Stewart's (2012: 9ff., 37ff.) call for the study of 'non-chronological' modes of historical consciousness, in which affect is a pertinent mode to be ethnographically explored. We can also read in a similar vein Kathleen Stewart's (2007: 4-5) experimental work in which affect is understood as "an idiosyncratic map of connections between a series of singularities." In turn, Ika's seemingly idiosyncratic story can serve as an example of affective modes of historical consciousness in which "affects highlight the question of the intimate impacts of forces in circulation. They're not exactly 'personal' but they sure can pull the subject into places it didn't exactly 'intend' to go" (ibid.: 40). This applies equally to the critical events of the war and its impact on ordinary lives in a post-conflict polity (Navaro-Yashin 2012). To return to the case discussed here, despite its monumentalization in the Srebrenica-Potočari Memorial and Cemetery and in public discourses on martyrdom, the critical event of the Srebrenica massacre intersects in multiple ways outside the official grand national narratives and the place as such through vernacular histories, witnesses, and their affective modes of engagement with the past that escape monumentalization.

Embedding Martyrs in the Sacred Landscape

The annual gathering known as Prayer for Martyrs in Solun (Šehidska dova u Solunu) belongs to a different scale of attention and monumentalization. In the verdant area (*harem*) around the local mosque, a graveyard for 140 martyrs from the region was systematically created after the war. If we use Wagner's framework, the gathering that has been organized here since the end of the war can be described solely as a commemorative one as it lacks any annual funerals (*dženaza*), unlike in Srebrenica. The great majority of bodies buried in Solun are not of formerly missing persons who were recently identified. On the contrary, the bodies are those of known martyrs who were buried here during the war because of an underground war hospital in its vicinity or were buried originally elsewhere and subsequently reburied in Solun. The graveyard in Solun is therefore a commemorative site that contains martyrs from various corners of the highlands, rather than a place witnessing anything comparable to the mass atrocities in Srebrenica, Korićanske Stijene, or Stupni Do.

The question that arises is how such gatherings, which do not index any singular, locally embedded event from the past but rather 140 micro-stories of sorrow and suffering, came to be framed or invoked in the present as a matter of history and collective remembering. If we were to adopt the conventional constructivist framework based solely on public discourses, we would arrive at the conclusion that this is just one of the many locally orchestrated politico-religious commemorations that mushroomed after the war to forge collective identity and national memory, although with less media attention and political publicity compared to Srebrenica standards. Yet it is probably the most important and emotionally charged annual gathering in the region that emerged after the war in the Zvijezda highlands, attracting hundreds of female and male Muslims from different walks of life. From the point of view that I pursue in this chapter, the question that arises is how such gatherings of collective prayers for martyrs have been animated as the realm of moral-cum-temporal orientations in which the acts of witnessing, enacted in prayers, relate the living to the dead and the present to the past and vice versa. To engage with this question, I suggest taking the local ritual calendar and practice of piety seriously as modes of historical consciousness.

It is not accidental that the commemorative gathering is called Šehidska dova (Prayer for Martyrs). Here attention needs to be paid to the word *dova*, which is usually translated as 'prayer'. However, the word *dova* is used interchangeably for a specific individual or collective prayer, as well as for indoor and outdoor prayers (e.g., for rain, *dove za kišu*). Outdoor prayers operate within a highly elaborated ritual calendar (cf. Henig n.d.) into which, as I will illustrate shortly, the commemorative gathering indexing the critical war events has been incorporated. Dating back to the Ottoman times, outdoor prayers have a long-lasting continuity in Central Bosnia, representing plural pasts in the present. The places of gatherings and worship, known as *dovišta*, can be found around the old Islamic tombs or mausoleums, but also around springs, caves, the tops of the hills, and lime trees (Hadžijahić 1978).

Furthermore, there is a fixed date for the annual prayer at respective sites in the local ritual calendar. The dates are reckoned by counting respective weeks either after Jurjevdan (6 May, derived from the Orthodox calendar) or Alidjun (2 August). Prayers reckoned after Jurjevdan are known as 'Jurjev's prayers' (*Jurjevske dove*). In the local figurative language, this period is associated with rain and water—hence prayers for rain (*kišne dove*)—and also with the processes of growing crops and grass and later with haymaking.[7] The mid-summer period is marked by Alidjun, and the prayers are known as 'Alidjun's prayers' (*Aliđunske dove*). The period around Alidjun is associated with sun, storms, and fires. Thus, activities after Alidjun are associated with work on the fields and harvest.

The cycle of prayers for rain and the days of Jurjevdan and Alidjun are a means of temporalizing ritual activities and commemorations, as well as work activities and the reckoning of time more generally. Yet the ritual calendar is codified. The official organization of the prayers is under the competence of the local office of the Islamic Community of Bosnia-Herzegovina. This office is also responsible for preparing a printed schedule (*raspored dova*) for all places where the prayers take place in the region. The schedules are distributed from April onward in the mosques during Friday sermons, although the majority of villagers know most of the dates by heart. The Prayer for Martyrs in Solun appears on the printed schedule of prayers for rain as well, namely, as the last (twentieth) *dova*, scheduled on 20 August.

Although the commemoration of the martyrs in Solun has been incorporated into a formalized scheme of temporal management by the Islamic Community, as in the case with the Srebrenica commemorative gathering, it cannot be interpreted solely as a matter of monumentalized memory. The prayer gathering in Solun is simultaneously a part of the ritual calendar and a mode of personal moral-cum-temporal orientation for Muslims in the highlands. Put differently, the Prayer for Martyrs in Solun belongs to a different temporal register—one that is embedded in vernacular histories and cosmologies. These are inseparable from a certain mode of action recognized as acts of witnessing (*svjedočenje*) through prayer (*dova*) as a means of invoking the past in the present.

This chapter, which started with a vignette about a prayer for rain, has shown that Muslims who venerate these sacred sites come to pray for the souls of martyrs to bear witness to the past in the present. At the same time, however, through the veneration of these sites and prayers, there is an act of vital exchange that earns good deeds, fortune, and blessing (or rain during the agricultural season) for the living. Put differently, vital exchange helps to maintain vital relations between the living and the dead and, in turn, between the past and the present. This cultural model of temporalization and engagement with the past into which the recent war events have been absorbed in the highlands, including the Prayer for Martyrs in Solun, has thus become part of the local vernacular histories. The annual gathering is now a commemorative event—part of the local tradition of veneration of a sacred site—that is also incorporated into the agro-ritual calendar associated with regenerative symbolism (cf. Bringa 1995). We can therefore observe that the Prayer for Martyrs in Solun has actually become a reversal of the monumentalizing process of martyrdom. What is at play here is a multiplication of temporalization, a topological dimension of time. War and post-war remembrances, rhythms of the sacred and the profane, the ritual calendar and memory politics, and their approximation into frames of reference—all of these shape the local historical consciousness and the relationships between the past and the present in multiple ways.

Conclusion

In this chapter I have outlined the manifold ways of making history in Muslim Bosnia. The chapter has focused on the 1990s war as a critical event and on the modes of historical consciousness that Bosnian Muslims produce to engage with it. There are undoubtedly a number of tensions and negotiations between the ways that the critical event has been subsumed into the hegemonic and grand nationalized historical narratives, on the one hand, and the grassroots historical consciousness, memories, and experiences of the past, on the other. To overcome these tensions and disjunctures, the chapter has taken the route of an ethnography of history to explore the nexus of memory politics with grassroots affective sensibilities, materialities, and practices as modalities of engagement with the past, which co-creates vernacular histories. I have argued that for Muslims in Central Bosnia, the act of prayer is a mode of engagement with the past, instantiated by interactions with specific materials and places, individual ethical conduct, and prayer economy. Specifically, I have traced two idioms of historical consciousness—witness and martyr—that emerge from the very act of prayer. The two idioms articulated in the prayers help Bosnian Muslims to reanimate the recent critical events as the realms of personal moral-cum-temporal orientations, rather than unreflectively partaking in an ongoing nationalization of the past.

To conclude, if we want to engage with the ethnographic specificity of the immanence of plural pasts of critical events in the present, what seems crucial to me is that we follow an analytical perspective that would not favor the forms of monumentalization of the past based on chronological and teleological models of time as the main foci of analysis. The process of monumentalizing violent critical events itself implicates the violence of forgetting. This is brought about by the fabrication, purification, glorification, and linearization of certain fragments of the past while silencing, ignoring, or deliberately excluding others. By participating in the monumentalization process, people perpetuate and maintain the process of purification of the past. In turn, anthropologists who engage solely with public discourses and public conversations, without paying attention to other interrelated domains and immanent modes of temporalization and plural pasts in the present, unreflectively perpetuate the monumental histories as well, as if this were the only way to produce knowledge about the past. I therefore concur with Charles Stewart's (2012: 9) suggestion to take the modes of invoking the past in the present—such as dreams, prayers, calendars, or affect discussed earlier—recursively (cf. Holbraad 2012) as a way to reformulate our own theories and assumptions as to what qualifies as the very notion of history.

Acknowledgments

I would like to thank first and foremost my friends in Bosnia-Herzegovina. I am grateful to Nicolas Argenti for inviting me to participate in the workshop "Balkan Topologies." Rebecca Bryant, Daniel Knight, Stavroula Pipyrou, and Charles Stewart have been important interlocutors over the years. Two anonymous reviewers provided very helpful feedback and suggestions. All shortcomings, of course, are mine. This research was supported by the Wenner-Gren Foundation.

David Henig is a Lecturer in Social Anthropology at the University of Kent. His research, conducted mainly in the Balkans and Central Asia, focuses on vernacular Islam, sacred landscape, diplomacy, and exchange theory. He has (co-)authored numerous articles on the Islamic dream tradition, dervish orders, everyday Islam, post-socialism, and anthropological research, including the co-edited special issue "Being Muslims in the Balkans: Ethnographies of Identity, Politics and Vernacular Islam in South-East Europe" (2013, *Anthropological Journal of European Cultures*). He is a co-editor (with Nicolette Makovicky) of *Economies of Favour after Socialism* (2017).

Notes

1. Due to limitations of space, the more distant Ottoman past cannot be discussed here. For a more detailed account, see Henig (2014).
2. Following Kapferer (1988), I use cosmology rather than ideology to study the relations between politics, imagination, and action in the context of Bosniak nationalized politics.
3. Thus, the collapse of the Yugoslav economy and the Federal Republic is related to the critical event of the war. The dysfunctional post-war federal state, the newly formed post-Dayton cantonal organizational structure, unemployment, privatization, reduced provision of health care—all are consequences of the war in one way or another.
4. Wagner (2008: 238) gives an illustrative example of Serbian counter-narratives and counter-temporalization.
5. For a similar argument on the recovery of missing persons in Cyprus, see Sant Cassia (2005). For the involvement of science in fabricating historical consciousness, see Charles Stewart (2012: 62). Verdery (1999) describes comparable instances of the political lives of dead bodies.
6. This is the same argument Muslims use when talking about the Hajj, the pilgrimage to Mecca that all Muslims are expected to make.
7. The Srebrenica commemorative gathering takes place at this time, accounting for villagers' frequent references to rain.

References

Argenti, Nicolas, and Katharina Schramm, eds. 2010. *Remembering Violence: Anthropological Perspectives on Intergenerational Transmission*. New York: Berghahn Books.
Bougarel, Xavier. 2007. "Death and the Nationalist: Martyrdom, War Memory and Veteran Identity among Bosnian Muslims." In *The New Bosnian Mosaic: Identities, Memories and Moral Claims in a Post-war Society*, ed. Xavier Bougarel, Elissa Helms, and Ger Duijzings, 167–191. Aldershot: Ashgate.
Bringa, Tone. 1995. *Being Muslim the Bosnian Way: Identity and Community in a Central Bosnian Village*. Princeton, NJ: Princeton University Press.
Das, Veena. 1995. *Critical Events: An Anthropological Perspective on Contemporary India*. Delhi: Oxford University Press.

Das, Veena. 2007. *Life and Words: Violence and the Descent into the Ordinary*. Berkeley: University of California Press.

Fortes, Meyer. 1987. *Religion, Morality and the Person: Essays on Tallensi Religion*. Ed. Jack Goody. Cambridge: Cambridge University Press.

Hacking, Ian. 1996. "Memory Sciences, Memory Politics." In *Tense Past: Cultural Essays in Trauma and Memory*, ed. Paul Antze and Michael Lambek, 67–88. London: Routledge.

Hadžijahić, Muhamed. 1978. "Sinkretistički Elementi u Islamu u Bosni i Hercegovini [Syncretic elements in Islam in Bosnia and Herzegovina]." *Prilozi za Orijentalnu Filologiu* [Contributions to Oriental philology] 28–29: 301–328.

Hayden, Robert M. 2007. "Moral Vision and Impaired Insight: The Imagining of Other Peoples' Communities in Bosnia." *Current Anthropology* 48 (1): 105–131.

Henig, David. 2012. "Iron in the Soil: Living with Military Waste in Bosnia-Herzegovina." *Anthropology Today* 28 (1): 21–23.

Henig, David. 2014. "Contested Choreographies of Sacred Spaces in Muslim Bosnia." In *Choreographies of Shared Sacred Sites: Religion, Politics, and Conflict Resolution*, ed. Elazar Barkan and Karen Barkey, 130–160. New York: Columbia University Press.

Henig, David. n.d. "The Embers of Allah: Cosmologies of Vital Exchange in Central Bosnian Highlands." Manuscript in preparation.

Henkel, Heiko. 2005. "'Between Belief and Unbelief Lies the Performance of *Salât*': Meaning and Efficacy of a Muslim Ritual." *Journal of the Royal Anthropological Institute* 11 (3): 487–507.

Herzfeld, Michael. 1991. *A Place in History: Social and Monumental Time in a Cretan Town*. Princeton, NJ: Princeton University Press.

Hirsch, Eric, and Charles Stewart. 2005. "Introduction: Ethnographies of Historicity." *History and Anthropology* 16 (3): 261–274.

Holbraad, Martin. 2012. *Truth in Motion: The Recursive Anthropology of Cuban Divination*. Chicago: University of Chicago Press.

Kapferer, Bruce. 1988. *Legends of People, Myths of State: Violence, Intolerance, Political Culture in Sri Lanka and Australia*. Washington, DC: Smithsonian Institution.

Lambek, Michael. 2002. *The Weight of the Past: Living with History in Mahajanga, Madagascar*. Basingstoke: Palgrave Macmillan.

Mauss, Marcel. (1909) 2003. *On Prayer*. New York: Berghahn Books.

Navaro-Yashin, Yael. 2012. *The Make-Believe Space: Affective Geography in a Postwar Polity*. Durham, NC: Duke University Press.

Sant Cassia, Paul. 2005. *Bodies of Evidence: Burial, Memory and the Recovery of Missing Persons in Cyprus*. New York: Berghahn Books.

Stewart, Charles. 2012. *Dreaming and Historical Consciousness in Island Greece*. Cambridge, MA: Harvard University Press.

Stewart, Kathleen. 2007. *Ordinary Affects*. Durham, NC: Duke University Press.

Verdery, Katherine. 1999. *The Political Lives of Dead Bodies: Reburial and Postsocialist Change*. New York: Columbia University Press.

Wagner, Sarah E. 2008. *To Know Where He Lies: DNA Technology and the Search for Srebrenica's Missing*. Berkeley: University of California Press.

Chapter 3

SURVIVING HRANT DINK

Carnal Mourning under the Specter of Senselessness

Alice von Bieberstein

In mid-January 2009, the Armenian youth organization Nor Zartonk put out a call to gather in commemoration of Hrant Dink, the former editor-in-chief of the bilingual Turkish-Armenian weekly *Agos*, who had been shot in central Istanbul by a nationalist youth two years earlier. A large photograph had been divided into nine equal squares and, like disjointed puzzle pieces, had been assembled on the wall. While a friend of the Dink family explained the development of the criminal trial against those who had planned and executed his murder, pieces of Hrant's photographed face kept falling to the floor, requiring members of Nor Zartonk to undertake the Sisyphean labor of guarding Hrant's facial integrity. The moment captured Hrant's almost sensuous yet unstable omnipresence. The Hrant Dink Foundation had published a book of photographs, and on every related occasion his image was projected onto walls, his favorite songs were played, and his articles were read out loud. At times, even voice recordings resounded. The day after this commemorative event, a flash mob brought together a number of people who went further than speaking about him, embodying him through the re-enactment of his murder. After they had gathered

Notes for this chapter begin on page 69.

silently, almost imperceptibly, in a central location, a shot resounded through the air, and the performers fell to the ground (see fig. 1). Journalists rushed around trying to take pictures that would resemble the iconic photograph of the murder: Hrant Dink, gunned down, his face on the pavement in front of his office, holes in his shoes. Hrant Dink was thus made to speak from the dead. His body, voice, and spirit were animated, kept alive, and his ghost slipped into many bodies.

This chapter concentrates on such conjurations in an effort to chart the entangled temporal, political, and intimate labor of responding to a loss that confronted an emergent community of survivors not only with the challenge of mourning a friend and/or role model, but also with the question of how to live on (or not) with what Lauren Berlant (2011: 1) calls the "fantasy of the good life" that he came to stand for and of whether it might have died along with him. Berlant describes such fantasies as affective modes of optimistic attachment to objects that promise endurance, well-being, and prosperity. These objects can take the form of concepts, ways of lives, projects, or scenes, and within the context of post–World War II political and economic transformations, they have tended to rally around ideas of liberalism and social democracy. With Turkey located on 'this' side of the Cold War divide, and with the case at hand being concerned mainly with Turkey's Armenian community, the fantasy of the good life under consideration attached itself historically to

FIGURE 3.1 Flash mob restaging Hrant Dink's murder in January 2009

Photograph © Alice von Bieberstein

a post-Ottoman constitutional promise of equality, belonging, and protection for non-Muslims and non-Turks in the Republic of Turkey after the 1915–1916 genocidal campaign that destroyed Armenian life in the provinces. Hrant Dink's own entanglement with this fantasy is therefore part of a struggle against the much more forceful fantasy of national homogeneity as propagated by the institutions and historical narrative of the Turkish nation-state. Thinking about Hrant Dink's life and the responses to his death provides an occasion to dwell on the temporal dynamics of living with or against these fantasies. This is because they emplace hopes and promises within a temporal economy that defines what counts as gains and losses—in short, that allocates value to what comes into (and goes out of) being. My intention is therefore to discuss the intersection and interaction between temporal genres as related to fantasies of the good life, mourning as a response to loss that encompasses processes of reattachment, and political activism through which such reattachments might get channeled into renewed or altered political commitments.

Encountering the Minority

Much of the pain of loss centered on Hrant Dink's voice, which, for many, emblematized a charismatic man's ability to effectively reach and affect others less through reasoned speech than through more visceral and affective channels. The event of his murder was therefore all the more critical because this forcefulness as an imagined motor of change could not be recuperated. Dink was referred to as a *gerçek anlatıcı*, a truth-teller, who spoke with a simple 'Anatolian' tongue in a way that unsettled all dogmatism. According to a friend, "There was no one who was not touched."[1] What made him so extraordinary, she continued, was that he broke with the old Armenian habit of presenting himself as a happy and grateful subordinate. He was critical toward Turkey, and he was critical of Armenians, as well as of the West, while practicing a lived form of ethics.

Hrant Dink founded *Agos* together with three companions in Istanbul in 1996. It was set up as a community paper, but one that took an editorial distance toward the Armenian Patriarchate and responded to the reality of decreasing numbers of Armenian speakers by publishing mostly in Turkish. Dink was committed to the vision of changing Turkey from inside. He placed *Agos* in a position of solidarity and alliance with other human and minority rights struggles in Turkey. Within a network that included journalists and academics, research institutes, community associations, and broader civil society organizations, *Agos* emerged as the central node and organ for efforts toward changing the terms of public discourse, asserting a self-determined Armenian presence, and providing a platform for the production and sharing of knowledge on the Armenian community and its history in Turkey. It thus also became an important channel for Turkish liberal and leftist circles eager to revive a post-Ottoman sensibility for ethnic and religious plurality and difference.

Elizabeth Povinelli (2011) has complemented Berlant's concern with the temporal emplotment of hopes and expectations of a good life by emphasizing the economizing role of value within such temporal orientations. Forms of killing and "making die," Povinelli argues, are subject to "modalities of expenditure and abandonment" (ibid.: 167). The question of sacrifice "opens the events of suffering and dying ... to the problematic of being and tense" (ibid.), to a particular articulation of the relation between violence and redemption. When such a relation is narrated in the social tense of a future perfect, suffering and death can be understood "as a mode of birth, as a way of bringing new being into existence" (ibid.). In Turkey, the dominant historical narrative features genocide denial, the nationalist and militarist cult of soldiers and martyrs, and the disavowal of ethnic, religious, or otherwise conceived difference beyond a depoliticized affirmation of folklore.[2] Its teleological temporality casts the death and expulsion of 'non-Turks' during the founding of the Republic as necessary birth pains of the nation and projects redemption onto a future moment when the social field will be inclusive and harmonious. Against a horizon of disappearing difference, the death and loss of Armenians, Greeks, Assyrians, and others are rendered unrecognizable.

It is against this background that an archaeological passion evident among some Turkish leftist and liberal circles to unearth and move stories hitherto privately withheld into the wider public appears as part of an oppositional memory work.[3] These efforts question the conclusive 'pastness' of these histories of violence and open for interrogation their contemporary legacies. The assessment as 'critical memory work' appears even more self-evident when considering the reflex-driven dynamic of repression and censorship—well and alive in Turkey—that characterizes what Taussig (1999) has called 'public secrecy'. Taussig makes the important point to complicate the relationship between truth and authority by placing the fetishist powers of state and ideology at the center of his discussion. He alerts us to the economy of desire and identification that find their expression less in a politics of representation than in the thrills and joys of transgressing boundaries and challenging state power. Processes of reassessing an oppositional politics in the fields of history can thus entail (possibly disavowed) investments in the state project. But it can also create room for modes of reflexivity. Rather than adopting the lens of power/knowledge to follow the emergence, establishment, and contestation of various historical narratives in public—a framework most commonly adopted in anthropological memory studies (cf. Climo and Cattell 2002; Halbwachs 1992; Hodgkin and Radstone 2003)—I emphasize the reflexive dimension of the 'turn to the past'. From the perspective of a Left dominated by an ideology of anti-imperialism, the discovery of a history of the Other is the flip side of a process of working through previously unacknowledged investments in a dominant ideology of state nationalism. By recharting the terrain of complicity, the project also reworks a field of relations.

Hrant Dink became a mediator for many liberals and leftists seeking to shift their ideological commitments toward a political grammar of human and minority rights and the imperative to confront the past. As an 'internal Other', he mediated the encounter with the emergent discourse and practice of 'confronting the past' (*geçmişle yüzleşmek*) and permitted relating to the loss of Turkey's pluralist past.[4] He thus assisted in the imagination of a past beyond state-sanctioned parameters and thereby also of a different future. As a political actor/activist, he was himself marked by a kind of temporal ambiguity as he performatively sought to bring about and make present the future he dreamed of.

Giving Body to Another Time

In resonance with the temporal horizon of the nation-state, in which differences are conceived as always in a process of vanishing, Meltem Ahıska (2007: 157), in her reflections soon after Hrant Dink's murder, reminds us that nationalism in Turkey emerged as "a way of subjecting differences to a logic of equivalence in order to unify them under the sign of a general name, Turkishness." The abstractly unifying aspiration of the project of nationalism found its expression in a secular modernist commitment to inclusion, that is, the position of citizenship as envisaged by the law. Yet the conception of citizenship remains subject to an exclusionary delineation according to language, ethnicity, and religious heritage. In the context of this contradiction, which Kader Konuk (2010) has linked more specifically to cultural and racial fears of becoming an unsuccessful copy of Europe, any plurality in identity is met with intolerance and anxiety, and minorities are pressured to *become* Turkish, to disappear through assimilation, even though they can never be 'truly' Turkish.

This contradiction stood at the center of Hrant Dink's life. He had been pleading and thereby trying to make it a livable possibility to be both Armenian and a Turkish citizen. In 2002, Dink (2008: 162) said during a conference: "I am not a Turk. I am a citizen of Turkey and also Armenian." For this he was charged under the infamous Article 301 of the Turkish Penal Code, which at that time made it a crime to "insult Turkishness."[5] He worked for a vision of Turkey where Armenians are more than historical remnants, where they are bearers of rights to the present. He laid a bodily claim to what lay outside normative categorical relations. His ceaseless affirmation of an enduring internal plurality rendered him a target of nationalist persecution. The hate campaign that finally led to his murder started in response to an article he had written about Sabiha Gökçen, Atatürk's daughter and Turkey's first female pilot. Hrant Dink revealed that she had been an Armenian orphan who had been adopted and converted to Islam by Atatürk himself. Dink thus highlighted the denial at the center of the Republican state project, emblematized in the figure of a disavowed Armenian orphan. By pushing the limits of the speakable, he became personally entangled with the prospect or reality of living in a post-genocidal era.

Were his writings and interviews a sign that Turkey was moving toward a post-genocidal era? Berlant (2011: 23) describes an object of desire as a "cluster of promises" in relation to fantasies of the good life. In the case of Hrant Dink, this object appears in a metonymic chain in that by embodying the possibility of living a different kind of life as an Armenian in Turkey, Dink could incarnate the Republican fantasy of eventual justice and equality realized on the basis of an inherent institutional reformability. This is how Hrant Dink's life was marked by temporal ambiguity: was it a future approaching, even made present through his body, or a 'meantime' that continuously deferred this future's arrival? This temporal equivocality was arrested, at least temporarily, on 19 January 2007.

Giving Sense to Survival

Ahron remembers how his friend's phone had rung that day, how his friend's face had gone blank. He had thought that someone in the family had died. But then his friend told him, and suddenly his nose started to bleed. He ran to *Agos*, where Hrant's body was still on the pavement, and passed the barrier, saying he was a member of the family. "And then I was suddenly part of it," Ahron recounts. "I took over some duties, was supposed to do some job in the church, and then I suddenly found myself there with Hrant's coffin, and they had put an edition of *Agos* under my arms. And then I sat there in front of the car, driving the coffin." The sense of being overcome is echoed by Tataryan (2012), who describes how the site of the murder became a gravitational center for an always already melancholy and mournful Armenian community. People drifted in shock to the site, lighting candles, leaving flowers, crying. This was the moment of a mediating and mediated affect that Berlant (2011: 16) describes as the "historical moment" that emerges—is sensed—before it becomes orchestrated into an event or era. From the initial affective resonance, from the collectivity magnetized around a spontaneous memorial in front of *Agos*'s office building, the murder turned into an event.

When people recounted their experiences to me, few failed to remark on how these initial days, weeks, and months radically altered their field of relations: new friends were made, old ones were lost, lovers broke up, family bonds came under strain. Many became involved, often for the first time, in platforms and political projects and went through an intense phase of politicization. New associations were formed, initiatives kicked off, exhibitions organized, and radio stations launched.[6] A new commemorative calendar emerged. Accordingly, many of my friends and informants narrated their lives in terms of a time before and a time after 19 January 2007.

Much anthropological writing about the 'event' has followed an interpretation of Alain Badiou's (2005) seminal work, conceiving of it as a break in modes of intelligibility by reconfiguring the possible and proposing new truths (see, e.g., Bensa and Fassin 2002). This is echoed by Ahıska (2007: 155) for whom the murder opens a "gap between 'what is no longer' and 'what is yet to come.'" Caroline Humphrey (2008: 360), in her interpretation of Badiou, adds that the event has no content in and of itself, but exists to the extent that it is acclaimed by a collectivity of witnesses "who constitute themselves as immortal subjects by their fidelity to its truth." The very eventfulness is therefore not settled; rather, it is what is at stake for many of those who became politically active in the aftermath of the murder. Humphrey's point alerts us to the labor of this activism, an activism intimately entangled with mourning.

Before attending to this mournful activism or 'carnal mourning', as I will call it, I want to return to the collectivity of witnesses in order to unsettle any presumption regarding the temporality of the date itself. As a hate crime, Hrant Dink's murder cast a shadow over the entire Armenian community, but it was also a blow to all those speaking up against past and present injustices. Echoing their semantic proximity, the witnesses are in this sense also survivors. As Caruth (1996: 7) argues, an encounter with death is also an encounter with survival and one that raises the question of ethical responsiveness. Because of Dink's entanglement with a Turkish Republican fantasy of the good life and the temporal ambiguity that this engendered in relation to his persona, his murder raises the question of survival in relation to the very fantasy itself: did his murder indicate that there was in fact nothing post-genocidal about this present moment? Survival thus implicates time: What has been survived, 2007 or 1915, again? And what survives?

The social tense of a future perfect that Povinelli makes out when loss is narrated in terms of possible future gains can be said, in this case, to open up a kind of meantime, as Robert Meister (2011: 12) spells out in relation to a contemporary human rights discourse, which he calls an "intermessianic (and implicitly antimessianic) secular theology." Its time is always a time between time, between "the end of evil and the establishment of justice" (ibid.). In this meantime of forever waiting for justice, during which neither eventfulness nor the temporal horizons of the murder has been settled, the community of survivors has to constantly adjust to the exigencies of "crisis ordinariness" (Berlant 2011: 10). Rather than examining and weighing the relative value of cognition, culture, practice, phenomenology, and ontology for an anthropological understanding of temporality (see, e.g., Gell 1992; Hodges 2008; Munn 1992), my concern is thus to highlight how the temporal impulses of mourning and activism engage with and play out in relation to politically charged temporal discourses in which violence, value, and time are always already articulated together.

Speaking Instead

Nor Zartonk underwent a fundamental change with the death of Hrant Dink. As Mihran, a member of the youth group, put it, Hrant had done the talking, but now they had to carry his work forward. Mihran's generation had come of age in the 1990s, and this first big experience of violence prompted them to take on Hrant's legacy. In the words of Mihran: "We want Turkey to become more democratic and more peaceful. Nor Zartonk wants to poke democratically minded people to wake up to the Armenian presence in Turkey. Armenians have always been silent, defensive, closed in on themselves, but what kind of life is that? We want to stand up and say we are here and alive!" Another friend, Hrair, had become active in the Friends of Hrant Dink group because he had felt guilty for not having stood by Hrant's side during the latter's trials. Now he feels alive when he stands up in public with a name and a face. If it means that he might get killed, so what? Yes, he has received many death threats, but Hrair feels that if he were to step down now, he would be dead, too. He believes that Hrant was so effective in changing things because he stood out there with his face and his name. Ahron, after becoming closely involved with the funeral and its reverberations, also started to make more frequent appearances in public. When I first asked him what he was doing in life, he responded: *"Ermeniyim*, I am Armenian. It's my job. Someone has to do it, to tell the truth. The people don't know any more that we exist. But there is a truth and I know it. My family was killed. It is the truth. And I want justice, so simple." Hrant Dink's death called for a responsiveness Ahron felt that he could not escape, although a great part of him just wanted to be with his family, hang out with friends, and lead an easy-going life.

Indeed, the racism and hate that had led to the murder remained virulent. On 23 January 2007, an overwhelming 200,000 people joined the funeral march across Istanbul toward the Armenian cemetery in Balıklı. A journalist from the Black Sea coast proceeded to file a complaint against the mayor of Şişli, a district in Istanbul, for having permitted the carrying and shouting of slogans that the journalist perceived as violating Article 301. In an article entitled "Honourable Prosecutor," he wrote: "They carried placards saying 'Hrant's murderer is Article 301.' They branded the laws of the Turkish Republic as murderers. Shouting 'We are all Armenian', they violated the constitution. They insulted the unity of the nation with separatism based on race. They caused traffic congestion. With live broadcasts, they encouraged others to take part in the demonstration. They did not even carry one Turkish flag. What else do you want? Treason, provocation, separatism and extreme disturbance. I am complaining and am a plaintiff. Honourable Prosecutor, please start an investigation."[7] The chief prosecutor in Şişli turned down the case. But the ethno-religious exclusionary delineations of Turkey's citizenship regime violently erupted again during the trial against Hrant Dink's murderers. A delegation of the Paris Bar Association attended the hearing on 20 April 2009 in solidarity with the lawyers of the Dink family. Although it was legal for these foreign lawyers to sit in any open case as observers and in their professional gowns, the president of the Istanbul Bar Association publicly stated that the significance of Hrant Dink's murder did not stem from his ethnicity. He had been a Turkish citizen, and his murder was therefore condemnable like any other. Yet the opposite appeared to apply to the lawyers, who were not identified by reference to their (French) citizenship. Because many of the observing lawyers had the same ethnicity as Hrant Dink, the statement of the Istanbul Bar Association suggested that their attendance likely violated the prohibition of race discrimination and revealed their intention to observe the trial for political reasons. The statement reiterated a principle of equivalence that denied the extent to which particularly marked differences were the target of murderous violence. Simultaneously, it banned recognition of difference to an outside that was thereby marked as threatening and illegitimate.

In such a context where the lives of those considered members of 'minorities' are cast as expendable, mourning in itself, when taken to the streets, becomes a "historically situated practice of dissent and alternative responsiveness" (Athanasiou 2005: 48). In the concrete gestures of speaking up 'instead', mourning takes on carnal qualities. Those whom I have described as having felt interpellated by Hrant Dink's death have sought to draw his voice near to theirs, to approximate his political ambitions for a more democratic Turkey, to multiply his presence through different media on the basis of an archive of images and sounds and through their own bodies. As a practice of dissent, their mourning is carnal in this performative, bodily, sensuous way. It defies the temporality of Hrant Dink's death. Against an impulse of letting go and moving on, commonly associated with mourning, Hrant Dink has been given a future. His time is still to come; his political vision did not die along with him. And to keep his vision alive means to keep him alive, to speak in his stead, which has transformed his name into the site of a battle of representation. Close friends and colleagues have expressed anger over the way that everyone claims to be Hrant's 'friend', wanting to legitimate their authority and various ideological projects by associating themselves with his name. In the process, a critical debate on Hrant Dink and his politics has itself been more or less silenced. But by referring to carnality, I also wish to emphasize how speaking up 'instead' means bearing the risk of becoming a target.

The activism that seeks to maintain Hrant Dink's vitality is tied up with investing in the eventfulness of his murder. By emphasizing the overwhelming response displayed by the funeral march on 23 January, Hrant Dink's fantasy of the good life is given a future again. Mourning is made possible and entails the making of sense, and sense is related to tense through acts of narration. Returning to Povinelli (2011), figurations of tense such as that of the future perfect, of what a murder will have been, pass into other discourses, into affective states and practices. When the quest for sense touches the question of theodicy, mourning becomes ambivalent. When the murder is narrated as having initiated a radical change, mourning enters into a contact zone with economies of sacrifice and abandonment. This specter of sense and value was also met with aversion.

Affirming Senselessness

While many responded to the murder by becoming more active, others did so by withdrawing into themselves. For many, it shattered the fantasy, the imagination of a trajectory that would enable living life as an Armenian and a Turkish citizen. When I arrived in Istanbul for my research, my old friend Anoush warned me that it would be difficult. Armenians would not want to talk, especially since the murder. As Anoush put it: "How they understand it, if you talk, you get killed." She told me that many families had considered emigrating after the murder. There had also been a lot of criticism within the community that Hrant had talked too much. Not that he deserved to be killed, but "this is how things work in this country: you are killed if you talk too much. So if you want to be happy, it is better to get along with these people and to live with them and not to speak up." As our conversation went on, we moved from topic to topic, ending with the story of a friend of her father who had gone to Urfa to reclaim property that had belonged to his ancestors and got killed.

The precariousness and vulnerability attached to the word 'Armenian' reaches further back in time than current Republican formations of citizenship. This is another temporal horizon within which Hrant Dink's life and death are inscribed. In some places, 19 January protest banners read "1,500,000 + 1," referring to the estimated number of Armenian victims of 1915 plus Hrant Dink. In Istanbul, such a link appeared on 24 April 2009, the central commemorative day for the Armenian genocide, when relatives of Hrant Dink and members of *Agos* went to his grave (see fig. 2) to lay down a wreath. Hrant Dink's nephew later explained the symbolism of the gravestone to me: "On the backside of the stone, underneath the pigeons are lots of crosses, some straight and some skewed. All are in the memory of the victims of 1915. And one of the crosses is slightly bigger than the others. That is the one for Hrant."

Hrant Dink's murder was thus a corrorobation for many that they do not yet live in a post-genocidal era. Some were also confirmed in their conviction that Hrant had been wrong to believe that Turkey could be changed from within. In their eyes, Hrant's struggle to assert an Armenianness in public, to reclaim an Armenian history beyond the confines of the family, the church, and the community and against a history of destruction, dispossession, and denial had been doomed to fail. No fantasies of a good life could be attached to the Turkish state project. The impulse was to withdraw even more into a form of inner exile.

Figure 3.2 Hrant Dink's grave

Photograph © Alice von Bieberstein

According to Nichanian (2003: 114), the Catastrophe of 1915 was characterized by a "violence without any assignable measure. That is why it forbids mourning." Beyond measurement and value, it resists integration into a narrative of sacrifice. No teleology or theodicy can encompass the Catastrophe, no sense can be reaped from it. Placing Hrant Dink's death within such a genealogy moves it from the horizon of a future perfect to that of a past perfect: it already happened. His murder will not enable a retrospective narrative of progression that will have transformed the political and social terms of living together. Within this perspective, it is Hrant Dink's political visions and his metonymic entanglement with the potential for an attainable change as promised by the idea of parliamentary democracy that become anachronistic. The resignation signaled by this approach partakes in neutralizing the eventfulness of his murder and thereby also in attenuating the pain of loss. In the absence of a horizon of redemption, the intensities of hopes and disappointments are dampened.

Conclusion

In this chapter I have approached the issue of time from a threefold vantage point: (1) the historically contingent form and availability of temporal genres that provide frames for postulating the durational presence or absence of beings, projects, objects, and the like, and that place that which has been, is, and will be not only in temporal relations, but also in relations of value to one another; (2) mourning as a multifarious response to loss that halts and calls into question routinized relations of attachment but might also appear in disavowed form or through gestures of dismissal or resignation; and (3) activism as a field of practice where such affective responses to loss are worked over as well as being made to work in possibly rearticulated commitments to political projects or other fantasies of the good life (themselves ripe with temporal discourses). I follow scholars of twentieth-century catastrophes in being cautious to assume too readily that all occurrences lend themselves to conventional forms of seeing and knowing and thereby to integration in temporal genres (Nichanian 2009; cf. Agamben 1999; Caruth 1995; LaCapra 2001). This is not to argue for an autonomous agency of time (cf. Das 2007), but to be attentive to the limits of perception, experience, and comprehension as conditioned by psychological, cultural, and political modes of apprehension and understanding. We can detect a hint of this in the responses to the loss of Hrant Dink that take him out of his own personal pathway by claiming that his battle had been lost before it had even started. While making him a victim of 1915 might appear as a cowardly and resentful surrender to the powers that be, it also declares—if in muttering—his death to be absolutely senseless. No future state or this-worldly moment can possibly redeem this death. By uplifting—or burying—his life and death into a *longue durée* of persecution, calculations of sacrificial worth are banned, and redemption is found, if anywhere, in an individual afterlife.

There is nothing mutually exclusive about the different impulses I have charted throughout this chapter. Declaring that one had always known that this could not end well—that Hrant Dink's murder had confirmed one's own strategy of silence and reclusiveness—was in equal measures a means of coping and affectively handling the loss by rhetorically diminishing its impact. Similarly, personally entangling oneself in Dink's lifework did not guarantee escaping the spectral possibility that no sense could be found, that no future better society could be made on the bones and ashes of so much destruction. The doubts flickered under the performative determination to not surrender to the intentions of the murderers and to defy a dominant temporal economy within which Hrant Dink's life was cast as not worth preserving, with no right to the future.

To this date, the logic of abandonment that targets non-Turks and non-Sunni Muslims and secures impunity for the murderers prevails. Localized campaigns for justice and against impunity, as well as carnal forms of embodied activist mourning, offer a political practice that complements the broader ideological shift in knowledge practices toward the discourse of *gecmişle yüzleşmek*—confronting the past. This temporal politics as knowledge practice presents itself in opposition to a national trajectory that has ossified through decades of authoritarian rule and Republican institutions such as the military, education, and citizenship. Hrant Dink's embodied dissent, his demand for recognition and inclusion within Turkey's citizenship regime as an Armenian, thereby calling on the alleged reformability of its institutions, made him a suitable candidate for this wider project of an alternative politics of time and history without abandoning altogether the Republic of Turkey as an object for the good life fantasy. Embodying difference for others, he could make palpable the imagining of a different past as well as the probability and reality of a different future. This was the contradictory positionality—standing outside yet bearing the promise of a better future—that catered to his power while heightening his precariousness and that continues to hold for all those that have followed in his footsteps.

Acknowledgments

An earlier version of this chapter was presented at the ESRC workshop "Balkan Topologies," which was organized in cooperation with and held at the British School at Athens on 19-21 May 2013. The research on which this chapter is based was made possible by the generous support of the William Wyse Fund and the European Research Council.

Alice von Bieberstein completed her PhD in Social Anthropology at the University of Cambridge in 2012 with a dissertation on the politics of history and citizenship in Turkey and Germany. Until 2015, she was a postdoctoral research associate at the University of Cambridge on an ERC-funded project entitled "Remnants," which focused on the material dimensions of the history of political violence in Mus, Eastern Turkey. In 2017-2018, she will be a fellow of the European Institutes for Advanced Study (EURIAS) at the Wissenschaftskolleg zu Berlin.

Notes

1. Throughout the chapter I have anonymized the identities of informants and friends by using pseudonyms. Unless otherwise noted, all translations are my own.
2. For critical studies on the denial of the Armenian genocide and on Turkish nationalist historiography more generally, see Bayraktar (2010) and Göçek (2006), among others.
3. For studies on the politics of memory and archive in Turkey, see Ahıska (2010), Mills (2010), and Özyürek (2007). For studies on governmentalizing difference in Republican Turkey, see, for example, Baer (2010), Brink-Danan (2012), and Konuk (2010).
4. For a longer discussion on 'confronting the past' in Turkey and its connections to Germany, see von Bieberstein (2017).
5. A legal reform in 2008 changed "Turkishness" to "the Turkish nation" and made the opening of legal cases dependent on approval by the Ministry of Justice.
6. An incomplete list of such associations and events includes 19 Ocak Kolektif (19 January Collective), Kronik Muhalif (Chronic Dissent), Hrant Dink Arkadaşları (Friends of Hrant Dink), Hrant Dink Vakfı (Hrant Dink Foundation), Nor Radyo (Nor Zartonk's radio station), the annual Hrant Dink Memorial Workshop, and the annual Hrant Dink Memorial Lecture.
7. See http://www.bianet.org/english/english/112468-no-trial-for-we-are-all-armenian-slogan (accessed 5 May 2015).

References

Agamben, Giorgio. 1999. *Remnants of Auschwitz: The Witness and the Archive*. Trans. Daniel Heller-Roazen. New York: Zone Books.
Ahıska, Meltem. 2007. "A Deep Fissure Is Revealed after Hrant Dink's Assassination." *New Perspectives on Turkey* 36: 155–164.
Ahıska, Meltem. 2010. *Occidentalism in Turkey: Questions of Modernity and National Identity in Turkish Radio Broadcasting*. London: I.B. Tauris.
Athanasiou, Athena. 2005. "Reflections on the Politics of Mourning: Feminist Ethics and Politics in the Age of Empire." *Historein* 5: 40–57.
Badiou, Alain. 2005. *Being and Event*. Trans. Oliver Feltham. London: Continuum.
Baer, Marc. 2010. *The Dönme: Jewish Converts, Muslim Revolutionaries, and Secular Turks*. Stanford, CA: Stanford University Press.
Bayraktar, Seyhan. 2010. *Politik und Erinnerung: Der Diskurs über den Armeniermord in der Türkei zwischen Nationalismus und Europäisierung*. Bielefeld: Transcript.
Bensa, Alban, and Eric Fassin. 2002. "Les sciences sociales face à l'événement." *Terrain: Revue d'ethnologie de l'Europe* 38: 5–20.
Berlant, Lauren. 2011. *Cruel Optimism*. Durham, NC: Duke University Press.
Brink-Danan, Marcy. 2012. *Jewish Life in Twenty-First-Century Turkey: The Other Side of Tolerance*. Bloomington: Indiana University Press.
Caruth, Cathy, ed. 1995. *Trauma: Explorations in Memory*. Baltimore: John Hopkins University Press.
Caruth, Cathy. 1996. *Unclaimed Experience: Trauma, Narrative, and History*. Baltimore: John Hopkins University Press.
Climo, Jacob J., and Maria G. Cattell, eds. 2002. *Social Memory and History: Anthropological Perspectives*. Walnut Creek, CA: Altamira Press.
Das, Veena. 2007. *Life and Words: Violence and the Descent into the Ordinary*. Berkeley: University of California Press.

Dink, Hrant. 2008. *Von der Saat der Worte*. Ed. Günter Seufert. Berlin: Verlag Hans Schiller.
Gell, Alfred. 1992. *The Anthropology of Time: Cultural Constructions of Temporal Maps and Images*. Oxford: Berg.
Göçek, Fatma M. 2006. "Defining the Parameters of a Post-nationalist Turkish Historiography through the Case of the Anatolian Armenians." In *Turkey Beyond Nationalism: Towards Post-Nationalist Identities*, ed. Hans-Lukas Kieser, 85–103. London: I.B. Tauris.
Halbwachs, Maurice. 1992. *On Collective Memory*. Ed. and trans. Lewis A. Coser. Chicago: University of Chicago Press.
Hodges, Matt. 2008. ""Rethinking Time's Arrow: Bergson, Deleuze and the Anthropology of Time." *Anthropological Theory* 8 (4): 399–429.
Hodgkin, Katharine, and Susannah Radstone, eds. 2003. *Memory, History, Nation: Contested Pasts*. London: Transaction.
Humphrey, Caroline. 2008. "Reassembling Individual Subjects: Events and Decisions in Troubled Times." *Anthropological Theory* 8 (4): 357–380.
Konuk, Kader. 2010. *East West Mimesis: Auerbach in Turkey*. Stanford, CA: Stanford University Press.
LaCapra, Dominick. 2001. *Writing History, Writing Trauma*. Baltimore: Johns Hopkins University Press.
Meister, Robert. 2011. *After Evil: A Politics of Human Rights*. New York: Columbia University Press.
Mills, Amy. 2010. *Streets of Memory: Landscape, Tolerance, and National Identity in Istanbul*. Athens: University of Georgia Press.
Munn, Nancy D. 1992. "The Cultural Anthropology of Time: A Critical Essay." *Annual Review of Anthropology* 21: 93–123.
Nichanian, Marc. 2003. "Catastrophic Mourning." In *Loss: The Politics of Mourning*, ed. David L. Eng and David Kazanjian, 99–124. Berkeley: University of California Press.
Nichanian, Marc. 2009. *The Historiographic Perversion*. Trans. Gil Anidjar. New York: Columbia University Press.
Özyürek, Esra, ed. 2007. *The Politics of Public Memory in Turkey*. Syracuse, NY: Syracuse University Press.
Povinelli, Elizabeth A. 2011. *Economies of Abandonment: Social Belonging and Endurance in Late Liberalism*. Durham, NC: Duke University Press.
Tataryan, Nora. 2012. "Armenians Living in Turkey and the Assassination of Hrant Dink: Loss, Mourning and Melancholia." MA thesis, Sabancı University, Istanbul.
Taussig, Michael. 1999. *Defacement: Public Secrecy and the Labor of the Negative*. Stanford, CA: Stanford University Press.
von Bieberstein, Alice. 2017. "Memorial Miracle: Inspiring *Vergangenheitsbewältigung* between Berlin and Istanbul." In *Replicating Atonement: Foreign Models in the Commemoration of Atrocities*, ed. Mischa Gabowitsch. New York: Palgrave Macmillan.

Chapter 4

THE MATERIAL LIFE OF WAR AT THE GREEK BORDER

Laurie Kain Hart

Fieldwork over the long term enables ethnographers to learn from, and be taken by surprise by, the effects of the passage of time. Social relations unthinkable at one historical moment are normalized two generations later. Here I focus on such time effects made visible in the material-infrastructural world. The presence of scores of abandoned but architecturally impressive buildings in the border zone landscape of the Prespa Lakes in northwest Greek Macedonia puzzled me on my first visit in 1993. The zone, I discovered, was the epicenter of the final phases of the Greek Civil War (1946–1949), and it testified physically to the disaster. I passed through two police checkpoints as I neared the lakes, where the international borders of Albania, Greece, and what had been, just two years earlier, Yugoslavia (and was now the independent Democratic Republic of Macedonia) intersect. The checkpoints were remnants of the special surveillance zone established during the dictatorship of General Ioannis Metaxas in the 1930s and maintained for the next 40 years to control internal movement on the Greek side of the boundary zone (Rombou-Levidi 2009). One checkpoint was

Notes for this chapter begin on page 84.

empty, but the other had been repurposed by the police as a roadblock to stop and detain unauthorized Albanian migrants. During the following two decades, I watched as pre-war buildings disintegrated and fell down, were demolished or were renovated, and as new buildings were constructed (Hart 2005). These ostensibly banal phenomena are, I argue, following Lefebvre (1991), the perceptible tip of an apparatus of power and property that constitutes the existential, world-historical, shifting infrastructural frame of everyday life. Key to the transformation of Prespa's local landscape over time are two critical facts: its geopolitical position at the borders of three nation-states, and its twentieth-century role as a theater of war and as a laboratory of Hellenic nation building.

Post-civil war studies focusing on specific ground zero conflict regions in Bosnia-Herzegovina, Peru, Cyprus, and elsewhere (see, e.g., Bougarel et al. 2007; Bryant, 2010, 2014; Kolind 2008; Papadakis 2005; Theidon 2013) draw attention to the material processes of entropy and building that contribute to the life (or death) of particular post-war communities. How does the work of inhabiting and the concreteness of things, which are also sometimes painfully "present but out of reach" (Garcia 2010: 84) due to the dispossession of property, affect the commutation of loss? The comparative study of infrastructural challenges to post-civil war communities reveals some common patterns and vulnerabilities across cases. In the everyday of what can be called 'territorial time', embedded segmentary oppositions and wounds can be inflamed by new conflicts at a distance, as occurred in northwest Greece during the 1990s ex-Yugoslav wars. By contrast, however, new generations may also, as Scott (2014) argues for Grenada, detach themselves from the melancholia associated with 'critical events'.

FIGURE 4.1 Abandoned settlement, 1994

Photograph © Laurie Kain Hart

The Greek Civil War and Its Precursors

The Greek Civil War ended in August 1949 when Greek government forces, reinforced by 51 bombers and napalm supplied by the US, obliterated the rebel army corralled in the mountains of northwest Greek Macedonia.[1] The conflict between Communist-led World War II resistance groups and the pro-West/monarchist Greek government began well before the end of the Axis occupation of the country in 1944 and continued in several rounds until October 1949 when the Communist forces (reconstituted after 1947 as the rebel Democratic Army of Greece or DSE) capitulated. The agro-pastoral villages of the northwest Greek border zone, where the DSE had established its final base of operations, were decimated. In the aftermath, citizens who were associated with actions, ideas, and persons connected with the DSE or were labeled subversive, leftist, socially progressive, internationalist, or non- or anti-Hellenic were pursued, persecuted, imprisoned, or executed.[2] The 1981 electoral victory of the Panhellenic Socialist Movement (PASOK) ended the persecution of former leftists, but not the suppression of 'non-Greek' minorities who were living at home or as political refugees abroad. Former civil war/Cold War polarities metamorphosed into the ethnic/nationalist targeting of Greece's Slav-Macedonian population well into the 2000s (Danforth and Van Boeschoten 2011: 292).

The 1940s war toll in Greece was immense. Between 1940 and 1949, more than half a million people, 10 percent of Greece's population of roughly 7 million, died or were killed (Nachmani 2016). Another 40,000–50,000 ended the decade as political prisoners in internment camps. Almost 500,000 houses were completely destroyed, nearly 2,000 villages were burned down, and roughly a million and a quarter people were rendered homeless (Hionidou 2012; Mazower 2001; Voglis 2002: 63, 44). During the civil war, villages in heavily targeted areas of northwest Macedonia were flattened beyond recuperation.

Population movements in this area were, of course, nothing new. The nineteenth-century implosion of the Ottoman Empire, propelled by new nationalisms, resulted in massive displacement, slaughter, and the destruction of property and cultural heritage. World War I 'peace' treaties converted de facto routines of displacement into international agreements with the methodical deportation of minorities and 'ethnic cleansing' of boundary zones. The Treaty of Versailles (28 June 1919) included a 'protection of minorities' provision to prevent forced removals (Cowan et al. 2001), while simultaneously the mass transfer of populations was legalized at the Neuilly Convention (29 November 1919) when Bulgaria and Greece mutually agreed to expel their minority populations in a 'voluntary' exchange. Yet half of the so-called (Christian) Bulgarian minority refused to abandon Greek Macedonia. The legal fiction of voluntarism evaporated after the 1919–1922 Greco-Turkish war: the Treaty of Lausanne (24 July 1923) mandated a compulsory transfer of Orthodox Christians from Turkey to Greece and of Muslims from Greece to Turkey. This second bilateral 'exchange of populations' meant that an influx of Greek refugees from Turkey would permanently recalibrate the Christian ethnic balance in Western Macedonia, as well as obliterate the Muslim presence. Such 'exchanges' ensured that members of targeted groups would forfeit their properties, enabling a state-controlled 'primitive accumulation' (Marx) of land and dwellings that could be distributed to new 'co-ethnic' immigrants (J.R. 1944: 579, 584, 585).

As Greece colonized its borders with vulnerable clients from Asia Minor, the Macedonian population, indigenous since the eighth century, was surveilled, policed, subjected to compulsory 're-education', and put under increasing pressure to Hellenize. Not surprisingly, Macedonian pro-autonomist sentiment was partially remobilized in the 1940s, especially among descendants of pro-Bulgarian fighters killed between 1903 and 1913 (Michailidis 2000). Villagers were drafted forcibly by both sides of the conflict. The local population that remained fled to Eastern Europe in the chaos of the final retreat of the Greek Civil War in the summer and fall of 1949.

In sum, the civil war took place in a landscape defined by the Ottoman transitions of the early twentieth century. State policies of ethnic engineering, if not ethnic cleansing, had been normalized. The Axis occupation—especially the brutal occupation of Thrace and Eastern Macedonia by Bulgarian forces in World War II that refueled earlier territorial concerns—was also a crucial factor in the anti-Slav-Macedonian post-war climate. Greece's Cold War government propaganda invoked the double threat of Ottomanism and Slavism and the specter of absorption into the borderless miasma of (Eastern) Communist internationalism to blackmail its citizens into compliance with its punitive post-war regime. In the early 1950s, poor transhumant Aromanian-speaking shepherds (Vlachs) were transported by the state to occupy properties belonging to evacuated ethnic Macedonians, again with the aim of establishing politically loyal clients. Like Pontians, Vlachs were stigmatized, vulnerable,[3] and recruitable border guards. The Slavophone population that had resisted expatriation to Bulgaria in the 1910s and 1920s was thus still "matter out of place" (Douglas 2005: 44) more than a half-century later. The "salience of ethnicity" (Van Boeschoten 2000: 40) in northwest Macedonia has persisted in a climate of continuing vigilance.[4]

Domestic Ghosts

Like persons, landed properties have, despite their emphatic appearance of material durability, unpredictable life spans.[5] The significance of landed property as symbolic and economic capital and its value to individuals may shift, sometimes suddenly, during a life-course. Affective attachments to place may ironically be intensified by forced displacement and diminished by forced confinement (cf. Green 2005). Vulnerable populations may have more at stake in the micro-politics of territory than do the powerful: the impact of living in one neighborhood of a city or another is greater for the well-being of the poor than it is for those who are relatively well off (Sampson 2012). In post-war circumstances, the pragmatic routines and the meanings of things and places of habitual life can be overturned and reformulated. Everyday acts of inhabiting, over time, can thus create new infrastructural facts on the ground.

For example, Vasso, an elderly woman of Vlach origin,[6] lives in a formerly Slav-Macedonian Prespa homestead that was transferred to her family by the government in 1953. Poor shepherds from Epirus, they had moved constantly to find pasture. "We lived," she noted with a laugh, "like gypsies." In Prespa, however, they became settled farmers, cultivating beans on land they owned or rented from absentees. Vasso and her husband had in fact been granted two local properties. Her son and daughter-in-law were now rebuilding the second property, half of a deteriorated stone house, reinforcing its walls with double courses of brick and with foam insulation and retimbering and retiling the roof. The north wall, however, abutted the still ruined half belonging to the heirs of the original owners who had fled abroad. Vasso's son dug a trench inside the absentees' part of the house to channel rainwater away from his new wall. This was a practical solution to an adjacency that commonly provoked disputes in the village, but it was also an objective material correlative to a break between the past and the future. The investments in home improvement that Vasso and her family were making gave material substance to the government program of ethnic engineering for the *longue durée*.

Vasso proudly gave me a tour of her house. The kitchen annex was built in the local mudbrick 'Macedonian' style, flanked by a wooden veranda opening into the yard. The newer wing of the house was more formal, appointed "with all the luxuries": television, video player, and display cabinet for china. The upper story was closed and locked, in waiting for Vasso's absent daughter. A large and very old cherry tree in the yard created a generous space for social gatherings. "You can't imagine the weddings and the parties here," Vasso said, as she urged me to climb the ladder and pick cherries, offering to cut down a whole branch. As I was leaving, she gave me a quarter loaf of bread. "It's good," she said, "to give."

Such generosity is a standard index of Greek well-being and self-regard, but the sharing of fruit from a tree also has bittersweet resonance locally. An ethnic Slav-Macedonian who had been orphaned during the Greek Civil War told me that when she and her sister returned to the village in the 1950s, her family property had been reassigned to new migrants. She remembers with a feeling of mixed gratitude that the new occupiers, Vlachs from Thessaly, gave her bread from her father's fields and fed her walnuts from her father's trees. Many surviving Pontic refugees from the 1923 Greco-Turkish 'population exchange', who had been resettled in Prespa, recounted nostalgic tales of requesting or being offered, on return visits to Turkey, a taste of the fruit from trees planted by their forefathers. One Pontic family, twice displaced themselves, in turn remembered an Albanian Muslim whose father had planted the pear tree in their garden: the youth visited once during World War II and wept. My Pontian octogenarian friend Maro knew a host of tales about the former owner of her plot of land, a quasi-mythic Turkish *sultana* who had been expelled in the exchange. Maro lived in the 2000s much as she had lived since the 1940s, with no interior toilet or shower. She could have asked for a government grant to renovate her property, but she was not interested. She suspected that her grandson's girlfriend would then seize the house and, more important, her flourishing, hard-worked garden.

Histories of dispossession run deep, tingeing the affective realms of kinship. During part of my fieldwork I lived in a large stone house owned by a native-born ethnic Slav-Macedonian family. My landlord had inherited a half-share in the house from his father's widow, whom they had cared for in old age. The other half-share was, technically, split between his two brothers, one now deceased. It was a typical local situation. Suddenly, the long-silent brother who had emigrated to Canada in the 1960s contested their de facto ownership, throwing my landlady into a state of anxiety. When her son in Athens insisted that year on renovating her reception room, she also grew suspicious of her in-laws' intentions. Nonetheless, she and her husband continued to invest labor and capital in the estate, reconstructing an outbuilding to house the undocumented seasonal Albanian laborers they needed annually to harvest beans.

These brief and ordinary accounts of infrastructural inertia and change expose the invisibilized effects of twentieth-century state violence on everyday acts of dwelling in the long term. In his remarkable study of the transmission of 'grievous loss' after mass political catastrophe in twentieth-century China, Taiwan, and Germany, Stephan Feuchtwang (2011) distinguishes several forms of temporality governing different arenas of post-conflict social engagement. To oversimplify, state, family, and religion differently shape the critical event into linear, recursive, or circular imaginaries. In the interaction of these temporalities of recognition and erasure, Feuchtwang locates our way of coping with the "collective historical demons" of irreparable loss (ibid.: 226). We might theorize territory—the ground on which such demons materialize and transform—as a fourth force in shaping temporality. Heonik Kwon (2008) powerfully shows this for the case of Vietnam, where the presence of the dead bodies of Americans, South Vietnamese forces, and other exogenous Vietnamese in village landscapes opens up a third category of ghost that cannot be contained within the protocols of (ancestral) kinship or (politically approved) state ritual. The local, material claims of the dead ignore "the political and moral border of inside and outside": the demands of village spatial intimacy engender a memorial process that liberates these dead souls from the "incarcerating history" of enmity (ibid.: 164; see also Feuchtwang 2011: 211) and through ritual hospitality turn the unincorporated Other into a *genius loci*. For Kwon, Antigone's burial of her outlawed brother, in Sophocles's Theban plays, does not place the law of kinship above that of the state but to the contrary invokes a universal ethics of any dead soul's right to burial: "Death longs for the same rites for all" (Sophocles, *Antigone*, quoted in Kwon 2008: 163).

As Murray Last (2000) observes in his reflections on the aftermath of the Nigerian/Biafran Civil War of the 1960s, ordinary people in small places keep discrepant understandings of the causes of civil war to themselves. In the interests of living a functional everyday life, hurt and anger are absorbed into private memory (ibid.: 316). The tension between remembrance and forgetting is differently managed in public and private arenas. Kwon's concept of hospitality, in contrast, brings the split community into the same space, if never on equal terms (cf. Papataxiarchis 2014). In one border community, I accompanied Eleni, born in Prespa, to put flowers on the grave of her mother in a capacious, wind-blown graveyard above the village. Her mother, a shepherd from Epirus, had immigrated in the

1950s. Eleni was unusually respectful of the displaced former inhabitants of the area. In the spirit of Kwon's Vietnamese villagers, she explained that, like the natives, she had buried her dead in this place. That meant, to her, that their painful history was becoming her history too.

Global-Local Borders and the Spatial Signature of Civil War

In the early 1990s, I confronted the remains, or phantasm[7] (cf. Navarro-Yashin 2012; Vidali 1994, 1997), of one civil war in the midst of another in full force. Sarajevo was under siege. The Greek side of the former Cold War border was in a state of apprehension provoked by the influx of migrants from a disintegrating Albania and by reanimated tensions with the bordering Republic of Macedonia. Empty hamlets were now not only indexes of a violent past but also shelters exploited by destitute migrants. Rumors of theft and rape contributed to a general unease in the countryside.

The fact of the Yugoslav break-up demonstrated to the local border population once again that modern states are fragile. The NATO air strikes from 24 March to 20 June 1999 against the Serb assault on Kosovo Albanian Muslims struck especially close to home—literally and figuratively—in northwest Macedonia, stoking conspiracy theories concerning US plots against Greece and Eastern Orthodoxy.

On a midsummer afternoon in 1999, the husband of a woman I was interviewing (about cross-ethnic marriages) exploded in anger over US interference in Kosovo and globally. The settlement in which he lived had been built by Muslim Albanian farmers, abandoned with the 'exchange' of populations, and then relocated and rebuilt in the 1920s by Pontic refugees. During the civil war, the Pontic residents were evacuated by the government to temporary camps; after the war, they were allocated property in a more favorably located village that formerly belonged to Slav-Macedonians now living as refugees abroad. Their old settlement was then resettled by Vlachs, like himself, from Thessaly. Aware of the multiple displacements wrought by international politics on local claims, my interlocutor did not want outside interference in Balkan affairs to wreck his security or devalue the currency of his Hellenist credentials in this former special security zone.

The simultaneity of my fieldwork in northern Greece with the Bosnian War provided a comparative lens on the radical spatial effects of civil war, as I tracked the post-1995 (post–Dayton Agreement) repatriation process. In collaborative research in Stolac, Bosnia-Herzegovina, an ethnically 'mixed' Croat (Catholic)-Bosniak (Muslim) community, Aida Premilovac and I looked at the post-war material environment (Hart 2006; Hart and Premilovac 2002).[8] What happened in Stolac is paradigmatic of the material-spatial transformations that follow ethno-political violence. The aftermath is composed of intimate experiences of dispossession and colonization importantly molded by the local-regional balance of power. It has a distinct, chronic, spatial signature constituted by both deformations of the material environment and techniques of the body

FIGURE 4.2 Stolac, ruined house and defaced monument, 2003

Photograph © Laurie Kain Hart

that are expressed in taking detours, observing silences or making noise, and occupying or evacuating space. Such public silences and detours are observed in Prespa and elsewhere in contemporary Greece (see Gefou-Madianou, this volume).[9] In Stolac, those who had seized power built new houses, cafés, and other structures on the ruins of the buildings owned by minority Bosniaks. Federal architectural heritage protection or other legal proscriptions or guarantees, where they existed, were ignored; metropolitan rulings on the legality of new construction were unenforceable (Hadjimuhamedovic 2002). New housing developments were established for Croat immigrants on municipal land, and Croat nationalist insignia (flags, colors, crosses, crucifixes, graffiti) were rampantly displayed. The repair or rebuilding of minority historical and religious monuments was obstructed, and imported (and invented) Italo-Catholic-style monuments were bankrolled. The preferential distribution of employment, separate and unequal school systems and nationalist curricula, and violent intimidation produced brute physical segregation. Former ethnically heterogeneous street names were replaced by generic/nationalist plaques.[10] Patriotic symbolic markers were compulsively reinscribed in squares, streets, cafés, municipal buildings, forts, monuments, and hillsides, and marginalized inhabitants were subjected to nerve-racking levels of vigilance in public space in which the spatial practices of everyday life were ideologically monitored.

Like Kwon above, philosopher Edward Casey (1996: 26) argues that the chief attribute of 'place' is its quality of gathering conflictual things together such that inhabitants of a common space are made manifest and gathered into "one arena of common engagement." Pluralist local culture is in this way historically constructed in the interaction between different social groups and is inherently 'distributive' (Keesing 1981). With its reductivist hypersymbolism, hyperdefinition, and hyperawareness of the proximities of others, ethnonationalism disables this syncretic force of place-based life. The sector of local society that 'wins' thereby cuts its roots and loses its localism and the substance of the very claim to territory it has so bloodily asserted.

These antipathetic affects also corrode ties between disenfranchised locals and their own ancestral properties. Bosniak former property owners who returned to Stolac after 1995 had no means of compelling squatters to vacate seized property. They were obliged to be bystanders in a process beyond their control. Arko, a young Bosniak waiting in the wings while a squatter considered if and when he might relinquish the house built by Arko's grandfather, told us that he wished the house would just burn down. Writing of the 1960s and 1970s in Prespa, architects Maria Culi and Dimitra Babalis (1980: 23; my translation) noted that some locals who emigrated a second time after the war often destroyed their own property as they left "as if to make sure they would have no possibility of returning again."

By the 2000s, the former town of Stolac had, it seemed, been lost in the war, apparently permanently. It was under the mantle of a 'sad' atmosphere, still being 'unmade': "[F]or everybody, Stolac is a new town, virtually nothing is as it was, personal contacts are gone, and the town has become ugly" (Kolind 2008: 69). Planners in Bosnia-Herzegovina observed that even the reconstruction of former Ottoman landmarks (e.g., in neighboring Mostar), so eagerly supported by foreign NGOs, turned into a further insult, a farce to please tourists, reminding locals of the 'irretrievable' character of the past (Calame and Pasic 2009).

In the immediate 1950s aftermath of the Greek Civil War, the villages in Prespa that had survived at least partially intact (several having been destroyed entirely) were sparsely populated. Some civilians who had been evacuated by the national army within Greece returned, as did men drafted as government soldiers, but political refugees and members of the DSE were unable to do so. Two convoys of child refugees from Yugoslavia were repatriated. During the next decade, more minors would return from other parts of Eastern Europe. The social, ethnic, and political complexion of the villages was radically changed due to this wartime and Cold War 'selection' among the indigenous and Pontian population and the arrival of new Vlach settlers. The re-sorting of houses and fields that ensued, combined with government land redistribution in 1958, confirmed the appropriation of houses and fields by new occupiers and the displacement of some locals from their wrecked natal hamlets to better-preserved villages, establishing the new status quo over the next decades. Some political refugees later returned from Eastern Europe, although their legal claims had been refused, while some new settlers, disappointed by paltry government grants, migrated again. Villagers remember a period in the 1960s when settlements recuperated a modest form of agro-pastoral life. But the rural population dipped again with out-migration to Germany and Australia, influenced by the persistent link between the disappointments of the local economy and the ethno-political repressions of the post-war period.[11] Culi and Babalis (1980: 140) note that in the 1970s only one village in the Prespa area—the central administrative village, which had been a minor settlement before the war but had experienced the bulk of development afterward—lacked this signature of pervasive *tristezza* (bleakness). After more than two decades, the afflicted zone was still 'unmade'. In the 1970s, Greece's military dictatorship built irrigation works to pump lake water into lacustrine fields, spurring the monoculture of white beans that eventually enabled local farmers to dig out of a marginal subsistence economy and keep a foothold in the border zone.

Common Inhabiting

To return to my initial question, how does the material act of common inhabiting over time affect the commutation of the injuries of the past? The last few decades have brought both intensifying and countervailing social forces to bear on the potential for co-existence in a common space. First, it is clear that divisive questions concerning the seizure of land and houses inflect the tone of public social events and kinship relations, sustained by persistent awareness of relative politico-ethnic or familial deprivation and hierarchy. A conscious sense of grievance re-emerges where there is a triangulation of past disenfranchisement with a cascade of aftershocks and insights provoked by contemporary inequalities. But dispossession and relocation are also collectively normalized features of local experience, widely shared among groups and absorbed as common sense. A villager remembered (with some admiration) the "German houses" she had lived in as a political refugee in Poland in the 1950s: she was referring to the houses vacated by Germans expelled from Poland in the Soviet advance—a triple displacement she found retrospectively unsurprising, given her own experience. Another former refugee remembered cheerfully how strangers were allocated half of her (paternal grandfather's) house after the war: it was nice, she said, to have more people around.

Ethnic intermarriage and out-marriage, locally rare in the 1940s, is increasingly common in the 2000s; hence, many villagers publicly embrace a 'counterdiscourse' (Kolind 2008)—if not consistently a counterpraxis—that de-emphasizes past politico-ethnic history. Poor agricultural communities, in what they see as an unsympathetic economy driven by metropolitan and international forces, also share a common local solidarity of marginalization. The generations with first-hand experience of war and disenfranchisement are dying out, and despite the continuity of familial (Vidali 1994) and structural effects of trauma, the vividness of loss fades underneath a new generational temporality (cf. Scott 2014). Residents from exogenous ethnic and class groups also disrupt social hierarchies and complicate the terrain of conflict (Rombou-Levidi 2012), while temporary residents such as European community youth volunteers naively disrupt and prod local habitual spatial and social boundaries.

The domestic investments described in my opening vignettes presume some kind of future and contribute to a sense of contemporaneity that increases the value of local fixed capital, not only to individuals but also to the shared community. The half-ruined mudbrick houses that dot the landscape, romantic to

FIGURE 4.3 Building under reconstruction, Prespa, 2010

Photograph © Laurie Kain Hart

outsiders, are depressing to villagers who would rather see them, and their stories of abandonment, gone. Preoccupation with the aesthetics of ruin belongs to foreigners.[12] The relentless curiosity of outsiders in villagers' catastrophic past is often resented. At the same time, what is desirable to insiders has changed as entrepreneurs rehabilitate structures that had stood empty for years. These tokens of past violence have metamorphosed into projects of modernity. Two villages near the lake are under architectural preservation regulations that affect domestic buildings and restrict the freedom to build but create capital resources in the form of a tourist nostalgia economy and a kind of local gentrification. Such historical resources, however, are unevenly shared among individuals and villages, potentially reinflating disputes over what was formerly worthless.

Monuments also play their role in the conservation and rupture of a history of violence. Busloads of pilgrims and tourists visit early Christian cave hermitages in the cliffs of the lakes and celebrate the Akritic[13] functions of the border in the defense of Byzantium, ignoring the period of imperial Slavic hegemony reflected in the zone's most impressive basilica (Hart 2012b). Local roads are lined with the busts and heroic sites of the Makedonomachoi, the bands who from 1904 to 1908 fought Turks, Bulgarians, and Serbs for union with Greece. In village centers there are stelae to the local nineteenth- and twentieth-century war dead, but these exclude the dead *komitadjes* (partisans of the Bulgarian Exarchate in the Balkan Wars of the 1910s) who are, of course, also among local *genii loci*.

The end of the Soviet bloc and the neutralization of communist internationalism, however, began to open the landscape to manifestations of the formerly hidden dead. In 1992, the youth of the Communist parties of Greece and the Balkans joined hands across the tri-state borders in a symbolic "human chain for peace" (Strevina 2001; my translation). In the mid-2000s, on a road some distance from any village, a faction of the Greek Communist Party (KKE) erected a monument to dead partisans of the defeated DSE. Paths were opened to the rebels' field hospital and headquarters, which now attract sporadic visitors. The Greek press now reports on 'Red tourism' that features battle sites associated with the civil war, especially its final stages on Mounts Vitsi and Grammos. The suppressed past generates cultural-territorial capital. In 2008, a group of artists mounted a series of public art projects entitled "Visual March to Prespa" with the stated intention of bringing elements of the natural landscape into play with local memory of the civil war; an academic conference on the civil war was also held in the district town hall. These interventions make the 'conflictual' reality(in Casey's terms) of political history materially manifest, while at the same time carefully keeping out of direct view volatile local specificities concerning ethnicity and family that cut too close to the living bone.

In Stolac after the war, as the parceling out of the built environment into ethnic enclaves and the ethnic branding of historical monuments intensified, anti-nationalist Croat and Bosniak youth in solidarity created their own 'anti-history' by taking refuge in 'nature'. In reaction to the appropriation of the town swimming pool by a separatist faction, the solidarity group moved their socializing to the river. Powerful localist memories of pre-war summer holidays were folded into global moral values associated with ecology and heritage as they placed signs reading "Let's preserve the river" along the banks. Celebrating the common capital of a locally beloved nature provided what philosopher Michel de Certeau calls making 'room for a void'—here briefly restoring the unexamined life of pre-war sociality. By the 2000s, one local told a reporter: "You can't maintain this situation forever. Kids eventually meet. It's very hard to sell them this story of a national need for unification against the enemy" (Jennings and Dzidzic 2008). By 2016, a considerable number of monuments had been rebuilt, the historical fabric partially rehabilitated, and Stolac had regained a viable cultural life. Despite this, the elections of 2016 were marked by ballot irregularities, exposing an ongoing struggle for factional supremacy.

In Prespa, the establishment of a national park in 1974, and later of an NGO and government agency dedicated to environmental stewardship of the area, has been fraught with political controversy. But it has also gradually created a territorial imaginary around agro-pastoral production and wildlife conservation that exalts a shared form of life, at least for the consumption of local schoolchildren. There is also for the first time a local high school so that adolescents now share a common local formation. The young are part of a new generation whose school friends are a mixed population of disparate older regional ethnic groups and new immigrants. Conflicts among ecologists, developers, hunters, fishers, and cultivators are serious, but new solidarities also emerge. One farmer who despaired to a reporter of the difficulty of small-scale agriculture in the twenty-first century encouraged the journalist to hike up to see local old growth trees "so broad it would take three men to encircle their trunks." He, like everyone

FIGURE 4.4 Stolac, river, 2002

Photograph © Aida Premilovac

else the reporter met on this visit to Prespa, was imagining a future for himself in ecotourism. In 2009, the center-left party of George Papandreou initiated a tri-state international agreement with Albania and the Republic of Macedonia for cooperative management of the lake resources.[14]

In the northwest border area, a long-term weariness, an impatience with the effects of past conflict, competes with the entrenchment of these effects in the social and topographical fabric (cf. Danforth and Van Boeschoten 2011; Hart 2012a; Myrivili 2004). The 1990s panic concerning Albanian labor immigration (now semi-regularized and desperately needed) has paled in the face of a broader Mediterranean migration crisis. A few Albanian immigrants are now local settlers with local stakes. And yet Rombou-Levidi (2012, 2016) has shown how gendered intimate violence builds locally on old hierarchies of state violence as Albanian brides are recruited by poor and socially marginalized farmers. In the general crisis around youth unemployment, the sense of ethnically stratified life chances strongly persists. The asymmetries of the international border, drawn in 1913 for nineteenth-century aims, take on a twenty-first-century role in post-socialist drug, arms, and human trafficking: a Prespa-born border guard was shot and killed in the hills in 2013, and a village youth died of a heroin overdose. The passage of time is nonetheless delicately persistent at creating new facts around the material infrastructures of the past and the common work of living together, and this makes a less foreclosed future also imaginable.

Acknowledgments

Research was supported by the Haverford College Faculty Research Fund, the Stinnes Research Fund, a Summer Research Grant from the National Endowment for the Humanities, the School for Advanced Research (SAR), and the National Endowment for the Humanities Resident Scholarship. I thank the anonymous reviewers for their helpful critique; the 2013–2014 cohort of scholars at the SAR for a happy year of companionship and collective work on borders; Akis Papataxiarchis for invaluable colloquia at the University of the Aegean in Mytilene; Jane Cowan and Maris Gillette for critical insight; fellow Prespa scholars Marica Rombou-Levidi and Lenio Myrivili for fellowship and inspiration; Aida Premilovac and Tasoula Vervenioti for generous ethnographic and archival collaboration; Philippe Bourgois for exacting and, as always, on the mark readings of this chapter; and Nicolas Argenti and the contributors to the 2013 "Balkan Topologies" conference for their visions of time and the post-Ottoman world. Many thanks also to Shawn Kendrick and the editorial staff of *Social Analysis*.

Laurie Kain Hart is a Professor of Anthropology at UCLA. She holds a Master of Architecture from the University of California at Berkeley and a PhD in Social Anthropology from Harvard University. Her research areas include Greece, the circum-Mediterranean area, and the US inner city (Philadelphia), with a focus on violence, ethnicity, kinship, population displacement, urban segregation, social inequality and health risk, architecture and housing, and border theory. She is the author of *Time, Religion, and Social Experience in Rural Greece* (1992) and the editor of *Good People in an Evil Time* (2004). She is currently co-authoring (with Philippe Bourgois) a forthcoming book on the carceral and psychiatric management of US poverty titled "Cornered."

Notes

1. See http://www.marxists.org/subject/greek-civil-war/.
2. High numbers of political detainees were sustained until the end of the military junta in 1974 (Vervenioti 2009).
3. Aromanians had seen their own ethnic movement in Greece crushed in the early twentieth century.
4. Van Boeschoten (2000: 31) identifies three central factors in this dynamics of inequality: differential access to resources among co-resident groups (influenced by the relative lack of extra-local social, political, and economic capital among Slav-Macedonians compared to Pontic and Vlach settlers); preferential and punitive state policies; and national and international political events of the late twentieth century.
5. The presumption of permanence is not universal. Among the West African Batammaliba, houses are tied to the life span of their builder-owners, and are left to disintegrate when the latter die (Blier 1987).

6. Two older settlements of Vlachs exist near Prespa, but most Prespa Vlachs immigrated in the 1950s.
7. As Vidali (1994: 23) explains, following Deleuze, a "phantasm" is "the ghostly reappearance of the event" in narrative, a singular "copy" that is not the same as the original but inflected by the temporal and contextual distance of the "copy" from the "original." I borrow the meaning for the case of events inscribed in buildings and landscapes.
8. Primary fieldwork for this project was carried out by linguist Aida Premilovac, a native of Stolac, in collaboration with the author.
9. Kolind (2008: 76) notes that Croat domination of "official public space" means that Bosniaks literally fall silent in public zones (cf. Hart 2005: 391–392). On architectural domination, I am grateful to Amra Hadjimuhamedovic, assistant minister of physical planning and environment for Bosnia-Herzegovina, whom I interviewed on 23 March 2002.
10. This same renaming process took place in Prespa after the tri-state border was imposed following the Balkan Wars, and Slavic speech was criminalized over the next few decades (cf. Karakasidou 2000).
11. From 1951 to 1971, the rural area of the Florina district lost 27 percent of its population (Van Boeschoten 2000: 44).
12. As Last (2000: 325–326) writes about Nigeria: "[I]t is those with a history who suffer … watchers of violence, in interpreting suffering unasked, are seen as trespassing into territory that is either past or private (or both)."
13. The Akrites were seventh to eleventh CE guardians of the eastern frontiers of Byzantium adjacent to Arab zones.
14. Sadly, the subsequent coalition government led by the conservative New Democracy Party failed to ratify the transboundary agreement.

References

Blier, Suzanne P. 1987. *The Anatomy of Architecture: Ontology and Metaphor in Batammaliba Architectural Expression*. Cambridge: Cambridge University.

Bougarel, Xavier, Elissa Helms, and Gerlachlus Duijzings, eds. 2007. *The New Bosnian Mosaic: Identities, Memories and Moral Claims in a Post-war Society*. Aldershot: Ashgate.

Bryant, Rebecca. 2010. *The Past in Pieces: Belonging in the New Cyprus*. Philadelphia: University of Pennsylvania Press.

Bryant, Rebecca. 2014. "History's Remainders: On Time and Objects after Conflict in Cyprus." *American Ethnologist* 41 (4): 681–697.

Calame, Jon, and Amir Pasic. 2009. "Post-Conflict Reconstruction in Mostar: Cart before the Horse." Divided Cities/Contested States Working Paper #7. http://www.conflictincities.org/PDFs/WorkingPaper7_26.3.09.pdf (accessed 13 January 2014).

Casey, Edward S. 1996. "How to Get from Space to Place in a Fairly Short Stretch of Time: Phenomenological Prolegomena." In *Senses of Place*, ed. Steven Feld and Keith H. Basso, 13–52. Santa Fe, NM: School of American Research Press.

Cowan, Jane K., ed. 2000. *Macedonia: The Politics of Identity and Difference*. London: Pluto Press.

Cowan, Jane K., Marie-Bénédicte Dembour, and Richard A. Wilson, eds. 2001. *Culture and Rights: Anthropological Perspectives*. Cambridge: Cambridge University Press.

Culi, Maria, and Dimitra Babalis. 1980. "Prespa nella Macedonia Grece: L'uso delle risorse locali nella prospettiva della riconstituzione del rapporto uomo-ambiente." PhD diss., University of Florence.

Danforth, Loring M., and Riki Van Boeschoten. 2011. *Children of the Greek Civil War: Refugees and the Politics of Memory.* Chicago: University of Chicago Press.

Douglas, Mary. 2005. *Purity and Danger: An Analysis of Concept of Pollution and Taboo.* London: Routledge.

Feuchtwang, Stephan. 2011. *After the Event: The Transmission of Grievous Loss in Germany, China and Taiwan.* New York: Berghahn Books.

Garcia, Angela. 2010. *The Pastoral Clinic: Addiction and Dispossession along the Rio Grande.* Berkeley: University of California Press.

Green, Sarah F. 2005. *Notes from the Balkans: Locating Marginality and Ambiguity on the Greek-Albanian Border.* Princeton, NJ: Princeton University Press.

Hadjimuhamedovic, Amra. 2002. "Through the Ashes of Cultural Memory: Suffering and Survival in Bosnia and Herzegovina Portrayed by Images of Architectural Heritage." Lecture, Department of Anthropology, Haverford College, 24 March.

Hart, Laurie Kain. 2005. "How to Do Things with Things: Architecture and Ritual in Northern Greece." In *Greek Ritual Poetics*, ed. Dimitrios Yatromanolakis and Panagiotis Roilos, 383–404. Cambridge, MA: Harvard University Press.

Hart, Laurie Kain. 2006. "Violence and the Revision of Place." Paper presented at the panel, "The Violence of Tradition and the Traditionalization of Violence." Meetings of the Western States Folklore Society, University of California, Berkeley, 20 April.

Hart, Laurie Kain. 2012a. "Expectations of the State: An Exile Returns to His Country." In *Contesting the State: Dynamics of Resistance and Control*, ed. Bruce Kapferer and Angela Hobart, 225–259. London: Sean Kingston.

Hart, Laurie Kain. 2012b. "Pictures at a Transnational Basilica." Paper presented at the Center for Hellenic Studies, Harvard University, Washington, DC, and Cambridge, MA.

Hart, Laurie Kain, and Aida Premilovac. 2002. "Reconstruction, Pluralism, and Syncretism of Place in Post-war Bosnia-Herzegovina." Paper presented at the Annual Meeting of the American Anthropological Association, University of California, Berkeley, 19 November.

Hionidou, Violetta. 2012. *Famine and Death in Occupied Greece, 1941–1944.* Cambridge: Cambridge University Press.

J.R. 1944. "The Exchange of Minorities and Transfers of Population in Europe since 1919—I." *Bulletin of International News* 21 (15): 579–588.

Jennings, Simon, and Denis Dzidzic. 2008. "Stolac: A Town Deeply Divided." Institute for War and Peace Reporting. http://iwpr.net/report-news/stolac-town-deeply-divided (accessed 29 January 2014)

Karakasidou, Anastasia. 2000. "Protocol and Pageantry: Celebrating the Nation in Northern Greece." In *After the War Was Over: Reconstructing the Family, Nation, and State in Greece, 1943–1960*, ed. Mark Mazower, 221–246. Princeton, NJ: Princeton University Press.

Keesing, Roger M. 1981. *Cultural Anthropology: A Contemporary Perspective.* New York: Holt, Rinehart & Winston.

Kolind, Torsten. 2008. *Post-War Identification: Everyday Muslim Counterdiscourse in Bosnia Herzegovina.* Aarhus: Aarhus University Press.

Kwon, Heonik. 2008. *Ghosts of War in Vietnam.* New York: Cambridge University Press.

Last, Murray. 2000. "Reconciliation and Memory in Postwar Nigeria." In *Violence and Subjectivity*, ed. Veena Das, Arthur Kleinman, Mamphela Ramphele, and Pamela Reynolds, 315–332. Berkeley: University of California Press.

Lefebvre, Henri. 1991. *The Production of Space*. Trans. Donald Nicholson-Smith. Oxford: Blackwell.
Mazower, Mark. 2001. *Inside Hitler's Greece: The Experience of Occupation, 1941–44*. New Haven, CT: Yale University Press.
Michailidis, Iakovos D. 2000. "On the Other Side of the River: The Defeated Slavophones and Greek History." In Cowan 2000, 68–84.
Myrivili, Eleni. 2004. "The Liquid Border: Subjectivity at the Limits of the Nation-State in Southeast Europe." PhD diss., Columbia University. http://academiccommons.columbia.edu/item/ac:139129 (accessed 16 April 2014).
Nachmani, Amikam. 2016. "The Greek Civil War, 1946–1949." Origins. https://origins.osu.edu/milestones/march-2016-greek-civil-war-1946-1949.
Navarro-Yashin, Yael. 2012. *The Make-Believe Space: Affective Geography in a Postwar Polity*. Durham, NC: Duke University Press.
Papadakis, Yiannis. 2005. *Echoes from the Dead Zone across the Cyprus Divide*. London: I.B. Tauris.
Papataxiarchis, Efthimios. 2014. "Unthinkable Racism: The Politicization of 'Hospitality' in the Time of the Crisis." [In Greek.] *Synkhrona Themata* 127: 46–62.
Rombou-Levidi, Marica. 2009. "Dancing beyond the 'Barre': Cultural Practices and the Processes of Identification in Eastern Macedonia, Greece." PhD diss., University of Sussex.
Rombou-Levidi, Marica. 2012 "Here, the End: Boundaries, Migration, and Mixed Marriages in Prespa after 1989." [In Greek.] Manuscript.
Rombou-Levidis, Marica. 2016. *Life under Surveillance: Music, Dance, and the Formation of Subjectivity in Macedonia*. [In Greek.] Athens: Alexandria Publishers.
Sampson, Robert J. 2012. *Great American City: Chicago and the Enduring Neighborhood Effect*. Chicago: University of Chicago Press.
Scott, David. 2014. *Omens of Adversity: Tragedy, Time, Memory, Justice*. Durham, NC: Duke University Press.
Strevina, Yianna. 2001. "The 'Journey' of the Youth Coalition: Every Year More Powerful." [In Greek.] *Rizospastis*, 1 July.
Theidon, Kimberly. 2013. *Intimate Enemies: Violence and Reconciliation in Peru*. Philadelphia: University of Pennsylvania Press.
Van Boeschoten, Riki. 2000. "When Difference Matters: Sociopolitical Dimensions of Ethnicity in the District of Florina." In Cowan 2000, 28–46.
Vervenioti, Tasoula. 2009. *Representations of History: The Decades of the 1940s through the Archives of the International Red Cross*. [In Greek.] Athens: Melissa.
Vidali, Anna. 1994. "Forbidden History and/as Subjectivity." PhD diss., Goldsmith's College.
Vidali, Anna. 1997. "Identification and the Transmission of Trauma." *New Formations* 30: 33–46.
Voglis, Polymeris. 2002. *Becoming a Subject: Political Prisoners during the Greek Civil War*. New York: Berghahn Books.

Chapter 5

(Re)sounding Histories
On the Temporalities of the Media Event

Penelope Papailias

At 10:30 AM on 28 May 1999, an Albanian migrant worker, 24-year-old Flamur Pisli, known in Greece as "Antonis," boarded a bus in a town at the outskirts of Thessaloniki where he had been living and working for several years. With a Kalashnikov rifle and two grenades in hand, he took the driver, ticket collector, and passengers hostage. He claimed that he was driven to this action because three local men (a security guard, a policeman, and a shoe factory owner) had framed him on charges of weapon smuggling and that while in detention for those charges at a police holding station he was beaten and raped. Pisli thus appears to have hijacked the bus in order to clear his name regarding the smuggling charge, as well as to assert his masculinity in the wake of the rape.[1]

By hijacking the bus, Pisli also hijacked Greek national television time, which indeed may have been his aim. In unprecedented 'live' coverage, viewers of Greek television followed the bus on its zigzag course through northern Greece

Notes for this chapter begin on page 102.

while eavesdropping on journalists' conversations (and negotiations) with the hijacker. After midnight, the bus crossed the Greek-Albanian border as it headed toward the hijacker's natal village in northern Albania and disappeared for the night from Greek television screens. Early the next morning, the bus was ambushed outside the central Albanian city of Elbasan. At 7:15 AM, Albanian snipers fatally shot the hijacker and, accidentally, a Greek hostage, 28-year-old Yiorgos Koulouris. The bloody denouement of the 20-hour ordeal was captured on camera by a Reuters television crew based in Albania.

This event radically rearranged time, space, and bodies. The temporal and spatial punctuality of the bus route was interrupted, stretching time and redirecting movement across a new terrain. A chance mix of bodies was thrown together on the bus, which was trailed by a phalanx of police, reporters, families, and bystanders. Through media transmission, this event, in turn, opened into other event-spaces: the viewing public in Greece, at home in front of their television sets or watching in public spaces, became mobilized at the time of the hijacking, while a re-enactment of the event in a cassette-recorded memorial song for the hijacker would later infiltrate and charge spaces of Albanian male migrant mobility, such as vans shuttling migrants from the border to their hometowns.

The temporality and spatialitiy of media events is radically multivalent; each act of mediated and mobile witnessing decomposes and reconfigures time and space (Reading 2011). Rather than producing a (mere) copy of the original 'here and now', mediated witnessing encompasses both the 'instance' (repeatability) and 'instant' (singularity) of the media event (Frosh and Pinchevski 2009). Less a point connected to others on a timeline, the media event emerges at the intersection of several lines, 'complicated' or folded over so many times that it cannot be unfolded: the attempt to explicate it only creates another fold, as new histories open up in history (Deleuze 1993; Rajchman 1998: 16; 2000: 60–61). Pierre Lévy (1998) has used the metaphor of the Möbius strip to describe the topological, rather than chronological, nature of this ongoing virtualization of the event's 'here and now', which flips outsides and insides, twists the personal into the public, and turns audience into author, and vice-versa.

This chapter proposes to unfold (again) the above media event, one that the author herself inevitably, if unintentionally, has played her own role in complicating. By tracking aspects of event virtualization in relation to the hijacking, I suggest what might be at stake in thinking about media events in terms of perception rather than representation. Briefly, this includes taking into account the production of event-spaces and author-effects, the transformation of private moments into public broadcasts, the bringing together and dispersing of disparate temporalities and spatialities, as well as the implications of all the above for anthropological engagements with (media) events.

This perspective does not bypass the intensities unleashed by the hijacking in order to deduce competing national-cultural viewpoints 'on the event', but dwells on the affective field (of loss, fear, anger, vengeance, shock) that kept opening this particular event in Greek and Albanian media flows. In retrospect, this was a critical period in which national borders, ideological discourses, social networks, and labor regimes were being violently unsettled, dismantled, and (re)placed, following the collapse of European communism and preceding the consolidation of neo-liberal governmentality in the Eurozone.

A Cassette Hero and a Tabloid Anthropologist

When the hijacking occurred, I remember being shocked and concerned about how the coverage contributed to the anti-immigrant fear mongering that had been growing since the influx of immigrants to Greece began in the early 1990s. However, I probably would not have written anything about the incident if I had not happened to learn about the existence and popularity of an Albanian mourning song for Pisli from an Albanian builder working in Greece. His father, he told me, had been listening to the song obsessively as he worried about his many sons then working as migrant laborers.

The song, entitled "Kengë per Flamur Pislin" (Song for Flamur Pisli), which circulated as an audiocassette, lionized the hijacker's attempt to 'speak back' to the Greek people concerning the violence and exploitation he had experienced at the hands of his boss and the police. In reality, Pisli had been the scapegoat for his brother, who had fled town after getting his employer's wife pregnant. Yet the song, written in Albania, far from the actual events, did not mention this incriminating context; instead, it presented Pisli as a victim of his boss, who had not paid him for his labor, or 'sweat' (djersën), and who had destroyed Pisli's identity papers when he had asked for his wages.

Many Albanian migrants (particularly northern Albanian men) with whom I spoke identified with Pisli even though—or probably because—they themselves had silently endured such losses without protest. The media spectacle of Pisli's extermination by Albanian police blatantly exposed migrants' precarity: even the homeland was no refuge. While the song hails Pisli as a 'hero of migration' (heroi kurbetit), the word 'martyr' better captures how his suicidal gesture transformed him into a symbol for a generation of 'lost sons' caught up in the maelstrom of post-socialist transformation and the exploitative labor relations of a neo-liberal Europe.

I ended up writing an article about this song (Papailias 2003), which reopened this media event in the Greek public sphere despite the fact that four years had passed since the hijacking. A reductive summary of the article was published as a spread in a major Athenian daily with the provocative title "Criminal for the Greeks, Hero for the Albanians" (Mihas 2004: 20–21; see fig. 1). A strident tabloid piece, entitled "The Bus Murderer a National Hero for the Albanians" (Tsigaridas 2004), was then produced on the basis of the Greek newspaper article, with excerpts of the song quoted in my article sutured together to produce a supposedly full script of the song. Soon after, a major Greek television channel tracked down a copy of the song and played it on Greek television, along with footage of the memorial in Elbasan I had mentioned in my article. Although this memorial was erected at the site of the shooting by the hijacker's family, in heated public discussions following the broadcast it was widely understood to be a monument erected by the Albanian state.

FIGURE 5.1 "Criminal for the Greeks, Hero for the Albanians": Article in the Greek newspaper *Eleftherotypia*, 2004

Photograph © Penelope Papailias

In 2005, Constantine Giannaris, a well-known filmmaker, made a feature film entitled *Omiros* (Hostage) about the incident. After the film was completed, Giannaris told me he had read and drawn on a draft of my article while preparing his film.[2] Despite his intention to loosely reconstruct the hijacking as an allegory of contemporary Greek and European society, most Greek and Albanian viewers saw the film not as fictional but as a 'docudrama' re-enactment of the event (cf. Sturken 1997), which shockingly foregrounded the death of the hijacker—migrant death—rather than that of the Greek hostage and 'host' (the focus of television coverage).[3] The film was decried by nationalists, protested outside the cinemas by the father of the murdered hostage, and only lukewarmly defended by leftist intellectuals and film critics.

The unsettling experience of getting caught up in this media spin forced me to rethink this incident as a media event—one that I could not simply examine critically, given my own immersion in its energies and lack of control over them. On a methodological level, I questioned how I had treated the song as a text to be transcribed, translated, and interpreted and started thinking more rigorously about the perceptual experience of hearing in the context of mediated and mobile witnessing, as well as the way those experiences were (re)produced across media formats and performance contexts. I also realized that I had taken the television coverage for granted (as hegemonic media discourse, not ethnographically 'exotic') and awoke to the stunning novelty of the production of a 'live' televisual event at that particular historical moment. Broadcasting a subject-in-motion outside the studio and off-script represented a significant technological breakthrough at the time, enabled by the availability of technologies such as portable video cameras, satellite links, and, most importantly, passengers' cell phones, which recently had become a widespread personal technological device and enabled voice transmission from inside the bus. Lastly, given the way my own authorship was stripped, as the 'primary sources' (the song, the memorial) were extracted from my article and my name gradually removed (misspelled in the first article, unmentioned in the tabloid piece, and not credited in the film), I also became attuned to when and how author-effects are produced (or not) in a media event.

In this chapter, I focus on the Albanian memorial song, treating it less as a counter-narrative than as yet another virtualization of the 'here and now' of Pisli's 'speaking back' during the hijacking. I analyze how this particular re-enactment of the hijacking in the mediated witnessing and mourning of Pisli's death by his family in Albania reverberates with the public mourning of unrelated witnesses through the cassette-mediated circulation of the song. In his discussion of 'event-transitivity' and 'event-spaces', Brian Massumi (2002: 84–85) speaks of the unpredictable 'repotentializing' of the gender dynamics and violent reflexes of the home during the televisual transmission of a sporting event. In this case, I argue that the event-spaces imagined by the song (ritual sites of mourning, such as the hijacker's home, the cemetery, the memorial at the site of the hijacking) were supplemented, or even superseded, by other performative contexts (jails, public van transport), thus generating a significantly expanded space of public mourning for a migrant death not recognized as worthy of mourning by either the Greek or the Albanian state.

A Post-Ottoman Bandit and the Televisual Live

One day, a well-known Greek investigative television journalist, Tasos Telloglou, slipped into my office on campus. Without wasting any time on formalities, he told me that he had read my article and wanted to discuss with me what had "really happened." Making a distinction between my work and his ("You do reflection, I reconstruction"), he presented his thoughts regarding Pisli's act, which he described at the outset as "pre-modern" and thus quintessentially "Albanian." His comment, though, begged a fundamental question: what *was* Pisli's act?

This journalist was hardly alone in viewing Pisli's decision to hijack the bus in culturalist terms, that is, as a reflex stemming from a Mediterranean honor-and-shame complex, much documented by early British social anthropology, which dictates that men should go to extreme lengths to defend their personal honor and family name. In this view, Pisli's act can be understood less in terms of whether he was guilty or innocent for violently seizing the bus and taking hostages, and more as a means to dispel the public disgrace of his imprisonment and rape. While the Albanian memorial song alludes directly to *besa* (the Albanian word for 'honor', also used in Greek), the Greek press consistently referred to the hijacking as a 'bus piracy' (*leoforeiopeirateia*). Related to *aeropeirateia* (airplane hijacking), this term, based on the word *peiratis* (pirate), evokes a pre-modern past of both lawlessness and agency. The use of the word 'pirate' is striking when one considers possible alternatives that were not chosen, or even mentioned, in Greek public discourse—notably, 'terrorist' (*tromokratis*). Although the hijacking occurred prior to the 11 September 2001 al-Qaeda attacks and the emergence of a global discourse regarding a 'war on terrorism', it is still noteworthy that a contemporary language of sovereignty, violence, and mobility was not invoked in the blatantly sensationalist media coverage.

For Greek householders, following this 'breaking news' on television actualized their media-shaped nightmares of capture by the new immigrants pouring into Greece in the 1990s from neighboring Albania. The passengers on the bus had been traveling to Thessaloniki, perhaps on their way to do some errands or to shop, but instead they were hurtled across the Greek-Albanian border and 'back' into an Eastern/Ottoman/Balkan/communist 'chaos' that European Greece supposedly had safely escaped. However geographically proximate that border, in Greek minds it was far distant—on the other side of history. A number of Albanians established in Greece told me that they too felt like hostages during the incident.

However, the image of Pisli with a Kalashnikov in one hand and a microphone in the other, as he 'spoke back' to his employer, the police, and the Greek people, suggests a more savvy understanding of the contemporary politics of mediation (and mediation of politics) than Ottoman period references imply. The striking transformation of the bus window into a stage recalls the 2002 Brazilian documentary *Ônibus 174* (Bus 174), directed by José Padilha and Felipe Lacerda, which presents an account of a similarly mass-mediated bus hijacking fiasco. At some point, the Brazilian hijacker takes off the hood covering his face in order to play to the television cameras. By contrast, Giannaris's film *Omiros*, based on the Pisli hijacking, simply pokes fun at the journalists' frenzied pursuit of the bus, rather than probing the workings of media spectacle. When the hijacker in the film pulls shut a curtain to block the journalists' view, the implication is that the spectacle-in-the-making is exterior to the event itself. The authentic story, it is suggested, resides in the interior, in the hostage experience, rather than with the mediated witnesses following the event on television or the radio.

Yet the bus hijacking as a media event crystallized not only the tensions and violence of the first decade of mass migration to Greece, but also the first decade of commercial television. In retrospect, the 'live' television coverage of the hijacking could be seen as emblematic of the heyday of what people then referred to sarcastically as 'teledemocracy'. Just prior to the emergence of Internet-based citizen journalism (with each user a potential 'channel'), television at this time appeared the best medium to expose injustice (inefficient bureaucracy, political patronage) by bypassing political mediation. It is no wonder that Pisli asked to speak to the journalist Nikos Evangelatos, known at the time as the pioneer of this genre of direct television, and through him the prime minister (something that did not happen), rather than press charges through the legal system.

While from the journalists' perspective Pisli wandered onto the stage of a modern media spectacle, I think we should ask how this event produced an atavistic figure within the rationalizing order of contemporary media time and on the eve of Greek Eurozone membership (in 2001) when the presence of migrants themselves seemed to testify to Greece's 'modernization' (*eksynchronismos*). Furthermore, given the positive valence of Ottoman-era bandit figures in the Greek national imaginary, it is also no wonder that a number of Greek viewers identified with Pisli as an underdog figure. *Peiratis* harks back to an era prior to the modern nation-state in which 'the people' (*laos*) were subjects of sovereigns rather than sovereign citizens. This ambivalence is evident in the figure of the *klefts* (lit., 'thieves'), self-appointed rebels against Ottoman rule who took the 'law into their own hands' and have been canonized as Greek national heroes.

Despite the journalists' attempts at relegating the hijacker to a surpassed cultural pre-history, the hijacker-as-pirate was uncannily familiar to Greek viewers, a ghost of past (male) selves, whether the brigand fighting the injustices of the (Ottoman) overlords or the migrant outsider of various waves of Greek migration. The intensity around this incident for Greek viewers reflects the reconfiguration of cultural identities and labor relations, as well as the imagining of a new European future in a historical conjuncture that saw the average (male) Greek householder morph (temporarily, as it turned out) from a potential immigrant into a 'boss'.

Other Times of (Im)mediation

Remarkably, Pisli did state on Greek television that he had been raped and then deported as a "half-person." But he stuttered and spoke haltingly in rudimentary Greek. He did not tell a chronologically ordered story and probably could not have formed his traumatic experience of betrayal and violence into a coherent narrative even if he had been allowed to speak freely in his televisual 'window' (*parathiro*) and had not been pressed by journalists' questions. As the reporting of the event proceeded, the footage of his confession was broken into sound bites and eventually replayed with the sound off, overlaid with journalists' voice-overs providing updates on the situation. In Greek televisual coverage, the hijacker was not a voice, but a face set up as an object of public scrutiny, sighted as prey to be hunted down.

The Albanian memorial song, based on the epic genre of 'heroic song' (*këngë kreshnike*), retells this snuffing out of Pisli as just another nameless Albanian migrant or, rather, as a generically renamed one. By situating the incident in the epic temporalities of national sacrifice, the song transforms the contingency of the hijacking into a "battle," casts chance death as heroic loss, and gives "Antonis" back his name. In the song, Pisli is even likened to the legendary Ottoman-era Gjergj Elez Alia, much celebrated in traditional song, who fought a mythical monster figure (invader, despoiler of local honor) despite having been wounded several times. The memorial song presents itself as the legitimate archive of Albanian history, a repository of truth in the media age. Lyrical slowness is held up as a virtue, as the painstaking mechanisms of oral tradition are contrasted to the hasty (and dishonest) conclusions of the Albanian press regarding "what really happened." A shorter song about the hijacking, "Flamur Pisli Rron Te Känga" (Flamur Pisli Lives in Song), written by the singer of the memorial song, describes the mediated witnessing of the hijacking thus:

> The radio and press report
> The refugee Flamur Pisli
> Strapped with grenades and automatic weapons
> Took hostages in Salonika
> Through the streets of Salonika
> He spoke with words of the soul
> Newspapers, don't rush to a conclusion
> The truth has come out in the squares.

Although the word 'square' brings to mind a village square, given the fact that the hijacker's own family found out about the hijacking from relatives living in Germany, this square, in fact, could be said to lie in diasporic networks of communication enacted beyond and between national media envelopes, with local knowledge being based in part on global and comparative media scanning.

The moral high ground claimed by the song in opposition to the television coverage, however, is hinged on claiming a status of 'im-mediation' in relation to the 'here and now' of the event. Anthropologist William Mazzarella (2006) describes 'immediation' as the 'fantasy' of transparency and immediacy that paradoxically is produced *through* mediation. Prioritizing sound over image, the naturalization and localization of singing in the hijacker's natal village, Patin, further enhances its authenticity, as we see in these lines from "Flamur Pisli Lives in Song":

> From the deep gorges of Patin
> A farewell gives sound
> For this brave man there is no place for mourning
> Flamur Pisli lives in the song
> For this brave man there is no place for mourning
> O! Flamur Pisli lives in song!

The song's refrain—O! Flamur Pisli lives in song!—conflates the song with an echo issuing from the mountain gorges of the hijacker's village, thus obfuscating the song's technological mediation.

The song as witnessing text is presented as enduring over time, given the potential for re-enactment—or (re)sounding—through ritual lament. The memorial song ends with this verse:

> This story, this story tells about an event
> but for Flamur Pisli this is a rebirth
> as many times as we sing this song
> Flamur Pisli we'll remember him
> As many times as we sing this song
> Flamur Pisli we'll remember him.

In safeguarding memory through future repetition and the collective sonic energies it generates, the song promises to transcend the ephemeral 'now' of the media event and preserve Pisli's memory in the long temporalities of traditional verse and national history.

The 'Albanian Folk Singer' as Character

In July 2002, after a bumpy van journey from Tirana, I arrived at the humble home of the traditional folk singer Ded Gjinaj in the northern Albanian village of Baz. Before I asked him anything, Gjinaj started to speak with bitter humor about the hard life of the Albanian folk singer (*rapsod*). I had seen cassettes of Gjinaj in stores in Tirana and northern Albania cities, as well as in an Albanian music store in Piraeus. Apparently, though, their sales did not bring him much income. He showed me a contract from a Tirana studio stating that he would be paid 10 euros in advance for every song as a deposit on their future sales. "Luckily," added his wife, "my husband is not a *lekist* [a lover of lek, the Albanian currency]." Responding to that comment, I took out my copy of the cassette featuring the "Song for Flamur Pisli." I noted that it probably was a pirated copy, judging from the cover image (a blurred photograph of a much younger and thinner Gjinaj; see fig. 2). Jumping out of his seat, Gjinaj exclaimed: "*All* those cassettes are pirated. There never was an original!" He even recounted how he had gone to the office of the company in Tirana that was distributing the cassettes. Taking out his passport and comparing it to the cassette cover, he had declared: "That's *me*." To bring home his point, he dug into his pocket and pulled out his passport, which he proceeded to brandish before my eyes: "Look! They even spelled my name wrong. I am Ded *Gjinaj*, not Gjini!"

Gjinaj's claims to ownership in regard to the memorial song might be futile, given the realities both of the folk music industry in Albania and of technological reproduction. What is notable, however, is that an author has been affixed to the text, thus suggesting that on an ideological level 'traditional' Albanian song is not legible in the absence of an author, with a name, a face, and a clear cultural-geographical origin. This desire to 'humanize' discourse and produce an author-effect contrasts sharply with the Greek television coverage of the event. When I interviewed one of the first television cameramen who had arrived at the scene of the hijacking, he rejected the idea that he had played a role in authoring the event. He told me that, in contrast to his documentary work, he did not keep footage from news reporting in his personal archive. Since he had shot the hijacking using a camera from the television channel for which he was working, in his view the footage belonged to the channel. To speak of authorship in this context, with its implications of subjectivity and artistry, would challenge the automatism of the camera and the objectivity of televisual news discourse.

While Gjinaj was angry that others were making a profit from the memorial song, under normal circumstances he would not have gone to any great lengths to claim it as his own. His research had included spending a long evening with

FIGURE 5.2 Cassette cover, "Song for Flamur Pisli" by Ded Gjini (*sic*)

FIGURE 5.3 Ded Gjinaj jotting down lyrics in Baz, Albania, 2002

Photographs © Penelope Papailias

the hijacker's father, who had commissioned him to write the song and who told him what (he heard) had happened. Many of the lines in the memorial song were taken directly from the many poems that friends and strangers had sent to Pisli's father (see fig. 4 and fig. 5). Like all his memorial songs, and in contrast to his commercial repertoire, this was a song that Gjinaj intended to sing only once. Unlike his studio-recorded songs, which are timely, sarcastic, and snappy, the memorial song for Pisli is long and solemn. While, according to Gjinaj, his commercial songs have 'political value' (*blerje politik*), his memorial songs are chiefly of 'poetic value' (*blerje poetik*).

As a virtualization of the hijacking event, the song centers on Pisli's act of 'speaking back'. Through the extensive use of direct discourse, the hijacker emerges as an agentive subject who succeeds in breaking the silence imposed on migrants in the societies in which they live and work. Throughout the song, Pisli constantly speaks: to himself, to the hostages, to his boss, to the Greek people, even to a minister. Ultimately, the song appears to be about voice—about the claiming of voice—in Greek society. The memorial song, thus, does not just

FIGURE 5.4 A poem for Pisli from his father's personal archive

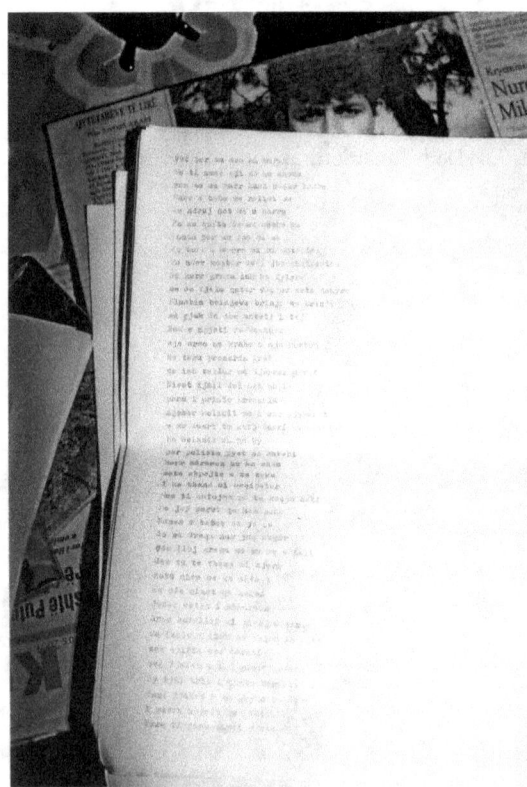

Photograph © Penelope Papailias

FIGURE 5.5 Another poem for Pisli from his father's archive

Photograph © Penelope Papailias

rewrite the event but, through the voice of the *rapsod*, re-enacts the hijacker's monumental act of 'speaking back':

> A journalist gets up the courage
> To interview Flamur Pisli
> Look at my wounds that are dripping
> It's my sweat I'm demanding.

When I expressed surprise at the stack of handwritten and typed poems for Pisli that his father took out to show me, he responded laconically: "In Albania we do not cry for our dead, we sing." This idea of 'singing as weeping' presents affect as embodied, pre-linguistic, and unmediated even given the material evidence of multiple acts and forms of mediation. Perhaps this paradox explains the need for an author figure. Serving as a conduit and surrogate for the dead hijacker's voice, Gjinaj/Gjini (re)unites body, voice, and place in a dream of unmediated presence with both the hijacker and the 'here and now' of the event. Furthermore, in a twist of the Möbius strip, Gjinaj/Gjini also becomes a character in his own right, playing the part of the *rapsod* singing/weeping for the dead in the event-space of the family's home as witnessed by unrelated mourners, such as northern Albanian migrant men listening to the cassette-recorded song.

Migrant Soundscapes and Mobile Listening

The fact that the memorial song was recorded on a cassette, of course, did not mean that hearing the song depended on owning the cassette. One Albanian migrant told me that he had first heard the song in a *fugon* (van), a quintessential emblem of male mobility and a site of congregation for 1990s Albanian migrants as they shuttled back and forth from the border to their hometowns. He heard it a second time in jail, where one of the hijacker's relatives sang the song from memory. This circulation of the song in spaces of migrant male sociality could be said to illuminate a small part of the soundscape of migration and demonstrate the way that hearing—a sensory experience much less scrutinized than viewing—contributes to shaping social memory and political identity.

The reception model inscribed within the song itself, however, is the *konak*, the room traditionally set aside in northern Albanian households for hosting guests and for male sociality where traditional singers, like Gjinaj, would be invited to perform at weddings and funerals. Yet, as we have seen, in the context of the spaces produced by mobility and mobile media, the song was being heard in new ways. Even though the song is presented as a long biographical narrative of the hijacker, interlaced with historical references, it is questionable whether the song was heard as a linear narrative or rather, as in the *fugon*, in the fragmented, distracted manner associated with televisual 'zapping' or Internet 'surfing'. This rushed and partial mobile listening troubles the song's bid to anchor Pisli's life in the narrative grid of epic temporality as a means to regain personal and national honor, to restore the patriarchal, heterosexual order, and to achieve class justice.

The song's transmission, however, did imbue these liminal spaces of migrant mobility with the intensities of private mourning. As a poor-quality recording, not meant to circulate, the recording gave the listener the impression of eavesdropping on a scene of family mourning through the voice of the *rapsod*. Hearing this song shifted relations of absence and presence, creating a sense of mediated co-presence in the mourning of Pisli's death. Thus, the witnessing of this event formed a public memorial node where unrelated mourners could attach their own multifarious experiences of loss—but also of vulnerability, anger, and violence—during the first wave of post-socialist migration. Gjinaj never expected that this song would be disseminated beyond the hijacker's family circle, reaching Albanian listeners across the Balkans and eventually being played on Greek television. Remembering his distinction between *blerje politik* and *blerje poetik*, we witness not only the twisting of personal mourning into public grief, but also the poetic into the political.

Conclusion

More akin to thresholds than to the linear series of film frames of which they are ostensibly comprised, media events can best be understood as affective contexts in which interiorities and exteriorities, the future and the past, are coming and going, meeting up and splitting apart. Media events, thus, are privileged sites in late-capitalist societies that enable us to consider how and when diverse pasts come to the surface in the present to be recognized, denied, or reworked for the future. The hijacking was a seminal event in late-twentieth-century Greek and Albanian societies. It opened up, among other histories, aspects of the pre-national Ottoman past (in relation to issues of sovereignty, masculinity, violence, labor exploitation) as part of an affective engagement with the social transformations of the immediate post–Cold War period. In addition, the transitivity of this particular media event across national media envelopes and media formats briefly produced a transnational 'Balkan event-space' not mediated through global media discourse—a rare event indeed.

The figure of Pisli as a migrant-cum-bandit was uncannily familiar for many Greek viewers, who saw him as a desperate adventurer possessing double vision concerning the injustices of global capitalism and the everyday ruthlessness of the local bosses. Yet the doubling of exclusivist national narratives also proved troubling to some. When I mentioned to a friend of mine, a high school philologist, the historical allusions in the memorial song to the Ottoman-era Albanian hero, she replied that she found it problematic since, unlike the *kleft*, Pisli was not in "his own place." The coming loose of the state-territory-sovereignty link, along with the emergence of internal 'enemies' and domestic 'wars', is not a pre-national but rather a post-national phenomenon characterizing late-capitalist globalization and neo-liberal democracies (Hansen and Stepputat 2005: 1–2). For some viewers, this seeing of the Self as the Other through the figure of the 'bandit' would trouble the givenness of such internal border making. Official reactions to the hijacking, however, were not ambivalent: the incident was treated as a crisis of international relations. It was not only Pisli who became a hero. A young Greek man who disarmed a second Albanian hijacker in the summer of 1999 was awarded a medal given for the first time when Greece was not at war. The militarization of migration resulted in the placing of the migrant (and the fact of migration) as forever outside Greek society. Shortly after the hijacking fiasco, the prime minister at the time, Kostas Simitis, authorized an unprecedented mass deportation of immigrants, tellingly referred to in Greek as a 'sweep' (*skoupa*).

The fragmented, dispersed experience of listening to the song on the move, as well as the journalists' voice-overs that obscured the hijacker's discourse in Greek televisual footage, troubles romantic notions of an autonomous and resistant soundscape in which the 'voice of the Other' was finally heard. I believe that the intensity and even visceral discomfort of Greek viewers when they learned about the memorial song for Pisli reflected an inability to accept that the hijacker—seen as an 'expendable' migrant Other—could be mourned as a son, a neighbor, and a citizen. Indeed, the journalist Telloglou mentioned above told me that when his investigative piece on the hijacking finally aired, data showed that viewership dropped precipitously when the interview with the hijacker's father was being played—a collective zapping away from a scene with which it was impossible to relate.

The version of the hijacking presented in the Albanian memorial song is radical in some respects: as a critique of unregulated labor markets at the beginning of the euro boom, as a comment on the crisis of political institutions in post-socialist states, and as an outcry against racist violence suffered by non-citizens at the hands of employers and police. Yet the song also celebrates violence as a response to conflict and presents migration as a battle of 'men against men', thus promoting as essentially (and timelessly) Albanian the values of a patriarchal, homophobic society and a militaristic nationalism (of heroes and martyrs). Nonetheless, the affective energies generated around this event certainly exceeded the script of the song, making the sonic re-enactment—the (re)sounding—of this hijacking a node for first-generation post-communist migrants to mourn the losses of migration and to articulate the dilemmas of social audibility, precarity, and citizenship.

Acknowledgments

I would like to thank Shkelqim Salkurti and Triandafillos Triandafillidis for their tireless support during the research phase of this chapter.

Penelope Papailias is an Associate Professor of Social Anthropology in the Department of History, Archaeology and Social Anthropology at the University of Thessaly, where she directs the Laboratory of Social Anthropology and the Pelion Summer Lab for Cultural Theory and Experimental Humanities. Her monograph *Genres of Recollection: Archival Poetics and Modern Greece* (2005) explores the politics of cultural memory and popular practices of historical documentation and archiving. She has also co-authored an online, open-access textbook in Greek, entitled *Digital Ethnography* (2015). In addition, she has written numerous articles on the cultural politics and media technologies of witnessing, focusing on topics such as affective publics, social grief, visuality and violence, and public death and necropolitics in the context of critical media events, network culture, and database aesthetics.

Notes

1. Pisli demanded that the police bring him the guns that had been planted on him. While Pisli believed these weapons would establish his innocence, this request was interpreted by the Greek public as a sign of escalating violence. Later in the evening, when Pisli was brought the weapons (but not the ones used to incriminate him), he refused to accept them. Needless to say, Greek viewers were shocked that the police presented guns to an armed man holding hostages. Pisli had also demanded 50 million drachma (approximately $160,000) and free passage to Albania, where he promised to release the hostages after treating them to a coffee in Tirana.

2. Interview with Giannaris, 12 May 2006, and comments at screening of *Omiros*, University of Thessaly, Volos, 5 April 2005.
3. While Greek television broadcast the hijacking 'live' for hours, Albanian television provided no coverage whatsoever. In order to deflect attention from the fact that a returning migrant had been shot by the police of his own country, Albanian newspapers initially reported that the hijacker had killed the Greek hostage and then committed suicide. When I visited Pisli's hometown, I found that copies of videotaped Greek television coverage of the hijacking were being sold at the local video shop. It is no wonder, then, that when the film *Hostage* was released, it circulated as a pirated videocassette in Albania with the title *The True Tragedy of Flamur Pisli*. In subsequent years, the film would be screened over and over on Albanian national television.

References

Deleuze, Gilles. 1993. *The Fold: Leibniz and the Baroque*. Trans. Tom Conley. London: Athlone Press.
Frosh, Paul, and Amit Pinchevski. 2009. "Crisis-Readiness and Media Witnessing." *Communication Review* 12 (3): 295–304.
Hansen, Thomas B., and Finn Stepputat. 2005. "Introduction." In *Sovereign Bodies: Citizens, Migrants, and States in the Postcolonial World*, ed. Thomas B. Hansen and Finn Stepputat, 1–36. Princeton, NJ: Princeton University Press.
Lévy, Pierre. 1998. *Becoming Virtual: Reality in the Digital Age*. Trans. Robert Bononno. New York: Plenum Trade.
Massumi, Brian. 2002. *Parables for the Virtual: Movement, Affect, Sensation*. Durham, NC: Duke University Press.
Mazzarella, William. 2006. "Internet X-Ray: E-Governance, Transparency, and the Politics of Immediation in India." *Public Culture* 18 (3): 473–505.
Mihas, Takis. 2004. "Hero for the Albanians, Criminal for the Greeks." [In Greek.] *Eleftherotypia*, 8 September.
Papailias, Penelope. 2003. "'Money of *Kurbet* Is Money of Blood': The Making of a 'Hero' of Migration at the Greek-Albanian Border." *Journal of Ethnic and Migration Studies* 29 (6): 1059–1078.
Rajchman, John. 1998. *Constructions*. Cambridge, MA: MIT Press.
Rajchman, John. 2000. *The Deleuze Connections*. Cambridge, MA: MIT Press.
Reading, Anna. 2011. "The London Bombings: Mobile Witnessing, Mortal Bodies and Globital Time." *Memory Studies* 4 (3): 298–311.
Sturken, Marita. 1997. *Tangled Memories: The Vietnam War, the AIDS Epidemic, and the Politics of Remembering*. Berkeley: University of California Press.
Tsigaridas, Ph. 2004. "The Bus Murderer a National Hero for the Albanians." [In Greek.] *Espresso*, 13 October.

Chapter 6

BETWEEN DREAMS AND TRACES
Memory, Temporality, and the Production of Sainthood in Lesbos

Séverine Rey

The monastery Agios ('saint' in Greek) Rafaïl was built in the 1960s on the northern Aegean island of Lesbos in Greece. Over the span of a few decades, it has become a well-known Orthodox Christian shrine that attracts many devotees and pilgrims, mainly Greeks and Cypriots, as well as tourists, especially over the summer. The monastery commemorates the 'newly revealed' (*neophaneis*) Saints Rafaïl, Nikolaos, and Irini, 'apparitions' attested to by a popular movement of veneration and quickly supported by the Orthodox Church. The Ecumenical Patriarchate of Constantinople officially recognized the saints in 1970.

In this chapter, I analyze the context in which this monastery was built. Apart from its religious dimension, it is worth examining what it has to tell us about history, memory, and temporality. The process reveals registers of time that are different from the usual unilinear chronology that characterizes contemporary Western societies: it combines the collective memory of violence

Notes for this chapter begin on page 115.

and displacements, historical consciousness, and the immanence of the past, themes at the core of the present collection (see in particular the chapters by Argenti and Stewart). After a summary of the main events of the saints' discovery, I discuss the role played in this story by the Asia Minor refugees and their descendants in the region. The analysis highlights the different experiences of temporality staged by this story, in particular through the saints' exemplariness in the post-Ottoman world.

An Anecdotal Find?

In 1959, a family living in the village of Thermi, located on the east coast of Lesbos facing Turkey, decided to build a small chapel in one of its olive groves.[1] As soon as they started digging the foundations for the building, the workers found pieces of marble carved with crosses and a grave containing a human skeleton, its jawbone replaced by a brick engraved with a crucifix. The exhumation of these unidentified remains amazed the local people, who wondered who the person might have been and why a Christian was buried there. Lesbos was under Ottoman rule from 1462 to 1912, and in the later period of Ottoman occupation the field had been the property of a *bey* (governor). Shortly after the skeleton's exhumation, some villagers said they had "seen dreams"[2] of a monk who explained that his name was Rafaïl and that the bones were his own, and who later provided details on his life and death.

Simultaneously, extraordinary and mysterious events occurred: a monk-like figure appeared, and dreams and miracles (curing, faith recovering, etc.) occurred. Various figures appeared in dreams and narrations, including well-known saints, such as Panagia (the All-Saint, the Madonna) and Saint Paraskevi, but also initially anonymous people, among them the monk Rafaïl and, later, Nikolaos (described as a deacon) and Irini (a young girl). In order to convince the Church authorities of the veracity of these dreams and to provide physical evidence to authenticate these stories, excavations were undertaken. After the first unearthing, other skeletons, ruins, and items (pieces of pottery, medals, gold coins) were discovered, among them some items that had been 'seen' in dreams. The archaeologists dispatched to the area dated some of these artifacts to the Byzantine era (the thirteenth to fourteenth centuries) and the architectural vestiges to Early Christianity (Charitonidis 1968).

For about a year, the religious authorities did not seem to be interested in this phenomenon and criticized it as a sign of imagination and credulity, a characteristic that they attributed to "simple people and above all women."[3] When the dreams began to be known, people belonging to the clergy or who were close to the Church supported the villagers. Together, they gathered a collection of dreams and testimonies (see Kontoglou 1962) to document the 'apparition' of the new saints and to convince the public of their legitimacy. The local church officials decided then to investigate, sending a priest to interview some of the persons who were seeing dreams. Thanks to this inquiry, the bishop of Mytilene[4] came to the conclusion that, first, the dreams matched the discovery of the excavations and, second, some miracles, such as the transformation of an atheist into a believer after sighting the apparitions, could be confirmed as real. He consequently launched the process of recognition of the saints by sending a report to the Holy Synod.[5] At the same time (in September 1962), without waiting for formal recognition, the Synod decided to build a monastery to commemorate the saints.

The story gradually revealed to the 'dreamers' is the following. Rafaïl was an archimandrite (head of a cloister) in a monastery located on the very same spot in which the family living in Thermi set out to build the chapel in 1959. On Easter Tuesday, 1463, the Ottomans had killed him along with Nikolaos, the deacon, and villagers who had gathered for the Easter celebration, including Irini, the daughter of a notable of Thermi. This slaughter supposedly occurred in response to a popular uprising against the 1462 annexation of the island, which had previously been under Genoese dominion, to the Ottoman Empire.

Asia Minor Refugees and Their Descendants in Lesbos

The main actors of the initial discovery were the nearby villagers, who then began to experience the dreams. The majority of these villagers, however, were not native to Lesbos but were refugees, or their children, who had arrived on the island as a result of the 1922 Greek exodus from Asia Minor. Their displacement and the violence they suffered were due to a collision of nationalisms at the end of the Ottoman Empire. On one side, the Greek government ardently wished to unify all regions inhabited by Greeks in the Middle East within the borders of a single state and to have Constantinople as its capital—the irredentist project called the 'Great Idea'. On the other side, Mustafa Kemal led the Turkish War of Independence in his bid to found the new ethnically homogeneous state of Turkey. Between 1919 and 1922, the war between Greece and Turkey raged, leading to massacres and culminating in a massive exchange of populations ratified by the 1923 Treaty of Lausanne. The Greeks refer to these events as 'the disaster' or 'the catastrophe of Asia Minor' (*katastrophē tēs mikras Asias*). More than one million people took refuge in Greece, which then had a population of approximately five million (Clogg 1992).

The first grave to be exhumed in Thermi gave birth to a double mystery: the revelation of the remains of an unidentified person and evidence of an inexplicable burial practice, as in Greece the ritual exhumation of bodies is performed two to five years after the burial. The Asia Minor refugees and their descendants living in the area quickly built up a close relationship with this anonymous deceased person, associating him with the slain kin whom they had had to leave behind in Asia Minor without a proper burial. Among them was Vasiliki Ralli,[6] who owned the field where the chapel was to be built. When gathering and cleaning the skeleton's bones with her mother, she recalled her father, who had disappeared in Turkey on the forced march that took place during the exchange of populations and was presumed dead: "'The sorrow of my deceased father oppressed us', confided Vasiliki. 'We did not bury him as befits a Christian, since he disappeared in Turkish captivity. So we thought we should fulfill our moral responsibilities regarding this unknown deceased person'" (Bishop of Goumenissa Dimitrios 1996: 48). What is meaningful in this case, as well as in many other examples I collected during fieldwork, is that even before knowing the identity and biography of the discovered bodies, the refugees seem to have inserted them into their own genealogy, regardless of chronology or geography. We see here "topological historicizing" (Stewart, this volume), which enables the expression of violence suffered and the remembrance of loss.

Subsequently, the identity of those who were to become saints was revealed, offering other occasions for such time loops. From then on, an interlacing took place between the life paths of both groups—the exhumed dead and the refugees. The past reappeared in the present in a double manner: the evidence from the excavation and the stories that arose from the dreams date back to the fourteenth to fifteenth centuries, and the memories and remembrances of the villagers go back to the 1920s. In an interview I had with her, Vasiliki described the dream she had had in October 1959 in which Saint Rafaïl told her: "Vasiliki, you ask to learn what my name is and who I am. I am the holy martyr Rafaïl. The bones you found ... are mine: the Turks killed me after torturing me like Christ. I am a saint ... and I will accomplish many miracles" (pers. comm., 2 February 1998).

Gradually, the graves and the discovered items came to be linked with the beginning of the Ottoman occupation in Lesbos. A brotherhood had been living in a monastery (at the same site as the discoveries), developing philanthropic activities and a peaceful connection with the neighborhood. A rupture occurred when the Ottomans entered Lesbos. After a villagers' rebellion, the occupying forces besieged the cloister, slaughtered the people who had gathered for the Easter celebrations, and set fire to the place before leaving it. In this reconstructed narrative, some survivors came later to bury the victims.

Conflation of Historical Periods and Expressions of Violence

The findings in the olive grove revealed a tragic episode of local history and also offered an opportunity for the Asia Minor refugees to express their own life paths and remembrance. A resemblance gradually emerged between their own destiny and that of the saints: "For all of us, the martyrs ... were not those who lived five centuries before us. We felt them to be alive among us, like our own beloved kin, and their martyrdom broke our hearts" (Ralli 1998: 81). Through this exhumation and what happened afterward, those refugees found a similarity with what they had experienced. When Vasiliki told her family about a dream she saw about Rafaïl escaping from Alexandroupolis[7] in a small boat, her mother burst into tears: "My daughter, we also came to Lesbos to take refuge, persecuted, and we did not know where to go and where to stay. Maybe it was the will of God to give this field [the olive groves where the discoveries were made] to me, the harassed woman devastated by the Turks, who has ... felt the desolation of exile … For me, these saints represent my beloved kin killed by the Turks" (ibid.: 70–71).

The refugees and their descendants never conflated the two events, but they saw strong similarities between them, as if they formed two sides of a parallel sequence. A good example is the explanation given for the local insurrection before the massacre. Some people doubted that it would have been possible under the Ottoman rule to organize a rebellion. Through dreams, they were informed that villagers had been waiting for help promised by 'the Franks' (Europeans)—help that never came. As Vasiliki related to me, Saint Rafaïl told one woman: "Myrta, the Franks deceived us: they promised to help us, but they forgot us! We rose in rebellion but they did not help us" (pers. comm., 2 February 1998). In this case, the parallel is explicit: "That is to say that the Franks did [in 1463] what they also did in 1922: during the war [against Turkey], they betrayed us and Asia Minor has been destroyed. The whole of Hellenism in Asia Minor fell into the depths of 'the catastrophe' because the Franks were our allies but in the end they betrayed us. They had already done the same in the time [of Saint Rafaïl]" (ibid.).

These events and discoveries bring the past back into the present. As Argenti so eloquently puts it in the introduction to this collection: "Where the past plays the role of an implacable social presence, we can conceive of it not only as remembered but also as immanent." The stories about the newly appeared saints express a discourse about other events lived by the refugees. In this way, the saints are interstitial figures linking the past and the present: existing outside of historical temporality, they enable the refugees to give their own story its place in history and to express an affective relationship to their new homeland. Often in the dreams, the saints make a comparison between both of their situations, as in the following example. A refugee saw in a dream the monks of the (old) monastery running frightened. One of them told him: "For us the time has come to flee. Do you know why Agios Rafaïl … brought you back on the path of God? Because you are also devastated by the Turks, who killed your father. We whom you see running are refugees like you" (Bishop of Goumenissa Dimitrios 1996: 210).

Such a conflation of historical periods creates "a chronology-busting historicity that provides a moral interpretation for the present" (Stewart 2012: 193). Beyond a resemblance of trajectories, some suggest an explanation: if a majority of dreamers were refugees, it is because they could better understand the saints' messages. When I asked Vasiliki about this, she replied: "[The saints] presented themselves to the Asia Minor refugees … most of whom had lost relatives … killed by the Turks, in order that they feel more, let's say, their own pain and that they believe more and bear witness … We commiserated with them … not only as saints … but we felt sorry for them as if they were our own beloved persons killed by the Turks" (pers. comm., 6 February 1999).

Sharing a destiny is key to the conviction that the discovery is not a coincidence. The whole process did not happen by accident, but by the will of God. If it is not fortuitous, then an explanation has to be found. The meaning is brought about by the actors of the events, referred to as 'appropriate persons' (*o katallēlos anthrōpos*), and by an 'adequate period' (*ē katallēlē stigmē*). Presented as tools of God's will, these persons are thus worthy of living the miraculous discovery. At the same time, those who wrote about these events (refugees, bishops, etc.) insist on the fact that people of the region who were not refugees also took part and saw dreams. Vasiliki described the atmosphere then as "full of pain, full of faith and piety," among all of the people around—dreamers, refugees, and villagers: "There were other people also, not only refugees from Asia Minor. Everyone believed, everyone suffered. Some of them, native villagers, did not believe at the beginning. In the end, they believed too because … they saw the findings … the dreams: everything has been confirmed" (pers. comm., 6 February 1999). The refugees are not the only ones to see dreams and to believe, even if their relationship to the saints is unique. As a collective experience, the discoveries and the sanctification movement pertain to the whole region and its population: the recent inclusion of Lesbos into the Greek nation-state and the search for a new nationalist narrative were of mutual concern to the island's refugees and natives.

The Search for Local Saints and Commemorations

The discovery of these saints happened in a context underscoring the reconstruction of the past in the present. Another relationship to the past—or, more precisely, another use of the past—is the discourse about religious and national identity in the post-Ottoman state. After the liberation of Lesbos in 1912, the local bishopric undertook to identify the figures who could meet the criteria of sainthood. In the 1930s, the calendar celebrating the saints of Lesbos included only five celebrations. There were 23 in 1958 and 37 in 1996, thanks to investigations and updates to the ecclesiastical history on the authority of the two bishops who succeeded each other during this period, particularly the second one, who served from 1959 to 1987 (Sotiriou 1996). The current calendar does not include each victim of the occupation, but mainly clergymen and monks whose tombs or relics had been found. Only some of them were identified as individuals who could not be declared saints during Ottoman rule: "There certainly was hazy information about other Saints of Lesbos [than the few already known] who, as it seems, were forgotten through the ages. There were testaments and indications, but it requires investigation, study, effort, in order that the wider public should come to know these forgotten Saints" (ibid.: 8). The initiative was therefore important, and the discovery of Saints Rafaïl, Nikolaos, and Irini is considered a "watershed" of local hagiography (ibid.: 9). In so doing, the Church emphasized the supposed tyranny of Ottoman rule and the risks associated with religious practice.

Because of their deaths, the newly identified saints of Thermi are considered to be 'neo-martyrs', a title attributed by the Church to those who died fighting for their faith during Ottoman rule. No written archives mention them or the monastery, and in this absence, the only record that could confirm the existence of the cloister is the medallion found during the excavations, a patriarchal seal given at that time to major monasteries. As reported in a local newspaper, the bishop of Mytilene stated: "Today we know only 18 of the 30 monasteries of Lesbos, and naturally it is not impossible that this one ... would be one of those that are unknown" (*Dēmokratēs*, 21 July 1960). This comment shows both his caution and the plausibility of the findings. Apart from the patriarchal seal, nothing can strictly confirm either the existence of the monastery at this site or the history revealed by the dreams and discoveries. Nothing has been found in historical or ecclesiastical archives.

The bishopric launched the process of canonizing the saints at the end of 1960. It thus played a major role in the celebrations organized in 1962 to commemorate at the same time the five hundredth anniversary of the Ottoman occupation, which began on 16 September 1462, and the fiftieth year of the island's liberation, which had taken place on 12 November 1912. The saints' martyrdom was considered particularly emblematic, as it represented the first killings under the occupation: "Just seven months after the island's occupation, we have the earliest known martyrdoms of the first neo-martyrs of Lesbos, possibly even of the enslaved Hellenism more generally" (Sotiriou 1963: 41). Through the saints, all of the victims of this period are commemorated and qualified as "anonymous heroes of the homeland and martyrs of the faith."[8]

For this occasion, diverse ceremonies were organized, among which was the founding of Saint Rafaïl's church. This commemoration marks the event as a key aspect of the regional (even national) history. It stages retrospectively the past as it is perceived in present time, in accordance with the issues of the present: "The very essence of commemoration is to make contemporary, by a theatrical fiction, the present time with the past time associated with the mythical time, on the one hand, and the future time, on the other. *Commemorating is first of all playing in the present the theater of the past*" (Namer 1987: 211; my italics). Commemorations are means by which memory is elaborated: they emphasize the temporal continuity with the past, even if a rupture occurred in the form of the occupation. The celebrations in 1962 highlighted both the community and the transcendence of the saints. From the present perspective, the neo-martyrs underlined the religious and resistant dimensions of the identity. The neo-martyr is considered a "worthy continuator of history" (Sotiriou 1971: 131), enabling the transition from past to present.

Heroes or Victims? Exemplariness in the Post-Ottoman World

Why are neo-martyrs needed in the twenty-first century? During the occupation, they could play the role of heroes who maintained their religious identity and therefore accepted their own sacrifice. The neo-martyrs of Thermi, however, were not known until their apparition in the 1960s. As stated above, no mention of them has been found in the archives, nor had they been commemorated, in contrast with the other neo-martyrs of Lesbos. Finding them is first of all meaningful for the ecclesiastical history and for the Church.

After the liberation, what does neo-martyrdom come to signify? In the post-Ottoman context, this figure is of particular interest as it underlies massacres and violence. Through their life story (and their death), these saints exemplify victimhood: they are said to have been assaulted and killed while they were gathered for a religious celebration. In the 1960s, their exemplariness is that of the victim, as pointed out by Christian Giordano (2006: 64): "[L]osing exemplariness, personified above all by hero-victims, is in the Balkans an essential component of the national identity and of the consequent definition of 'us' and 'them.'" The exemplariness of Saints Rafaïl, Nikolaos, and Irini is associated with the attempt to define national boundaries and identity.

The saints' relics lay buried throughout the Ottoman occupation in the same way as a treasure (to which I return below). They reappeared after the island's liberation and before the commemoration, as if they preserved an essential part of local identity from destruction, thus revealing the continuity between the past and the present. The monastery built in the 1960s, conceived of as a restitution of a pre-existing monastery, was erected on the site of the original edifice. It commemorates the story of those slaughtered and also the very presence of this former cloister. These references to the past establish the place in an extended duration. Each text or account about the discoveries underlines this continuity, as it is seen retrospectively. For example, in his booklet about the new saints, Bishop of Mytilene Iakovos Kleomvrotos (1968: 11) titled a chapter "Five Hundred Years Later, the Monastery Is Resurrected." One single monastery had crossed the centuries and was merely rebuilt in the 1960s. The bishop designated as "Commission for the renovation [*anakainisēn*] of the monastery" the Commission for its erection (*anegerseōs*) (ibid.: 14). In the same way, during the new church's inauguration on 6 July 1969, the bishop of Mytilene evoked the "revival" (*anaviōsē*) of the monastery and characterized this day of celebration as a "holy bridge" (*ieran gefyran*) between 1463 and 1963.[9] This attempt to erase the Ottoman hiatus that occurred during the era between these years reconstitutes a unity—of a country and of people living there—through a seemingly cohesive and unitary Christian reign.

Concretely, the building of the new monastery also creates a place of memory, a new heritage in the form of a building that shows the Christian presence and the power of faith. The retrospective turn to the past, necessarily anachronistic, celebrates a Christian and Greek identity and glorifies the martyrdom of the nation through the death of its neo-martyrs. Their case shows how the past is understood and incorporated into the present, an operation through which, as expressed by Mondher Kilani (1992: 46), "it is not a question of identification with the past but of identifying the past with oneself." This process associates victimhood and (present) exile with (past) martyrdom and, in doing so, offers a way to express (and perhaps to sublimate) the present.

The Immanence of the Past and the Intervention of the Future in the Present

The story did not cease with the discoveries of the 1960s. The dreams contained information about other items to be found and alluded to new developments.

The 1960s were, according to Vasiliki, the right time for the new saints: another moment will come for other findings. In dreams, the saints repeated that "the holy hill yet hides the Crypt of the ancient monastery: when the appropriate time and the appropriate person will come, only then will the Saints indicate the precise place" (Bishop of Goumenissa Dimitrios 1996: 276). Indeed, the old monastery crypt was not found during the excavations. Many had hoped to find it for the treasure it must contain. Mentioned in many dreams, the icon of Panagia, to whom the old monastery was dedicated, was never found. Vasiliki summarized her account with these words: "And now, I will tell you something else … Everything I have talked about so far is what was discovered. Other discoveries [*eureseis*] were not found" (pers. comm., 2 February 1998). The phrase "Other discoveries were not found" is paradoxical but eloquent: even though they remain to be excavated, some items are already named discoveries, waiting for the moment when they will be found. The time and/or the person(s) who will find them will not be up to chance in the religious reading of the events, but will depend on the will of God: "Another generation will find the crypt, in order that other infidels shall have faith" (ibid.).

On Naxos, an island in the Greek Cyclades, Charles Stewart (2003, 2012) has been confronted with dreams of treasure that present many similarities to the events in Lesbos. His deep analysis brings theoretical perspective to a case falling within 'lived temporality', rejecting 'temporal linearity' (Stewart, this volume). Through their connection of the present to the past, treasures "may also be past attempts to preserve and communicate a history to the future, like a message in a bottle or a time capsule in the cornerstone of a building" (Stewart 2012: 198). The fact that the crypt was not discovered in Lesbos is neither a deficiency nor a failure. It is instead a promise, "a constant reminder that more icons and treasures remain hidden" (ibid.: 206). The dreams reveal a type of relationship with the future, in particular as a support for belief. For Stewart (2003: 487), this is also "a mode of relating to historicity because treasures are, by definition, traces of the past in the present."

This medium establishes a continuity between past and present, making the former appear in the latter. The continuity is even more important than ruptures (invasion, occupation, war) that intervene in between. Such ruptures "are punctuation marks in the past that give rise to the sequences and time frames of subsequent historicizations" (Stewart 2003: 489). In Lesbos, the exhumation enabled the connection between two periods and, to a certain extent, closed temporal parentheses that had lasted for several centuries. Buried in the depths of the earth, the victims were, in a way, preserved during the period of Ottoman rule and reappeared uncorrupted in the present.

On Traces, Archives, and Sources

What about traces and archives? Historical studies usually rely on documentary evidence. In the context of this case study, marked by 'historical consciousness' and 'affective history' (Stewart 2012), what kind of proof has been collected and by whom? What remains from the initial discovery is at the same time a lot and almost nothing. The event has had a major impact on the region because of the construction of the monastery and the subsequent visits of pilgrims. Some archaeological relics have been put on display in the monastery or in museums, and a certain amount of texts and books have been written. However, there are no written archives besides the dreams collected by Kontoglou (1962). The first mention in a newspaper dates back to 16 June 1960, one year after the discovery. Some photographs document the main findings, but not the first grave, as the workers immediately collected the bones and put them in a bag. The only (official) archive is the report made by the archaeologist Seraphim Charitonidis (1960: 236), who spoke of finding "a number of architectural elements of a basilica" (i.e., an Early Christian church), following which a search occurred "with religious zeal and by private means." Its result was not the discovery of the basilica, whose location was never determined, but "only of graves from a later period and remains of a church" (ibid.). In another article, Charitonidis (1968: 12) dated the period to the late Byzantine Empire or to the post-Byzantine era. He stated that two discoveries were made: one archaeological and the other of a religious order. In the process of sanctification, the archaeological items were of no interest and were not mentioned. Charitonidis expressed regret that the excavations for the basilica had not been completed.

Upon what type of proof are these discourses and temporalities based? If the archaeologist looks for vestiges and remains, the believers use different evidence according to circumstance. In the process of conviction, the villagers turned to immaterial signs belonging to their faith: saints or deceased persons who appeared in the dreams and the content of these dreams. Between them, they could relate the dreams they had seen, share their questions and doubts, and support each other, without needing any evidence. However, when they had to convince other people, they used facts or traces, that is, discoveries that corroborated the dreams or references to historical events. Elisabeth Claverie (1990) convincingly highlights these different systems of understanding in her study about the Madonna's apparitions in Italy as well as in Bosnia and Herzegovina. The experience of pilgrims and believers is intangible by nature; it belongs to blessing and faith. They have recourse to this proof only through contact with other people. In my case study, obstacles and difficulties were interpreted as the will of God, as a test of faith. With the completion of the monastery and with the saints' recognition, the villagers could also demonstrate that nothing could have prevented the course of events. When necessary, they presented their discoveries as a convincing argument—not the archaeological vestiges, but items such as gold coins or medals.

The question of sources is also of interest in a self-reflexive perspective. What about the evidence collected by the anthropologist? I gathered all of the written documentation I could find (books, newspapers, archives, etc.) and conducted interviews. I tried to be in a position to verify the accounts that I had read or heard. Doing so, I was in a situation diametrically opposed to that of my interlocutors. Where I wanted to find a proof or a trace but found none, they saw signs. Some of the signs were material (items, vestiges), while others belonged to faith and divine mystery. After all, I had to analyze the strategy of belief and conviction. In this perspective, the fact that very few archival sources were available is not a problem. The lack of traces is not an absence of proof; the traces are of another type. They in turn adhere to the faith or refer to similar situations in the Church's history. The temporality of sainthood defies historical dating, inscribing it in non-human, divine, eternal time.

Conclusion

A grave and some ruins. The events triggered by these findings deserve attention. Beyond the belief and the sainthood emerges a relationship with the past and its revision according to the present. After the end of the Ottoman Empire and the exchange of populations that followed the Greco-Turkish War, this event gave a group of refugees the opportunity to inscribe their life in a new place. They duly recorded that they did not live anymore in Asia Minor, but through transposition a connection was created between them and their new homeland. This case demonstrates that the nature of time is not (always) linear: past and present co-exist. The past appeared in (or was called into) the present and was made to support a performative engagement that nurtured a collective memory of violence suffered. It facilitated the expression of that violence and promoted a new attachment to the place of exile.

These discoveries and the discourse to which they have given rise indicate different relationships to memory and history. Temporalities of variable dimensions are interlaced within them: the past intervenes in the present and marks the continuity of destinies (the juxtaposition of the trajectories of the new saints with the Asia Minor refugees) and of sacred places (the construction of a monastery on the site of the buried ruins of a previous one). Different temporalities co-exist about the discoveries in Thermi and the processes they brought about, demonstrating that experienced time falls within both a linear and a cyclical chronology. The manifestation of past events in the present and the way to interpret them and to interact with them show not only how the past is remembered but also its immanence. However, the cycle does not end there. In dreams, the past may also announce events to come and promises for the future: under the form of hidden treasures, the past may manifest its presence at any time.

Acknowledgments

Most of the information presented here was collected during field research in Greece, mainly between 1997 and 1999, conducted with the financial support of the Swiss National Science Foundation. I extend my deepest thanks to Nicolas Argenti for his offer to contribute to this volume and for his support and constructive comments.

Séverine Rey is a Professor of Social Sciences at the School of Health Sciences of the University of Applied Sciences and Arts Western Switzerland. Previously a Lecturer in Anthropology at the University of Lausanne, her doctoral thesis was an anthropological study of the shrine of Agios Rafaïl at Lesbos (Greece), which examined the process of sainthood making. She is the author of *Des saints nés des rêves* (2008). Her current research topics focus on gender and health professionals and on image and technology within the radiological practice.

Notes

1. For more details about this case of sainthood making and its stakes, see Rey (2008).
2. In Greek, the verb 'to dream' is *oneireuomai*, but the usual expression, which I always heard during my fieldwork, is "I saw a dream" (Eida ena oneiro), not "I had a dream." Here, I maintain the Greek phrasing to convey an aspect of being a viewer or of being visited by someone. Please note that I have provided the translations for non-English texts.
3. Excerpt from the bishop's report to the Holy Synod of the Church of Greece, cited in Mytilene's parish magazine, *Poimēn* 1961: 10. For an analysis focused on gender relations and everyday religious practice, see Rey (2012).
4. Mytilene is the county town of the island.
5. The Holy Synod is the highest authority in the Orthodox Church. In Greece, it gathers together all the bishops in office under the chairmanship of the archbishop.
6. Because Ralli has written a book about this story (see Ralli 1998), I have not observed the usual rules of anonymity here.
7. A town near Istanbul (then Constantinople), northeast of the current Greece, close to the Turkish border.
8. See *Poimēn* 1962: 195.
9. See *Poimēn* 1969: 139.

References

Bishop of Goumenissa Dimitrios. 1996. *Ē zōē ek taphōn: Hoi synklonistikes authentikes martyries tēs thaumastēs phanerōseōs tōn Agion Raphaēl, Nikolaou kai Eirēnēs* [The life out of the graves: The staggering authentic testament of the miraculous apparition of Saints Rafaïl, Nikolaos, and Irini]. Griva Goumenissis: Monastery Agios Rafaïl Goumenissa.

Bishop of Mytilene Iakovos Kleomvrotos. 1968. *O Agios Raphaēl kai ē Iera Monē tōn Karyōn eis tēn Mytilēnēn* [Saint Rafaïl and the Holy Monastery at Karies, Mytilene]. Mytilene: Bishopric of Mytilene.

Charitonidis, Seraphim. 1960. "Chronika." [Chronicle] *Archaiologikōn Deltiōn* [Archaeological Annals] 16: 236.

Charitonidis, Seraphim. 1968. "Palaiochristianikē topographia tēs Lesvou." [Early Christian topography of Lesvos] *Archaiologikōn Deltiōn* [Archaeological Annals] 23: 12–13.

Claverie, Elisabeth. 1990. "La Vierge, le désordre, la critique: Les apparitions de la Vierge à l'âge de la science." *Terrain* 14: 60–75.

Clogg, Richard. 1992. *A Concise History of Greece*. Cambridge: Cambridge University Press.

Giordano, Christian. 2006. "The Past in the Present: Actualized History in the Social Construction of Reality." In *Critical Junctions: Anthropology and History Beyond the Cultural Turn*, ed. Don Kalb and Herman Tak, 53–71. New York: Berghahn Books.

Kilani, Mondher. 1992. *La construction de la mémoire: Le lignage et la sainteté dans l'oasis d'El Ksar*. Geneva: Labor et Fides.

Kontoglou, Photios. 1962. *Sēmeion mega: Ta thaumata tōn Agiōn tēs Thermēs Raphaēl—Nikolaou—Eirēnēs* [A large sign: The miracles of the saints of Thermi Rafail, Nikolaos, and Irini]. Athens: Astir.

Namer, Gérard. 1987. *Mémoire et société*. Paris: Méridiens Klincksieck.

Ralli, Vasiliki. 1998. *Karyes: O lophos tōn Agion Raphaēl, Nikolaou, Eirēnēs: Ena chroniko tēs eureseōs tōn ierōn leipsanōn tōn Agiōn* [Karyes, hill of Saints Rafaïl, Nikolaos, and Irini: A chronicle of the discovery of the Holy Relics of the Saints]. Athens: Akritas.

Rey, Séverine. 2008. *Des saints nés des rêves: Fabrication de la sainteté et commémoration des néomartyrs de Lesvos (Grèce)*. Lausanne: Antipodes.

Rey, Séverine. 2012. "The Ordinary within the Extraordinary: Sainthood-Making and Everyday Religious Practice in Lesvos, Greece." In *Ordinary Lives and Grand Schemes: An Anthropology of Everyday Religion*, ed. Samuli Schielke and Liza Debevec, 82–97. New York: Berghahn Books.

Sotiriou, Georgios P. 1963. "Hoi prōtomartyres tōn chronōn tēs douleias eis tēn nēson Lesvon, 9 Apriliou 1463–9 Apriliou 1963." [The first martyrs of the servitude time in Lesbos, 9 April 1463–9 April 1963] *Poimēn* [Shepherd]: 41–43.

Sotiriou, Georgios P. 1971. "Hoi neomartyres ōs fōta pneumatika kata tous chronous tēs douleias." [The neomartyrs as spiritual lights during the years of slavery] *Poimēn* [Shepherd]: 130–134.

Sotiriou, Georgios P. 1996. *Myrties kai daphnes stous Agious tēs Lésvou* [Myrtle and laurel for the Lesbos's saints]. Mytilene: Bishopric of Mytilene.

Stewart, Charles. 2003. "Dreams of Treasure: Temporality, Historicization and the Unconscious." *Anthropological Theory* 3 (4): 481–500.

Stewart, Charles. 2012. *Dreaming and Historical Consciousness in Island Greece*. Cambridge, MA: Harvard University Press.

Chapter 7

"Eyes Shut, Muted Voices"
Narrating and Temporalizing the Post–Civil War Era through a Monument

Dimitra Gefou-Madianou

During my long fieldwork in a community in Attica, near Athens, which I call Messogia, I came across two secrets that had wounded the local society—secrets that had led to violently dismissive characterizations of the Messogites and to their political and economic exploitation. These were related mainly to the use of the Arvanitic language, which questioned the locals' Greekness, and the consumption of retsina wine, which turned them in the eyes of the 'Athenian elite' into 'drunkards' and 'uncivilized savages' (Gefou-Madianou 1992, 1999). During the long construction process of the Greek nation-state (from the 1900s through the beginning of the twentieth century), these characteristics of the Arvanitic speakers acquired ethnic connotations.

This exclusion, which Messogites still experience as a traumatically recurring critical event (Caruth 1996: 4; Das 2007: 7), reveals structures of domination and instances of inequality in relation to the state and the Athenian elite (Gefou-Madianou 1992, 1999; Kambouroglou [1889] 1959), as well as local authorities, who have embodied the dominant discourse. Under these conditions and for more than a century, the Arvanites of Messogia have been molded into a subaltern

Notes for this chapter begin on page 128.

community—until recently a politically conservative one—self-identified as *vasilochoria*, that is, communities friendly to the institution of monarchy.

In the context of these long and by no means linear processes of subjugation and acquiescence, this chapter examines a second critical event, enfolded in the first one: the torching of the village by the Nazis and the ensuing civil war. My interest in this issue was triggered by the raising of a monument in memory of the 'holocaust' or 'tragedy of 1944', referred to by locals as *to kako* (the evil). The monument was erected in 1995, when PASOK (the socialist party) was in government, to commemorate the torching, which brought together in the signifier 'German Nazis' all the evil associated with the war and the civil war that followed.

During the inauguration of the monument, many locals, including myself, believed that this would lead to reconciliation along the crude lines that had divided the Left and the Right since the civil war. This understanding made sense when seen from the vantage point of the post-junta socio-political opening toward democratization that included the official recognition of the 'Resistance'; the legalization of the Communist Party (1974); the burning of the security police files of the leftists (1989), who were considered 'dangerous citizens' (Panourgiá 2009); and, finally, the closing down of exile camps. Things, however, proved to go quite differently.

Irrespective of the tensions the monument had produced, the picture got more complicated due to the collapse of the Communist Albanian state in the early 1990s and the opening of the borders with Greece. Within a few years, massive numbers of Albanian migrants entered the country, veering toward Athens and especially nearby Messogia, where language and an implicit cultural proximity promised better work opportunities, especially with the construction, in the same period, of the new Athens airport (Gefou-Madianou 2010). This presence of migrants led to the (re)-emergence of discourses concerning the positionality of local Messogites-cum-Arvanites within the dominant Greek (Athens-centric) nationalist narrative.

From this point of view, the monument absorbs and crystallizes all these tensions and conflicts through which the evil of history is resurfacing. The memorial seems like a third critical event covering as a foil the previous two, around which knots of histories, both personal and collective, concerning past, present, and future situations are being experienced and anticipated.

The goal of this chapter is to understand how divergent local histories about loss, betrayal, and political violence, especially when filtered through the monument, were remembered, narrated, and experienced in a present as uncertain, unstable, and critical as the past. In other words, the chapter examines how the politics of the past informs present emic categories of memory and time.

Critical Events, Time, Temporalities

Critical events are not experienced in the same manner or with the same intensity by all. When people narrated the civil war (a subject prevalent at the time the monument was being erected), I could detect other histories, different from the nationalized official history, which offered alternative and contradicting versions of the 'same' event(s). At the same time, I realized that certain distant and disjointed past events also included pressing concerns and future orientations that were experienced by my informants as relevant and near. Indeed, the past was not "bygone" and "out-of-date," as argued by Serres (1995: 48) in a conversation with Latour.

Of course, approaching these events from a linear point of view is what makes them look distant and separate. Yet when seen as existing "in culture" (Serres 1995: 57), they seem very close. For example, when, each year on 9 October, local authorities commemorate in front of the monument the torching of the village by the Germans in 1944, they are trying to register in collective historical consciousness a naturalized temporality based on linear chronological events. On the other hand, family secrets and personal stories constantly disturb and undermine this linearity, revealing other histories or 'historicities' (Hirsch and Stewart 2005). These remembrances were more fluid and loose, often disconnected, contradictory, oblique, and confused, but they nonetheless assisted my informants in making sense of their world(s) in the present. Their pride in actively participating in the Revolution against the Ottomans; their bitterness over their betrayal and exclusion from the nation-building process; their loss, wounds, and violence suffered during the civil war (still 'unfinished' for some); and their present-day hardships due to the raging crisis—all these were intermingled in diverse temporal occurrences (Deleuze 1991: 38; Knight 2012: 353, 358; Stewart 2003: 487; 2012: 193).

The past, then, is possible only in present—and even future—terms. There can never be a past as it was. Adopting a Bergsonian approach to time, Deleuze (1991: 58) argues that the past "is 'contemporaneous' with the present that it *has been*." This contemporaneity has another consequence: "Not only does the past coexist with the present that has been, but, as it preserves itself in itself (while the present passes), it is the whole, integral past; it is *all* our past, which coexists with each present" (ibid.: 59; see also Argenti, introduction; Proust [1913] 1990; Seremetakis 1994: 31).

By trying to explain how time is experienced, Munn (1992: 112) has introduced the notion of "[t]emporalizations of past time," suggesting that people perceive and experience the past by "actualizing it in the present," which also contains dimensions of the future. Munn defines human temporalities as symbolic processes "continually being produced in everyday practices" (ibid.: 116). They are unavoidably tied up with these practices: they constitute them and give them form, yet at the same time they are the products of these practices (Hodges 2008: 406).

In this way, Munn (1992: 94) can also argue that time and space cannot be separated; instead, they collide in many different ways. We can say, then, that people live in dimensions of time and space simultaneously—in 'spacetime', as Hodges (2008) puts it—and this is what comprises social life. But time is always hidden from the picture; it is always invisible or, as Derrida (1994: 6) argues, "[i]t itself withdraws itself from visibility" despite the fact that paradoxically "nothing *appears* that does not require and take time." In that sense, time is not autonomous. It needs something else to make its presence felt, a medium through which it can be 'expressed'. Thus, time is always embedded in temporal dimensions and meanings and takes the form of the medium through which it is revealed, that is, practices and objects.

Following the ethnographic literature concerning the power of objects to channel and reorient memory and temporalities along different paths and in unexpected ways, where past, present, and future are condensed (Knight 2012: 358; Stewart 2003: 487; 2012: 206), I argue that the monument of Messogia represents a complex and dynamic assemblage of temporalities. The spatiality it evokes forces subjects to see time and space as inextricably entwined, thus informing their memories by the temporalities of culture (Munn 1992). This reveals that historical time is perceived in terms of culturally informed models rather than linearly (Argenti, introduction; Hirsch and Stewart 2005). Significantly too, these models allow one to consider not only the Nazi occupation and the ensuing civil war, but also historically more distant but equally formative pasts situated in the post-Ottoman era of Greek nation-building, when Albanian-speaking Christian Orthodox populations were not yet considered to be subaltern.

What Is the Monument?

The monument consists of a full-body bronze female statue raised on a marble pedestal, the front of which bears an engraving of a burning village and the names of the 47 people "murdered by the Germans on 9 October 1944" incised on its flanks. The statue depicts a standing woman, as if she is ready to take a step forward. Her hair is covered, and her right hand is elevated, holding a dove with open wings.

Shortly after the monument was erected, two books were published, one by a local schoolteacher and the other by a candidate for the municipal council. Exuding patriotic and nationalistic ideology, both books were based on an earlier account of the burning of the village that had been published in 1947 at the height of the Greek Civil War and was penned by a local royalist military prosecutor, the man mainly responsible for sending Communists into exile. Drawing from that official version of the event, the two books, which appeared in the late 1990s, maintained that it was the German troops who had torched Messogia, having been provoked by the incursion of partisans into the village.

More recently, the declaration of Messogia as a Martyr City by the local council on 9 October 2011, the date the village was torched by the Nazis,[1] and the claims raised against the German government on war indemnities have created more tensions and infighting in the community. This has been further intensified by the general anti-German climate associated with the recent severe economic crisis. It is indicative that during the 2012 commemoration ceremony, the German company that had constructed and managed the Athens International Airport was accused of polluting the area, yet another Germany-related by-product of the economic crisis (Gefou-Madianou 2014).

Alternatively, when one looks at versions of local history contrary to those described above, the picture gets even more complicated. During the last two decades since the raising of the monument, local history has been in a process of continual rewriting. *Lethe* (oblivion) and *aletheia* (truth/disclosure) are struggling for pre-eminence, just as different discourses and versions concerning the history of the era are struggling to attain prominence and legitimacy (Yalouri 2010). This is clearly shown in the three biohistories that follow, which reveal uncertain memories, disquieting politics, silenced sentiments, and secret meanings where opaque and faded pictures of the past mix and blur with present and future dreams and anticipations.

The First Story: "Eyes Shut, Muted Voices"

Thanasis Kiousis is a retired Army general living in the community with his family. Initially, he assisted in the raising of the monument, believing that it would "exorcise the evil"[2] of the civil war. He also had a personal motive: his father's brother—a left-wing law student and poet—was killed at the age of 20 during the dramatic events of 1944. His uncle had been a member of the United Panhellenic Organization of Youth (EPON), the youth wing of the National Liberation Front (EAM).

Kiousis realized that the monument had been given a title—the "Monument Dedicated to Liberty"—that was general enough to be harmless and malleable instead of commemorating the Resistance against the Nazis, something that the right-wing village elite would not allow. In 2003 he published a book, and a second one in 2006, with his own account of the 1944 events. Criticizing former publications, Kiousis presented his version of the story, which was based upon records and historical data collected from official archives,[3] interviews with partisans and officers of ELAS,[4] and local testimonies. Both books caused strong reactions among the authors of previous publications. A 'war' started, focusing on the monument's authenticity and what it represented. This dispute, conducted through local newspapers, evoked memories of the post-Ottoman split between those still identified as Arvanites and the non-Arvanitic local elite.

For Kiousis, the monument does not honor the memory of those killed in the events of 1944, nor of his uncle, who had been killed by a 'German' who spoke Arvanitika—that is, by a local collaborator who was his uncle's neighbor. This he realized when he put together all the half-spoken words, the disconnected and often uncertain memories, and the other information he had managed to collect. In his second book, he also proved that the village had not been torched by the Nazis, but by members of the Greek collaborationist security battalions (*tagmatasfalites*), who had been wearing German army uniforms and whose mission was to clear the area of partisans. This explains how the 'Germans' who torched the village were speaking Arvanitika, as certain eyewitnesses have testified. For the village, this was the beginning of the civil war.

More than anything else, Kiousis had been hurt by his grandmother, the very person who had first talked to him about his uncle's story through allusions and half-spoken scattered words, with gestures, facial expressions, and nods. She had never talked with the specific villagers involved since her son's death and had often taken Kiousis to his uncle's grave, always in tears, muttering curses and recounting what had happened back then. When the monument was raised just a few months before her death, this same grandmother changed her story, stating that she "agreed" with the official version of events proclaimed on the monument out of fear that Kiousis would take revenge.

After the books' publication, Kiousis himself became the Other: half of the community is no longer on speaking terms with him. What does he consider to be evil? The collaborators with the Germans, the local authorities, the same big families who are still pulling strings in the community, and those who, despite their Arvanitic origins, avoid calling themselves Arvanites, preferring the appellation 'Northern Epirots'. This invokes nationalistic and irredentist claims on Southern Albania as being Greek, bringing to the surface the post-Ottoman agonistic nation-building in the Balkans. "During all these years, my co-villagers had their eyes open but did not see: eyes shut, muted voices," as Kiousis put it.

The Second Story: "Time Is Turmoil"

Antonia is married with children and grandchildren. She comes from a wealthy and respected family of wine producers, as does her husband. According to Antonia, all her family's political orientation is right-wing. They belong to the local elite, who conceal their Arvanitic origin.

And yet her personal story is one of loss and unfulfilled love for a fellow pupil at school who was the son of a left-wing partisan. "I was hit, I was in pain, I felt fear, but in the end I understood why my father forbade this relationship," she explained. Everything then made sense when she recalled the violent gestures of her grandmother, who would pull her by her wrist when they were out, signaling that she should not talk to 'them' in the street, in the cemetery, or in the neighborhood.

Antonia transformed all this into courage and a strength that guided her when raising her children. While he was still a student, her son wanted to learn Albanian, just like their grandparents spoke Arvanitika (Gefou-Madianou 1999). She let him do so and even persuaded her husband not to react. As she explained: "Arvanitika was forbidden to us, even to listen to it. Not even our parents [could speak it], although they knew it." The monument woke up "unknown feelings" inside her: "The monument restored Costas [her young boyfriend] to me. I saw love—being in love—as a good thing again. Throughout my life I considered it a very bad thing that springs up where it is not needed and torments you … the fear, you see. For my parents, love was totally a bad thing, so it became bad for me as well. That's why now I dream that my own children will marry *only* out of love."

Antonia remembers Costas's school essay about his father who was in exile: "He was the best in his class, but was expelled from school for his ideas and eventually was forced to leave the country." She recalls the secret police looking for

Costas's uncle in the neighborhood: "Left-wingers were sent into exile—words so negative when I was young, but which have now turned sweeter and more tender inside me." Antonia explained her conflicted feelings about the monument: "What is the monument to me? A lie—just like my whole life is a lie. I feel moved and angry at the same time! I am divided in two. The monument made me angry but also made me stronger." She remembers attending her son's school parades when the pupils stopped at the monument to lay a wreath: "When I first stood in front of it during the ceremony, I felt pain and turmoil inside me. I thought, time has gyrations, turbulences; it turns everything topsy-turvy, time is turmoil [o kairos ehei gyrismata, fernei ta kato-pano, tarahi einai, bora]."

The Third Story: "The Civil War Never Ended for Me"

Locals call him by a Russian name; I call him Boris. He works as a small real estate agent, mostly in agricultural land. He enjoys speaking Arvanitika and, despite his wife's disapproval, is proud of being Arvanitis.

At the time of the torching of the village in 1944, Boris was 14 years old. He was a member of EPON and had an uncle serving as an officer with ELAS. For Boris, the torching of the village was a battle between ELAS and members of the Greek collaborationist security battalions. Some Germans might have been present, too. As he recalls: "No one knows, they were hiding, wearing hoods." He himself took part in the combat, carrying a gun. It was a fierce battle, which he described to me in detail.

The monument, which for him aimed at reconciliation and justification, was quickly invested with other meanings. First of all, he feels betrayed by the state. Although he was entitled to receive a pension as a member of the Resistance, he never did: "I am illiterate. I signed some papers ... but nothing. The files had been burned, I was nowhere." Moreover, Boris feels betrayed by the local people, who have imposed their own version of history as 'real' and dominant: "These people who got rich, whose houses were not burned, who looted other people's houses before they torched them, who collaborated with the Germans and sent leftists to exile ... these people are evil." They ridiculed him when, shortly after the monument was raised, he had paraded there as a member of the Resistance, together with a few old comrades. He explained why he never went to the parade again: "Fear! Things got messed up; they turned out rather badly." The monument became 'alien' to him.

Boris wants to remember local history in his own way, based on his well-educated ELAS uncle's claim that Arvanites were considered heroes during the Revolution against the Ottoman Empire when they had fought on the Greek side and had been considered "more Greek than the Greeks." But now Arvanites are considered "foreigners in their own place." As Boris explains: "In the old times the entire Balkan area was *one*. Now you need a visa to visit the villages in Southern Albania where our great-grandparents once lived" (cf. Argenti, introduction).

In Boris's view, the discussion over the torching of the village and the civil war that followed has not been opened: "The way they silenced Arvanitica, they silenced the monument and the war. From a memorial it has become a grave. I am just asking for an apology ... The civil war never ended for me." For Boris, the monument alternates between being seen as a lie, a tomb, a holy icon, and a sacred place. Boris makes the sign of the cross whenever he passes by it. Once he removed his grubby shoes before ascending the marble steps. "I don't want to soil them," he said to me. Visibly touched, he removed his hat, caressed the statue with his hand, and kissed it gently and affectionately.

In the early days of the summer of 2010, we returned to Boris's home from Water-Tank Hill, where he had shown me the battlefield scars. Elli, his wife, brought us coffee. As the discussion continued, she became increasingly troubled, asking me if I knew the schoolteacher who had written the book supporting the official story of the village torching. My positive reply worried her even more. She intervened in the discussion, agitated and muttering: "What's the point of all this? ... the Germans torched the village."

Elli tried hard to check her husband's explicitness. In the end, she went to another room and returned with a Christmas card. She smugly put it in my hand, saying: "We come from a good family" (meaning loyal, right-wing). The card depicted a photograph of the entire Greek ex-royal family (the monarchy having been abolished in 1974) with a handwritten inscription from the ex-king: "We wish you a happy 2010."

Multi-temporalities and Unfinished Pasts

How can one define the monument, then? Under the weight of the intensity and density of the topologies[5] that surround it, the monument ceases to be a concrete artifact made of bronze and marble. The memories of my informants become the topos of the monument. Multiple layers of time collide in it, lending its shattered remnants a new dynamism and essence, each time producing new knots and currents, new multi-temporalities (Munn 1992).

From a topological perspective, the 'monument-as-event' is still in the process of 'becoming' because it is constituted by the ways in which people have encountered it when experiencing critical events that have demoralized and disturbed them and threatened their world(s). In that sense, although the torching of the village and the civil war are of the past, their repeated presence in people's everyday lives does not reveal any feeling of "pastness" (Das 2007: 97). On the contrary, the present is shaped in new, unpredicted, and often surprising ways that reveal its dialectic, complex, and ambivalent relation with the past.

Temporalities and the Agency of Time

This is clearly evinced by the previously mentioned biohistories. For example, although Kiousis's project focused on facts belonging to the past, in reality it very much concerned his present and future orientations. He often questioned his present urgent concern, not only about what had happened then, but also about where he stands now. Why now, and what was so pressing about it?

Kiousis explained: "It was [the right] time for me to search, now! [Itan kairos na psaxo, tora!]." It was as if time had agency (Das 2007: 95, 98), compelling him to search and get involved. Also, by preparing his own archive, Kiousis was not simply recollecting and 'keeping alive' the village history, which he believed had been institutionally repressed into oblivion. More importantly, he wanted to make *present* (and *in the present*) an accurate picture of the past as clearly as possible.

Paradoxically, then, while searching the past, Kiousis actually was concerned with the future: his own, his family's, his community's. He was concerned about his younger daughter's recent visit (pilgrimage) to Southern Albania, to the land of her ancestors, which had to do with concerns about her present identity. At that time, Kiousis was alarmed by the government's decision to violently deport Albanian migrants who had been part of the community. In that period, questions of who was Arvanitis and who was Albanian (Christian Orthodox or Muslim) and who was Messogitis and who was 'native Greek' were of great concern and had caused heated debates in the area. The (Athenian) press referred to Messogitic villages as *Arvanitochoria*, once again, with denigrating remarks, which brought back all the 'heavy load' of Kiousis having an Arvanitic origin and carrying it all his life.

Time as Kairos

Narrating 'through' the monument, my informants frequently referred to time as *kairos*. In Greek, at one level *kairos* means time passing, weather, and era or epoch (Herzfeld 2009; Hirsch and Stewart 2005). At another level, it also implies and gives the sense of duration itself (Dimitrakos 1969: 724).

In her encounters with the monument, Antonia sensed time (*kairos*) as turmoil and storm, which caused her pain and turned her inside out. As Serres (1995: 59) argues, "time flows in a turbulent and chaotic manner." For Kiousis's grandmother, it was as if her son's murder had happened only yesterday. As she used to tell me: "Time is curing, but the grave stays fresh [O kairos giatros, ma o tafos freskos]." Indeed, it is difficult to determine when the event of her son's death began and when it ended. Time was flowing.

Similarly for Boris, the Greek Civil War was still unfolding: "The civil war never ended for me; I am still living [in] it" [Krataei kairo o emfylios gia mena, ton zo akoma]." Through the monument, he relived the wounds (physical and psychological) of the civil war and of his current treatment by the authorities. Being an Arvanitis and a leftist was viewed by local authorities as a double betrayal of the Greek nation-state and, until recently, had been considered 'dangerous' by some. The state's act of forced 'oblivion' (Liakos 2001; Papailias 2005) and the burning of the security files made Boris feel invisible and 'homeless'. In his talk, past-present-future are experienced in "formidable contemporaneity" (Serres 1995: 47) with "gaps" and "stopping points" (ibid.: 57), bringing together the Arvanitic post-Ottoman past during the building of the nation-state, the civil war, and the recent influx of Albanian migrants, whom Boris refers to nostalgically as brothers.

From such a point of view, critical events, especially the traumatic and violent ones, are in a sense "unfinished stories" (Das 2007: 108) as they continuously change over time, bringing to the fore new and dynamic temporalities and trajectories. The civil war, however, was not only about violence, but about the 'anticipation' of violence (see Bryant and Papadakis 2012: 2–3; Das 2007: 9, 98). Boris had been ridiculed once during the commemoration ceremony in front of the monument, and he never again attended another out of fear, as he told me. He constantly experiences fear in the street, in the coffee shop. For Boris, the anticipation of violence is a fearful "temporality of anticipation" (Das 2007: 9) that demands constant alertness for possible violent harassments and the continuous revival of past traumas. In that sense, it is not only the past that is 'unfinished' and constantly present for Boris; the bitter and frightening anticipation of violence brings the future into the scene for him as well.

For Antonia and Boris, the monument has offered a way of expressing images of past traumatic events that were transferred and maintained by ritual performances and that formulated a bodily "performative memory" (Connerton 1989: 124). Antonia often talked to the monument, about her dreams and lamented her 'lost life'. Fragmented pictures and shreds of her feelings encapsulated in different time bubbles suddenly came together, rewired and refreshed yet new and inherently unstable. Boris treated the monument as an icon, making the sign of cross when passing by. But it is not only the observed practices and the direct enunciations upon which the ethnographic gaze should focus. Equally significant are the unseen and the unuttered traumas, even the flows of time and subjectivities "embodied unconsciously" (Hodges 2008: 406). So, too, are the "unknown feelings," in Antonia's words (cf. Caruth 1996: 4), the muted voices and the closed eyes of my informants.

Family secrets and histories about the torching of the village and the civil war that emerged during my fieldwork do indeed disturb and dislocate the longer and more durable temporalities of the nation-state and the local authorities' unified history. They also question and clash with the official ideology about the critical event of the civil war and the split of the country and the community itself into two distinct parts: Left and Right. But the question is, who has the power to impose his or her own version of history as important? Whose temporalities are powerful enough to overshadow all the others and to be presented as the only 'natural' and 'correct' ones? As Munn (1992: 109) has expressed it: "[C]ontrol over time is … also a medium of hierarchic power and governance."

By Way of Conclusion

This chapter has focused on past critical events that in many ways challenge the notion of time's linearity. The turbulence of time has been exposed by the erection of a monument to commemorate the torching of the village by the German Nazis and the Greek Civil War, events that have been distinctively engraved on people's memories. Viewing these events in simultaneity has allowed narratives to be understood, not simply as recollections, but also as temporalities. As a result, past, present, and future events have been temporalized, transforming the monument from a stable and durable object into a hybrid entity that brings to the fore unconventional histories and experiences of time.

Munn (1992: 93) employs the metaphor of time as sand to describe time's "pervasiveness ... [in] all aspects of social experience and practice." I feel the same when I am analyzing these stories that concern the multifaceted and convoluted connections between time, critical events, and objects. They slip like sand through my fingers when I am trying to understand how they made sense in my informants' everyday worlds.

The chapter has also dealt with how past critical events, such as the civil war, have produced contradictory understandings of local histories, especially when one considers the role of the nationalized history. In Messogia, local authorities have produced a model of temporal distancing, implying that only some may experience time in the 'right' way (Fabian 1983).

Following the restoration of democracy in 1974, many publications and an active interest in civil war issues have since been observed.[6] However, the question remains as to why discussion about the Greek Civil War has been suppressed and muted for so long (Papailias 2005: 141; Van Boeschoten et al. 2008: 21–22). This paradoxical temporality of the civil war raises important questions concerning power relations in the politics of history production at both the local and national level. The oblivion imposed on the civil war has affected local temporalities and has brought up issues of identities that have past, present, and future concerns.

These concerns are also connected with topologies associated with the post-Ottoman condition and with the Arvanitic language and identity. In broad lines, there are those who consider themselves modern and identify with the state's hegemonic discourse of progress, adopting an attitude of "move on and get over it." Then there are those who often bring forward the anamnesis of the civil war, the torching of the village, and the Arvanitic past and who are considered anachronistic by the local elite. Having been subjected for more than a century to derogatory discourses perhaps explains the identification of the community's elite with the dominant state (royal) discourse, which can be seen in psychoanalytic terms as overcompensation, and also explains the appellation *vasilochoria* mentioned earlier. From the viewpoint of certain left-wingers of the civil war era, like Boris, this is experienced as a double exclusion and betrayal.

The ethnography makes it clear that such a significant violent experience as the civil war acquires a voice that is hardly heard and seems to be insignificant in the context of the contemporary linear official narrative of the issue. The local authorities have tried to impose a pseudo-unity of the community's past through a media-type representation, deploying an attitude of oblivion, resulting in the Monument Dedicated to Liberty. However, it seems that the more the authorities have made efforts to suppress the encounter with evil of the village torching and the civil war, the more this evil has returned (Ricoeur 2004), nurturing a critique that questions the neo-liberal understandings of the politics being imposed.

At the same time, the monument is seen as a topos that epitomizes the politics of memory and oblivion, accommodating divergent histories and even conflicting conceptualizations of evil. In a period of demographic changes related to massive immigration into the area, mainly from Albania, and in the midst of a raging socio-economic crisis, things have become even more complicated. It is in this context that the memorial produces the means through which multiple temporalities are revealed. The monument offers an umbrella that provides shelter for many opposing topologies to be expressed: emotional and personal, political, ethnic, linguistic, class, and gender-based.

Acknowledgments

I would like to thank Nicolas Argenti, organizer of the Athens workshop "Balkan Topologies," for his invitation to participate and for his critical reading of this chapter. I am also grateful to my colleagues Gerasimos Makris and Eleana Yalouri for their valuable comments.

Dimitra Gefou-Madianou is a Professor of Social Anthropology at the Panteion University. She has conducted fieldwork in Athens, Messogia-Attica, Thessaly, and Southern Albania. Her research interests include ethnicity, alcohol and gender, identity formation, drugs, migration, anthropological theory, culture and ethnography, anthropology and psychoanalysis, memory, and civil war. She has edited *Alcohol, Gender and Culture* (1992), *Alcohol and the Community* (1995), and *Current Trends in Anthropological Theory and Ethnography* (1998, in Greek). Her monographs in Greek include *Culture and Ethnography: From Ethnographic Realism to Cultural Critique* (1999), *The Self and 'Other': Conceptualizations, Identities and Practices in Greece and Cyprus* (2003), *Anthropology and Psychoanalysis* (2006), and *Facets of Anthropological Research: Culture, History, Representations* (2011). Recent book chapters include "Culture in the Periphery" (2010, in *Culture Wars: Context, Models and Anthropologists' Accounts*) and "Ethnography in Motion" (2010, in *Ethnographic Practice in the Present*).

Notes

1. This is hardly a coincidence. See Stewart (2012) on affective history.
2. Frequently referred to by my informants, evil is an emic category. Although I am not employing it systematically here, I reference it by adopting Ricoeur's (2004) aporetic stance of being open to uncertainties and contradictions.
3. Kiousis especially drew on the civil war archives that were opened to the public in 1998.

4. The acronym ELAS stands for Ellinikos Laikos Apeleftherotikos Stratos (National People's Liberation Army), the military arm of the left-wing EAM.
5. Although I draw partly from Leontis's (1995) dialectical approach in using topology, I fully adopt Argenti's (introduction, this volume) differentiation regarding the term's temporal dimensions.
6. Recent publications on the Greek Civil War include Danforth and Van Boeschoten (2012), Panourgiá (2009), and Van Boeschoten et al. (2008).

References

Bryant, Rebecca, and Yiannis Papadakis. 2012. "Introduction: Modalities of Time, History and Memory in Ethnonational Conflicts." In *Cyprus and the Politics of Memory: History, Community and Conflict*, ed. Rebecca Bryant and Yiannis Papadakis, 1–26. London: I.B. Tauris.
Caruth, Cathy. 1996. *Unclaimed Experience: Trauma, Narrative, and History*. Baltimore: Johns Hopkins University Press.
Connerton, Paul. 1989. *How Societies Remember*. Cambridge: Cambridge University Press.
Danforth, Loring M., and Riki Van Boeschoten. 2012. *Children of the Greek Civil War: Refugees and the Politics of Memory*. Chicago: University of Chicago Press.
Das, Veena. 2007. *Life and Words: Violence and the Descent into the Ordinary*. Berkeley: University of California Press.
Deleuze, Gilles. 1991. *Bergsonism*. Trans. Hugh Tomlinson and Barbara Habberjam. New York: Zone Books.
Derrida, Jacques. 1994. *Given Time: 1. Counterfeit Money*. Ppk. ed. Trans. Peggy Kamuf. Chicago: University of Chicago Press.
Dimitrakos, Dimitrios. 1969. "Kairos." *New Dictionary*. Athens: Yiovanis.
Fabian, Johannes. 1983. *Time and the Other: How Anthropology Makes Its Object*. New York: Columbia University Press.
Gefou-Madianou, Dimitra. 1992. "Exclusion and Unity, Retsina and Sweet Wine: Commensality and Gender in a Greek Agrotown." In *Alcohol, Gender and Culture*, ed. Dimitra Gefou-Madianou, 108–136. London: Routledge.
Gefou-Madianou, Dimitra. 1999. "Cultural Polyphony and Identity Formation: Negotiating Tradition in Attica." *American Ethnologist* 26 (2): 412–439.
Gefou-Madianou, Dimitra. 2010. "Ethnography in Motion: Shifting Fields on Airport Grounds." In *Ethnographic Practice in the Present*, ed. Marit Melhuus, Jon P. Mitchell, and Helena Wulff, 152–168. New York: Berghahn Books.
Gefou-Madianou, Dimitra. 2014. "Messogia, the New 'Eleftherios Venizelos Airport' and 'Attiki Odos' or, the Double Marginalization of Messogia." In *Crisis-Scapes: Athens and Beyond*, ed. Jaya K. Brekke, Dimitris Dalakoglou, Christos Filippidis, and Antonis Vradis, 18–22. Athens: Synthesi.
Herzfeld, Michael. 2009. "Rhythm, Tempo, and Historical Time: Experiencing Temporality in the Neoliberal Age." *Public Archaeology* 8 (2–3): 108–123.
Hirsch, Eric, and Charles Stewart. 2005. "Introduction: Ethnographies of Historicity." *History and Anthropology* 16 (3): 261–274.
Hodges, Matt. 2008. "Rethinking Time's Arrow: Bergson, Deleuze and the Anthropology of Time." *Anthropological Theory* 8 (4): 399–429.
Kambouroglou, Dēmētrios G. (1889) 1959. *I Istoria ton Athinon* [The history of Athens]. Athens: Papadimitriou.

Knight, Daniel M. 2012. "Cultural Proximity: Crisis, Time and Social Memory in Central Greece." *History and Anthropology* 23 (3): 349-374.
Leontis, Artemis. 1995. *Topographies of Hellenism: Mapping the Homeland*. Ithaca, NY: Cornell University Press.
Liakos, Antonis. 2001. "I neoelliniki istoriographia to teleftaio tetarto tou 20ou aiona" [Modern Greek historiography in the last quarter of the twentieth century]. *Synchrona Themata* 76 (7): 72-91.
Munn, Nancy D. 1992. "The Cultural Anthropology of Time: A Critical Essay." *Annual Review of Anthropology* 21: 93-123.
Panourgiá, Neni. 2009. *Dangerous Citizens: The Greek Left and the Terror of the State*. New York: Fordham University Press.
Papailias, Penelope. 2005. *Genres of Recollection: Archival Poetics and Modern Greece*. New York: Palgrave Macmillan.
Proust, Marcel. (1913) 1990. *À la recherche du temps perdu*. Paris: Puf/Etudes littéraires.
Ricoeur, Paul. 2004. *Le mal: Un défi à la philosophie et à la théologie*. Geneva: Editions Labor et Fides.
Seremetakis, C. Nadia. 1994. "The Memory of the Senses, Part II: Still Acts." In *The Senses Still: Perception and Memory as Material Culture in Modernity*, ed. C Nadia Seremetakis, 23-43. Boulder, CO: Westview Press.
Serres, Michel, with Bruno Latour. 1995. *Conversations on Science, Culture, and Time*. Trans. Roxanne Lapidus. Ann Arbor: University of Michigan Press.
Stewart, Charles. 2003. "Dreams of Treasure: Temporality, Historization and the Unconscious." *Anthropological Theory* 3 (4): 481-500.
Stewart, Charles. 2012. *Dreaming and Historical Consciousness in Island Greece*. Cambridge, MA: Harvard University Press.
Van Boeschoten, Riki, Tasoula Vervenioti, Efi Voutira, Vasilis Dalakvoukis, and Konstantina Bada. 2008. "Introduction." In *Mnimes kai Lithi tou Ellinikou Emfyliou Polemou* [Memories and the oblivion of the Greek Civil War], ed. Riki Van Boeschoten, Tasoula Vervenioti, Efi Voutira, Vasilis Dalakvoukis, and Konstantina Bada, 8-41. Athens: Epikentro.
Yalouri, Elena. 2010. "I dynamiki ton mnimeion: Anazitiseis sto pedio tis mnimis kai tis lithis" [The dynamics of monuments: Explorations in the field of memory and forgetting]. In *Amfisvitoumenoi Horoi stin Poli: Horikes prosegiseis tou politismou* [Contested spaces in the city: Spatial approaches to culture], ed. Yiannis Yanitsiotis and Kostas Yannakopoulos, 349-380. Athens: Alexandreia.

Chapter 8

UNCANNY HISTORY
Temporal Topology in the Post-Ottoman World

Charles Stewart

In this chapter I explore the poetics of history in the post-Ottoman world by examining how people configure the connections between events past, present, and future. Mental maps of time exist everywhere (Zerubavel 2003), and they do not come in discrete cultural packages as Eliade's (1971) typology of archaic (static, circular), Christian (teleological), and modern (linear, random) might lead one to think. They are not singular within any given society, but multiple and often in competition. They may alternate as Leach (1961) observed in his classic essay on the symbolic representation of Western time, where anxiety about linearity is moderated by images of cyclicity on a regular basis; or one type of time may suppress another as in Bloch's (1977) argument that rituals reproduce the ideological status quo of the past, thereby obscuring novel practical ideas arrived at through everyday activity. Even anthropology itself is not immune to conflicts

Notes for this chapter begin on page 142.

over time models as evidenced by Robbins's (2007) claim that a fascination with cultural continuity has prevented the study of discontinuity.

Usually, one particular conception of historical time predominates in a given society as the unmarked or taken-for-granted assumption. For contemporary Western societies, this concept is linearity, which governs everyday rationality, science, and historiography (Burke 2001), and it is conventionally recognized by the term 'historicism' (e.g., Chakrabarty 2000: 7). The historicist timeline emerged visually in the eighteenth century in the diagrams of Priestley, who plotted the lives of great thinkers as lines running horizontally across the page (Rosenberg and Grafton 2010: 18f.). The ascendance of linearity cast alternative ideas into higher relief (as anomalies), an example being the time charts printed in Laurence Sterne's *Tristram Shandy* (published in nine volumes between 1759 and 1767). In the sixth volume, Sterne presented diagrams of the story line in each of his preceding five books (fig. 1). The loops and squiggles indicate digressive narrative leaps going backward and forward in time in what might be the earliest graphic representation of temporal topology.[1] These diagrams arose as a comic foil to linearity, yet they captured the non-linear human engagement with time, which continued in the shadow of linearity.[2] This example opens the theme I intend to pursue below, namely, the affective, political, and existential attributes of topological time and its juxtaposition to linear time (Rosenberg and Grafton 2010: 244).

The concept of 'the uncanny' reflects a further stage in the naturalization of linear temporal thought and also the effects of parallel Enlightenment tenets, such as objectivity (the value of tangible evidence), the scientific method, and the ideal of dispassionate inquiry. According to the *Oxford English Dictionary*, the term 'uncanny' did not become common in its current meaning of "partaking of a supernatural character; mysterious, weird, uncomfortably strange or unfamiliar" until 1850. It could be understood as the residue formed by the expansion of science at the expense of religion, a crepuscular category where eerie and unsettling phenomena gradually accumulated (García Marín 2015; Royle 2003: 22).

The transformation of Enlightenment reason into intuitive ontology has not, however, been unidirectional or complete. In Latour's (1993) formulation, we have never been modern but rather continue to fluctuate between the expectations of post-Enlightenment reason and sensitivity to experiences where these expectations are violated. 'We' are ontologically 'multimodal' (Harris and Robb 2012: 676) with respect to history, as are post-Ottoman societies and every other society that has internally produced, or come into contact with, competing systems of thought. The "Uncanny History" of my title refers to cases of post-Ottoman topological historicizing where the past is not in its expected place. This may evoke an affective response not through intellectual surprise alone, but, as Freud contended, on account of the shocking immediacy of the encounter with powerful ideas and emotions from the past.[3]

The post-Ottoman world has no monopoly on uncanny histories, yet the violent recent past of the region has contributed to making local histories a "perpetual calendar of human anxiety" (Kermode 1967: 11). Displacement,

FIGURE 8.1 Laurence Sterne, *The Life and Opinions of Tristram Shandy, Gentleman*, vol. 6, 1762 original

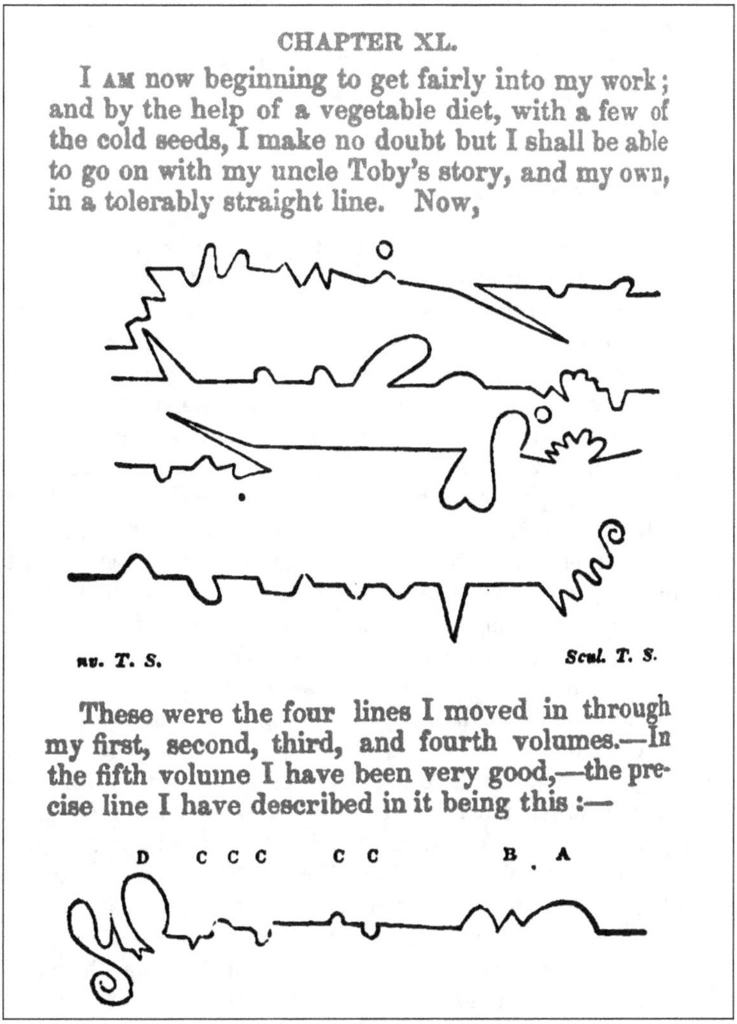

> CHAPTER XL.
>
> I AM now beginning to get fairly into my work; and by the help of a vegetable diet, with a few of the cold seeds, I make no doubt but I shall be able to go on with my uncle Toby's story, and my own, in a tolerably straight line. Now,
>
> *Inv. T. S.*   *Scul. T. S.*
>
> These were the four lines I moved in through my first, second, third, and fourth volumes.—In the fifth volume I have been very good,—the precise line I have described in it being this :—
>
> D   C C C   C C   B A

Note: This image can be found in the public domain at https://archive.org/details/lifeandopinions03stergoog. See also Rosenberg and Grafton (2010: 20).

persecution, or subjugation have left pulsating communal complaints whose slow decay prompted Loizos (1999) to describe them as 'Ottoman half-lives'. On all sides, fantasies of restitution percolate in the imagination, stymied from realization not only by political realities but also by the sheer impossibility of recovering the past. Compensation is not the same as restitution; it unsatisfactorily converts prized objects into other terms. But the originals no longer exist, either in themselves or in their contextual moment. They are past and can be restored only in counterfactual imaginings. Even should the original be recovered in a hypothetical act of restitution, the insult and pain of its having been taken in the first instance can never be undone. This restitutive imaginary suffuses the post-Ottoman world, informing a present that, in various modes of consciousness, probes the loss of the past, readily entertains temporal topology, and produces uncanny histories.

Myth and History

For the most part, topological histories have been studied under the rubric of 'myth' as opposed to history. Topological histories do differ markedly from linear histories, which emphasize objective verification over affective assertion, yet they also share much in common. Interest has accordingly turned to the continuities and commonalities between what were formerly conceived as polar-opposite categories. Mali (2003) examines the catalytic role of myth in the formation of modern historiography, and Samuel and Thompson (1990) consider how historical events can take on moral or gnomic significance, thereby becoming myths that people live by. Anthropological works such as Peter Gow's (2001) *An Amazonian Myth and Its History* show that myths respond to social change and attempt to comprehend it by creating new analogies between the present and the past, including myths from/about the past (ibid.: 279). If representing and understanding the past is the goal of history, myth becomes very hard to distinguish from history in such cases. Myth is then a form of history.

I adduce a contemporary example from the United States to open up the study of the features of myth and topological history and also as a reminder that these are not unusual forms found only in peripheral places such as Amazonia or the post-Ottoman sphere. Jackie Robinson was the first African American major league baseball player. On 15 April 1947, he broke through the color barrier to play for the Brooklyn Dodgers. Like other great players, he was voted into the National Baseball Hall of Fame. But in 1997, 25 years after his death, things took an unprecedented direction when his number was retired for all of baseball. No one on any team can now wear the number 42. Then, starting in 2004, a Jackie Robinson Day (15 April) was instituted during which all players on every team wear the number 42, and in April 2013, the film *42* was released to coincide with Jackie Robinson Day. Jackie Robinson's life story has become a parable about the struggle for equality and the demise of racism—a story that America likes to tell itself, with more and more fanfare.

Many outstanding baseball players played alongside or against Jackie Robinson, and there are even books and films about some of them. But for the most part they are past personages with no particular afterlife except in the minds of those interested in baseball history. They are the past past. The Jackie Robinson story is certainly history in that it has past factuality, but it operates now more as myth, buttressed by an annual ritual. The difference between history and this particular type of myth, which grows out of historical factuality, is that the emphasis has shifted from a focus on the past per se to a set of images and stories that inform understanding of life today, guiding morality in the present and into the future. Standard history operates as present thought about the past, while myth operates in a timeless present. I say 'timeless' because these sorts of mythical formulations have a durability that is not subject to the normal decay of criticism and forgetting. Of course, people know that Jackie Robinson lived in the past, but the truth and meaning of that life now float free from pastness; indeed, it is made present and pointedly so for every player who wears 42 on 15 April. If new historical information should emerge, this will not necessarily affect the myth. The film shows Robinson breaking his bat in the tunnel after being abused by fans. When his wife pointed out that this never happened, the film director responded that it well could have.[4] Such poetic license works in line with a coherence theory of truth that resonates with assumptions and feelings about the case at hand, not by a correspondence theory that requires external evidence as a basis for statements. Standard history can grow with new interpretations of existing facts, and it undoubtedly grows when new factual sources, such as a trove of letters or an archaeological discovery, come to light. Myth is always internally growing as the core message continually receives enhancement while remaining impervious to factual criticism.

The everyday semantic difference between myth and history takes myths to be false in contrast to histories. In the view I am taking here, myths and histories can both be true and can overlap, but myths are true at a level different from the scientific methods of evidence and probability that underwrite historiography. History aims for the truth, whereas myth begins as truth. Yet a history can escalate into a myth, and a myth can contract back to history and be largely forgotten. Documentary evidence may not kill myths, but changing times do. Jackie Robinson will be less necessary when racism in America becomes less problematic. "All meaning is answerable to a lesser meaning, which gives it its highest meaning," as Lévi-Strauss (1966: 255) put it.

In their account of children during the Greek Civil War (fought between 1946 and 1949), Danforth and Van Boeschoten (2012: 37) expose the power of the term *paidomázoma*. This word, which literally means the 'gathering up of children', refers to *devshirme*, the Ottoman practice of selecting Christian children from subjugated peoples throughout the empire and raising them to be loyal Muslim subjects known as Janissaries, who could rise to high public office. During the latter phase of the Greek Civil War, as fighting intensified in northern Greece, both the government army and the resistance forces evacuated children from war zones. The government placed children in care at various institutions in Greece, while the Communist Party evacuated children from its area of control into Eastern Bloc countries, such as Yugoslavia, Romania, and Hungary. Up to the present day, the government and its mainstream supporters refer to the Communist evacuation of children as *paidomázoma* (rendered as 'abduction' or 'kidnapping' in English), while the government's evacuation is labeled 'child protection' (*paidophýlagma*). This usage of *paidomázoma* collapsed the Communist evacuation of the late 1940s with an oppressive Ottoman practice, which had ceased by 1700. People were reaching back for an analogy from a distant past—not an episode that anyone knew first-hand, but one that had been passed on in collective memory, very likely through history textbooks, as a quintessentially evil action perpetrated by the archetypal enemy against a helpless Greek nation. This offers another example of history being amplified into a myth that can guide moral action in the present. It resembles the even older myth of the tribute of Athenian youths to King Minos of Crete to be fed to the Minotaur.

The historical practice of *devshirme* contained negative moral potential above and beyond the theme of kidnapping. It also involved conversion to Islam and service to the enemy, themes that came to guide interpretations of latter-day events: the children taken to the Eastern Bloc during the civil war were being converted to communism and/or becoming de-Hellenized and turned into Slavs. To this day, some of these children, now adults, are not allowed to return to settle in Greece as they are not considered ethnic Greeks. It could be argued that the mythicized image of the *paidomázoma* still animates government policies even though one of the 'deeper meanings' supporting it—the Cold War—has disappeared.

No matter how much evidence Danforth and Van Boeschoten (2012) produced to document the *paidomázoma* as a well-intentioned evacuation program—and they give details of their public engagement—they could not dislodge the entrenched opinion that the evacuation was a nefarious abduction. The *paidomázoma* shows how myths may be immune to historicization, while at the same time provoking more and more detailed historiography, such as Danforth and Van Boeschoten's volume.

The life cycle of the mythicized *paidomázoma* appeared to be winding down after the fall of the military junta in 1974 and the rise of a center-left government, PASOK, which did much to defuse and move beyond the right-left polarization that plagued Greece throughout the twentieth century. This, combined with the end of the Cold War mentioned above, would seem to have eradicated any 'deeper meaning' holding the myth in place. Indeed, Greek children born in the 1980s and 1990s grew up unfamiliar with the term *paidomázoma*. However, with the new polarization in Greek politics brought on by the rise of the extreme right-wing Golden Dawn political party in the twenty-first century, the term has resurfaced and the younger generation are coming to comprehend it. The mythical past may come back, disappear, and then come back again, raising the question of whether powerful historical events such as wars are ever over.

Other mythicizations have difficulty getting off the ground at all. Yannis Hamilakis (2012, 2013) wonders how Zeus Xenios (hospitable Zeus/god of hospitality) could have been adopted as the official code name for the Greek government crackdown on illegal immigrants last year. Was this mistaken mythology? In an even more disturbing development, the Golden Dawn party has likened itself to ancient Spartans. At one of their rallies, a speaker compared their mission to the Spartan initiation rite called *krypteia* (hidden things) in which young Spartans murdered unsuspecting helots (a subjugated serf population) in stealthy attacks. This historical analogy possibly emboldens attacks on innocent migrants such as 26-year-old Shehzad Luqman, a Pakistani who was knifed by motorcyclists. The assailants unscrewed and hid their number plates before speeding away in a modern-day version of *krypteia*. Mythicization can be ill-conceived or offer a template for criminal violence and still potentially recruit followers.

Historians can never capture the past as it actually was; they can only aspire to that. They must be selective. And they can never eradicate presentism from their accounts, although they do recognize the danger of anachronism and work hard to avoid it. History is always history for a certain time and a specific audience. History is organized by temporal sequence; chronology is its deep structure, as Lévi-Strauss (1966: 258ff.) pointed out in *The Savage Mind*. Myth of the sort under consideration here—that is, the sort bordering on historiography—is structured by affect. The affective resonance of particular events brings them into relationship with other events in an allusive, analogical system.

Daniel Knight (2012), for example, has shown how the biting realities of the current economic crisis in Greece have caused images of the World War II famine and the Greek Civil War to surface in contemporary Greek consciousness. These historical images amplify public apprehension that the sufferings of the past will be repeated in the future. They do so through analogical thinking in which, for example, the German occupation of Athens and the ensuing death by famine of some 300,000 people in the early 1940s are paralleled with the current austerity imposed by the European Central Bank. Current German opposition to a lenient bailout is bitterly felt in Greece, and many political cartoons have cast Germany's chancellor, Angela Merkel, as Hitler. German businesses have taken the lead in loaning Greek farmers the money to buy photovoltaic panels to lay over their fields in order to produce electricity rather than food (see Knight, this volume). Farmers in Thessaly, Greece's breadbasket, complained about the disadvantageous long-term contracts and accompanying loss of control over their land, comparing it to the Ottoman period when they were landless serfs working on large estates known as *tsiflíkia* (Turk. *ciftlik*). As one man expressed it: "Greece has become the *ciftlik* of Europe" (see Knight 2012: 64).

The foreboding and fear that Ottoman times, Nazi occupation, and civil war incite by their eruption into the present is consistent with Freud's ([1919] 1955: 219, 240) definition of the uncanny as once familiar matter, encountered by surprise, and with unsettling effect. This historical uncanny is produced by temporal pollution (*sensu* Mary Douglas)—matter not in its correct temporal place. The year 2013 in Greece was not supposed to be another Ottoman period or a 1942 or a 1948. Greek people have long found these painful pasts hard to contemplate and had consigned them to a twilight of partial memory. The malnutrition endured during famine not only left marks on the bodies of people, but also gave rise to numerous deep psychological reactions to food, such as parents inordinately concerned that their children eat. I always interpreted the refrain *pháei, pháei* (eat! eat!) as anxious hospitality, but it possibly stems from a basic worry about food itself. Currently, the affective resonances of the Greek present give this past new vitality. It is very different from the Jackie Robinson feel-good story, which has undergone steady amplification. Robinson is a topologically bent story as well as a myth, but it is not uncanny because people want him and have never really forgotten him. By contrast, the stories told to

Daniel Knight are feel-bad stories, evil mythology, stories people do not like telling themselves about themselves, but which they cannot stop themselves from contemplating—and telling.

Autonomic History

Walter Benjamin (1968) offers a perspective on the sudden and surprising aspect of the uncanny apparition of the past. He conceptualizes the past as "an image which flashes up" (ibid.: 255) to consciousness in moments of danger, while Taussig (1984: 88) describes it as "history [forming] analogies and structural correspondences with the hopes and tribulations of the present." This imagery of the past comes into mind unexpectedly and "set[s] thinking in motion" (Adorno, cited in ibid.: 89).

Whereas in the contemporary Greek case documented by Knight (2012, this volume) the imagery of the past instigates fear, frugality, melancholy, or even suicide, Benjamin and Taussig see the analogical use of the past as empowering and redemptive. The past comes to hand as a weapon to be used in the fight against injustice, as if there existed "a secret agreement between past generations and the present one" (Benjamin 1968: 254). The spontaneous arrival of the past characterizes a particular moment of social potential, which Benjamin terms the *Jetztzeit*, the now time, when the oppressed can slip the noose of traditional domination off their necks. The past dead become a source of power in this case, a moral sword in the present, not a premonition of suffering and doom.

The past does not come into mind only when one intentionally decides to think about it. The past is in and around us all the time, cognitively distributed among persons, objects, and landscapes (Birth 2012: 12). Yael Navaro-Yashin (2012) describes this as a situation where people and external objects are also affectively entangled. Affect circulates between them, prompting a posthumanist analysis that does not posit the person as the locus of control (ibid.: 41, 133). Seeing a bullet hole, for example, or passing a grave or massacre site can provoke feelings. This is necessarily a diachronic relationship between the present moment and traces made in the past. Navaro-Yashin points out that in the case of Cyprus this past goes back to the 1974 Turkish invasions and partition of the island and therefore lies within living memory.

By contrast, in Kóronos, a settlement in the mountains of the Greek island of Naxos, villagers came into contact with a previously unknown past (Stewart 2012). They dreamed of a buried icon calling out to be unearthed. This was an autonomic, surprising intervention of the past in the life of the community. The history produced in these dreams related to a distant past undocumented by any historical record. The dreams informed people that Egyptian Christians fleeing persecution over a thousand years earlier had deposited the icons. The dreamers vacillated over whether these Egyptians were fleeing Roman persecution in the third century or iconoclasts in the eighth century. Basically, objects representing a compression of past moments of persecution were coming to the surface in order to protect the villagers in a current moment of persecution.

In the 1830s, when these dreams first occurred, the Greek state was in the process of nationalizing the local emery mines, thereby impoverishing the people of Kóronos. In these dreams, as again in later dreams during the Great Depression in 1930 (Stewart 2012: 70), saints and material objects spoke to the villagers, and the villagers spoke back to them in their dreams. The historical (Egyptians) and the meta-historical (saints and scenarios of redemption) combined to offer orientation in moments of crisis. The villagers at the time of the Greek War of Independence had not yet been exposed to historicism; they held a Romeic Christian temporal orientation, which assumed the possibility of the past returning to redeem the present. The histories produced were topological but, in a Christian context, not necessarily uncanny in the sense of 'weird', since such returns were hoped for. As Freud ([1919] 1955: 244) observed, the uncanny emerges according to rules of genre: "[O]ur own fairy stories are crammed with instantaneous wish-fulfilments which produce no uncanny effect whatever." After the installation of Otto, the Bavarian prince who became king of Greece in 1832, however, Christian dreams caused friction with the emergent historicist suppositions of the state, which duly accused the Naxos dreamers of fraud. The Enlightenment had come later and more abruptly to Greece, and its oppositional attitude of suppression soon began to freight topological histories with ambivalence, thus tilting them toward the uncanny.

Post-Ottoman Topological History

I earlier referred to Lévi-Strauss's (1966) view that myth is structured by affective resonance and history by chronology, but that was not his ultimate conclusion. He continued on to make the case that history is also constructed by affect and that this comes along with the idea of history as history *for* something (ibid.: 257). National histories collect a series of emotional moments—wars, violations, victories, and celebrations are assembled on a timeline. The major historical periodizations are most often the epochs that follow wars or other disasters: the Pax Romana, the post–World War II period, or post-Katrina New Orleans. Societies orientate themselves in relation to disruptive events and then reorientate after new cataclysmic events. The philosopher of history Frank Ankersmit (2002) contends that this is because traumatic events throw people into a direct relationship with reality, which reveals its radical strangeness. Trauma is thus the beginning of historical consciousness because it "is the sublime and vice versa and at the bottom of both is an experience of reality that shatters to pieces all our certainties, beliefs, categories and expectations" (ibid.: 75–76). I take Ankersmit's use of 'trauma' in the sense of emotionally overwhelming, rather than in the psychiatric PTSD sense. Historical consciousness establishes links, whether analogical or chronological, between these accumulating sublime experiences.

Reactions to the burning of the Madımak Hotel in Sivas, a central Anatolian town, illustrate this last point. A mob set fire to the hotel in 1993, killing 37 visitors who had been invited to attend a cultural festival. An Alevi association—Alevism being a minority branch of Islam in predominantly Sunni Turkey—had organized the festival. Most of those who perished were Alevis, and they are mourned by the Alevi community and viewed as martyrs. Their martyrdom has been commemorated over the years by public demonstrations in Sivas on the anniversary of the events, accompanied by demands for government accountability. These demonstrations have become very large gatherings of Alevis and their supporters from all over Turkey and Europe. The state approaches their day of commemoration with heavy security precautions in the form of barricades that prevent the crowd from coming close to the Madımak Hotel site, which supporters want to see converted into a memorial to the martyrs. Every year, then, police containment strategies cause those attending the demonstration to re-experience sensorially the authority of the state in conditions approaching those of the original incident—a form of political historical re-enactment.

There is a history of contestation and mutual suspicion between Alevis and state authorities in Turkey, and this context disposes the Alevi community to conceive of the "Sivas Massacre" as "one in a long chain of atrocities" (Çaylı 2014: 20), exhibiting an "ethnohistorical ideological conflation" (Mandel 2008: 255). This iterative relationship to martyrdom is evoked and inculcated in the central Alevi ritual known as *cem*, which involves emotive identification with the Twelve Imams, or martyrs, represented by candles that are extinguished at the climax of the ceremony (ibid.: 280; see also Tambar 2011). Past, present, and future atrocities are activated (or anticipated) and rolled into one timeless post-Ottoman topological experience during the *cem*.

The Sivas Massacre has been fitted into this structure of historical consciousness and placed in strong relation to one particular preceding martyrdom: the execution of Pir Sultan Abdal, a sixteenth-century minstrel who was accused of fomenting revolt against Ottoman authority. As Çaylı (2014: 20) explains:

> [Pir Sultan Abdal] is believed to have later been hanged in Sivas by the governor. The 1993 culture festival in Sivas, whose guests were targeted by the arsonist mob, was named after Pir Sultan, while also a state sponsored sculpture reputedly depicting him was erected in a public square in Sivas the night before the festival. On July 2nd, prior to setting the hotel on fire, the arsonist mob defaced this monument and demanded its toppling … [In an attempt to reduce tension] the local municipal and state authorities decided to meet the mob's request and brought them the toppled monument as proof. This is believed to have further encouraged the perpetrators.

The Sivas martyrs and the martyrdom of the sixteenth-century Pir Sultan are thus intimately linked, and the Pir forms part of a larger martyrology extending back to the martyrdom of Husayn at Karbala in AD 680. It is as if the martyrdom of Husayn in the past were like a huge star, with other events of lesser magnitude within its gravitational field. The Sivas Massacre will perhaps grow in size inside collective historical consciousness as time goes by and exert its own pull on future events. Experientially, all of these events can be felt as compacted into one present swirl: a "time-knot," to use Chakrabarty's (2000:

112) Bengali expression, a vortex, or even a black hole, to remain consistent with the galactic imagery. Each phase is co-present, embedded into the others, giving a multi-temporal emotional resonance to the present moment.

Uncanny History

As Karl Mannheim ([1924] 1952: 85–86) put it: "Historicism ... is a *Weltanschauung* [that] not only dominate[s] our inner reactions and our external responses, but also determine[s] our forms of thought. Thus, at the present stage, science and scientific methodology, logic, epistemology, and ontology are all moulded by the historicist approach." The central idea of historicism is that time is divided into past, present, and future. The past is over with and knowable, and the future is yet to come and unknowable, although predictable to a certain degree. As time goes by, society builds on its past, and this past becomes recognizably past. The uncanny arises as a scandal to this certitude. Freud's essay on the uncanny, written around the same time as Mannheim's diagnosis of pervasive historicism, rests on the bedrock of this historicism. The uncanny surprises and shocks because it violates the intuitive temporal ontology of modernity. The uncanny arises as a stark identifiable figure against the background of historicism.

Mannheim was not, however, entirely accurate. Historicism had become hierarchically dominant in his time, but other forms of relating to the past continued to exist in its shadow. Spiritism, for example, flourished in the 1920s as a bereaved population attempted to communicate with those killed during World War I. In any case, human beings constantly produce other relationships to time. Temporal linearity may be an objective system of measurement, but it does not necessarily capture the quality of lived temporality. Phenomenologists beginning with Husserl have shown that temporal experience can be fused in a past-present-future where knowledge from the past collides with projections of the future in present perception and action (Gell 1992: 221). Heidegger expanded this in his particular existential ontology where Being is orientated to the future, the past, and then the present, often in that order, although in principle human beings experience temporality in any order. At different times people live profoundly toward the future, whether hopefully or anxiously, and at other times are burdened by the past or not able to supersede it.

The view suggested by phenomenology is that experiencing the past or the future in the present is a perennial human trait, not an optional or easily suppressible feature. Linearity has not obliterated other temporalities, but rather co-exists with them unstably in the multi-modal ontology referred to earlier. Paul Ricoeur (2004: 393) takes up this point when reflecting on the challenge that school history poses for collective memory.[5] Personal, familial, and communal histories transmitted by known people in relation to familiar places and objects make sense. These local histories may, as exemplified by the cases considered above, resort to topological time structures and affective connections in order to impart their messages. School history textbooks come as 'externalities'—not only written but also couched in hard-to-assimilate terms of chronology and names. Scholastic historiography can present the community with novel facts, but my point is that it challenges them with an odd way of knowing.[6]

For Ricoeur (2004: 394), learning from schoolbooks involves gradual familiarization with "the uncanniness of the historical past." At first, historicism is itself uncanny in the sense of disturbing or disquieting, even shocking, when introduced into non-historicist settings. In time, however, people bring historicist structures into relation with local, perhaps more topological and affectively driven forms of historicizing, such as the dream apparitions of saints on Naxos or the emotive historical consciousness of martyrdom among Alevis in Turkey. Ultimately, uncanny histories are not just the product of a historicist measuring stick. It is the tension and instability between local non-historicism and historicism (often purveyed by the state or other authorities) that continually produce experiences of uncanny histories (Bryant 2014: 682). Uncanny histories expose the incomplete synthesis between two different genres of history. At the same time, unresolved grievances or disputes over facts keep uncanny histories vital as the necessary mode of grounding alternative pasts in the certitude of experience.

Acknowledgments

I wish to thank Eray Çaylı and Ruth Mandel for commenting on an earlier draft of this chapter.

Charles Stewart is a Professor of Anthropology at University College London. He has conducted field research in Greece (Naxos, Athens, Thessaloniki) on the topics of religion, dreaming, and local forms of historical practice. He is the co-editor, with Eric Hirsch, of a special issue of *History and Anthropology* titled "Ethnographies of Historicity" (2005), and he is the author of *Dreaming and Historical Consciousness in Island Greece* (2012).

Notes

1. As a branch of geometry, topology allows consideration of shapes that have been bent and not merely stretched, as in standard geometry. A plate and a bowl made out of wet clay can be shaped back and forth into one another without the need to break any lines, and they are therefore topological variations of one another.
2. As Sterne (1760: 163) put it: "Digressions, incontestably, are the sunshine;—they are the life, the soul of reading!—take them out of this book, for instance,—you

might as well take the book along with them;—one cold eternal winter would reign in every page of it."
3. Freud ([1919] 1955: 223; italics in original) quoted Schelling to make this central point in his essay: *"Unheimlich is the name for everything that ought to have remained ... secret and hidden but has come to light."*
4. One of the actors in the film commented: "At some point he had to break, and the fact that Rachel Robinson didn't fight us to take [the scene] out [of the film], to me proves that it is true." See http://www.historyvshollywood.com/reelfaces/42-movie-jackie-robinson.php (accessed 5 January 2014).
5. Bryant's (2014) study of property in occupied territory after the partition of Cyprus applies Ricoeur's ideas and comes to conclusions about the 'unhomeliness' of history that inform my discussion.
6. This parallels the reaction to the imposition of dogmatic theology on local religion. In reaction to reformist imams pronouncing on proper practice, a local Bosniak Muslim objected to "the dead tradition contained in books" (Henig 2012: 761).

References

Ankersmit, Frank R. 2002. "Trauma and Suffering: A Forgotten Source of Western Historical Consciousness." In Rüsen 2002, 72–84.
Benjamin, Walter. 1968. "Theses on the Philosophy of History." In *Illuminations*. Ed. Hannah Arendt; trans. Harry Zohn, 253–264. New York: Schocken.
Birth, Kevin K. 2012. *Objects of Time: How Things Shape Temporality*. New York: Palgrave Macmillan.
Bloch, Maurice. 1977. "The Past and the Present in the Present." *Man* 12 (2): 278–291.
Bryant, Rebecca. 2014. "History's Remainders: On Time and Objects after Conflict in Cyprus." *American Ethnologist* 41 (4): 681–697.
Burke, Peter. 2001. "Western Historical Thinking in a Global Perspective—10 Theses." In Rüsen 2002, 15–30.
Çaylı, Eray. 2014. "Architectural Memorialization at Turkey's 'Witness Sites': The Case of the Madimak Hotel." In *Contemporary Turkey at a Glance: Interdisciplinary Perspectives on Local and Translocal Dynamics*, ed. Kristina Kamp, Ayhan Kaya, E. Faut Keyman, and Özge Onursal Beşgül, 13–24. Berlin: Springer.
Chakrabarty, Dipesh. 2000. *Provincializing Europe: Postcolonial Thought and Historical Difference*. Princeton, NJ: Princeton University Press.
Danforth, Loring, and Riki Van Boeschoten. 2012. *Children of the Greek Civil War: Refugees and the Politics of Memory*. Chicago: University of Chicago Press.
Eliade, Mircea. 1971. *The Myth of the Eternal Return: Or, Cosmos and History*. Trans. Willard R. Trask. Princeton, NJ: Princeton University Press.
Freud, Sigmund. [1919] 1955. "The Uncanny." In *The Standard Edition of the Complete Psychological Works of Sigmund Freud, Volume XVII (1917–1919): An Infantile Neurosis and Other Works*. Trans. James Strachey, 217–256. London: Hogarth.
García Marín, Álvaro. 2015. "The Origin Is Already Haunted: Greece as the Uncanny of Modernity." *Modern Greek Studies Online* 1: A1–A22. http://www.moderngreek.org.uk/journal/content/garcia2015.
Gell, Alfred. 1992. *The Anthropology of Time: Cultural Constructions of Temporal Maps and Images*. Oxford: Berg.
Gow, Peter. 2001. *An Amazonian Myth and Its History*. Oxford: Oxford University Press.

Hamilakis, Yannis. 2012. "Hospitable Zeus." LRB blog, 8 August. http://www.lrb.co.uk/blog/2012/08/08/yannis-hamilakis/hospitable-zeus (accessed 20 June 2015).

Hamilakis, Yannis. 2013. "Spartan Myths." LRB blog, 14 February. https://www.lrb.co.uk/blog/?s=Spartan+Myths (accessed 20 June 2015).

Harris, Oliver J. T., and John Robb. 2012. "Multiple Ontologies and the Problem of the Body in History." *American Anthropologist* 114 (4): 668–679.

Henig, David. 2012. "'This Is Our Little Hajj': Muslim Holy Sites and Reappropriation of the Sacred Landscape in Contemporary Bosnia." *American Ethnologist* 39 (4): 751–765.

Kermode, Frank. 1967. *The Sense of an Ending: Studies in the Theory of Fiction.* Oxford: Oxford University Press.

Knight, Daniel M. 2012. "Turn of the Screw: Narratives of History and Economy in the Greek Crisis." *Journal of Mediterranean Studies* 21 (1): 53–76.

Latour, Bruno. 1993. *We Have Never Been Modern.* Trans. Catherine Porter. Cambridge, MA: Harvard University Press.

Leach, Edmund. 1961. "Two Essays Concerning the Symbolic Representation of Time." In *Rethinking Anthropology,* 124–136. London: Athlone.

Lévi-Strauss, Claude. 1966. *The Savage Mind.* Chicago: University of Chicago Press.

Loizos, Peter. 1999. "Ottoman Half-Lives: Long-Term Perspectives on Particular Forced Migrations." *Journal of Refugee Studies* 12 (3): 237–263.

Mali, Joseph. 2003. *Mythistory: The Making of a Modern Historiography.* Chicago: University of Chicago Press.

Mandel, Ruth. 2008. *Cosmopolitan Anxieties: Turkish Challenges to Citizenship and Belonging in Germany.* Durham, NC: Duke University Press.

Mannheim, Karl. [1924] 1952. "Historicism." *Essays on the Sociology of Knowledge: Collected Works Volume 5.* Ed. Paul Kecskemeti, 84–133. London: Routledge.

Navaro-Yashin, Yael. 2012. *The Make-Believe Space: Affective Geography in a Postwar Polity.* Durham, NC: Duke University Press.

Ricoeur, Paul. 2004. *Memory, History, Forgetting.* Trans. Kathleen Blamey and David Pellauer. Chicago: University of Chicago Press.

Robbins, Joel. 2007. "Continuity Thinking and the Problem of Christian Culture: Belief, Time, and the Anthropology of Christianity." *Current Anthropology* 48 (1): 5–38.

Rosenberg, Daniel, and Anthony Grafton. 2010. *Cartographies of Time: A History of the Timeline.* New York: Princeton Architectural Press.

Royle, Nicholas. 2003. *The Uncanny.* Manchester: Manchester University Press.

Rüsen, Jörn, ed. 2002. *Western Historical Thinking: An Intercultural Debate.* New York: Berghahn Books.

Samuel, Raphael, and Paul R. Thompson, eds. 1990. *The Myths We Live By.* London: Routledge.

Sterne, Laurence. 1760. *The Life and Opinions of Tristram Shandy, Gentleman.* Vol. 2. London: Dodsley. https://archive.org/details/lifeandopinions03stergoog (accessed 20 June 2015).

Stewart, Charles. 2012. *Dreaming and Historical Consciousness in Island Greece.* Cambridge, MA: Harvard University Press.

Tambar, Kabir. 2011. "Iterations of Lament: Anachronism and Affect in a Shi'i Islamic Revival in Turkey." *American Ethnologist* 38 (3): 484–500.

Taussig, Michael. 1984. "History as Sorcery." *Representations* 7: 87–109.

Zerubavel, Eviatar. 2003. *Time Maps: Collective Memory and the Social Shape of the Past.* Chicago: University of Chicago Press.

INDEX

abandoned settlement, 72f
abduction (*paidomázoma*), 135, 136
adolescents (*pallikaria*), 35
affective history, 112
agency of time, 124–125. *See also* time
Agios Rafaïl (monastery), 104–115
Agos, 57, 59, 62, 66. *See also* Dink, Hrant
Ahıska, Meltem, 61
Albania, 71, 76; bus hijacking, 88, 89, 90–92; Communist Albanian state, 118; media events, 89 (*see also* media events)
Albanian folk singer (*rapsod*), 96–99
Albanian memorial song, 88–102
Alia, Gjergj Elez, 94
Alidjun's prayers (*Aliđunske dove*), 52
al-Qaeda, 93
Althusser, Louis, 5
Amazonian Myth and Its History, An (Gow), 134
Amin, Idi, 15
Anderson, Benedict, 11
Ankersmit, Frank, 139
archives, 112–114
Argenti, Nicolas, 45
Armenian community (in Turkey), 57–69
arms, trafficking, 83
Article 301 (Turkish Penal Code), 61
Arvanitic language, 117
Asia Minor, 12, 17, 74, 106–107, 108, 109
Athanasiou, Athena, 64
Athens, Greece, 29
Athens International Airport, 120

Australia, 12
autonomic history, 138–139
Axis occupations, 29. *See also* World War II

Babalis, Dimitra, 79
Badiou, Alain, 62
Bahloul, Joëlle, 15
Balkan Topologies (workshop), 3
Balkan Wars of 1912 and 1913, 29
Benjamin, Walter, 138
Bergson, Henri, 16, 17, 119
berićet (divine blessing), 44
Berlant, Lauren, 58, 61, 62
besa (honor), 92
bleakness (*tristezza*), 80
blerje poetik (poetic value), 98, 100
blerje politik (political value), 98, 100
blessings, 44
borders, 71. *See also* Greece
Bosnia-Herzegovina, 43–55; embedding martyrs in sacred landscapes, 51–53; martyrs, 48–51; memories of war, 47–48; Muslims, 44; prayers as history, 44–45; Srebrenica massacre (1995), 48, 49; war as critical events, 46–47
Boym, Svetlana, 4
Braudel, Fernand, 7, 38
broadcasting, 89. *See also* media events
Brown, Keith, 37
Bryant, Rebecca, 32
Buddhism, 15
building under reconstruction, 81f

Note: Page references with an *f* indicate figures.

Bus 174 (*Ônibus 174*), 93
bus hijacking, 88, 89, 90–92, 92–94
"Bus Murderer a National Hero for the Albanians, The" (Tsigaridas [2004]), 90
bus piracy (*leoforeiopeirateia*), 93
Byzantine Empire, 105, 113

carnal mourning, 63, 65
Caruth, Cathy, 63
Casey, Edward, 78
castes, 1
causality, 51
Chakrabarty, Dipesh, 140–141
Charitonidis, Seraphim, 113
China, 76
Christianity, 1, 11, 111, 138
chronology, 15, 16, 51
civil wars: Greece, 31; Greek Civil War (1946-1949), 36, 71, 73–74; post-civil war Greece, 117–128; post-civil war studies, 72; remains of in the present, 77–80. *See also* specific civil wars
Claverie, Elisabeth, 113
co-existence, 13–18
Cold War, 58, 74, 77
collaboration, 35
collective identities, 48
collective memory, 31–32, 39, 104, 105, 136
common inhabiting, 80–83
Communist Albanian state, 118
Communist Party, 118
confronting the past (*geçmişle yüzleşmek*), 60, 68
Couroucli, Maria, 2
Cowan, Jane, 37
crisis experience in central Greece, 28–40; energizing objects, 33–36; tangible histories, 31–33; topographies of time, 36–38; topologies of, 30–31
critical events, 50; exclusion of Messogites, 117; Greece, 118–120; wars as, 46–47
Culi, Maria, 79
cultures: temporality of, 2–9, 120; of trauma, 9
Cyprus, 72

Danforth, Loring, 136
Das, Veena, 46, 50

de Certeau, Michel, 82
de Coulanges, Fustel, 5
Deleuze, Gilles, 16, 17, 119
democracy: Greece, 127; Turkey, 67
Democratic Army of Greece (DSE), 73
Democratic Republic of Macedonia, 71
Derrida, Jacques, 119
devshirme (gathering up of children), 135, 136
Dink, Hrant, 57–69; affect of after murder, 65–67; change of Nor Zartonk after death of, 63–65; grave of, 66, 66*f*; mourning, 62–63; murder of, 58, 58*f*, 64, 68; nationalism in Turkey, 61–62; temporality, 61, 62; as victim, 67
disasters, 139
divine blessing (*berićet*), 44
Douglas, Mary, 10, 137
dovište (outdoor prayers), 43, 52
drugs, 83
durée, theory of, 17
duše (souls), 45
dženaza (Muslim funeral), 49

Early Christianity, 105
earthquakes, Greece, 29
economic crisis in 2009, 31
Egyptian Christians, 138
eksynchronismos (modernization), 94
energy, 33, 34
Enlightenment, 4, 5, 14, 139
ethnicity, 2, 74
European Central Bank, 33, 137
European Commission, 33
Evangelatos, Nikos, 93
event-spaces, 92
event-transitivity, 92
evil, the (*to kako*), 118
exclusion of Messogites, 117

Feuchtwang, Stephan, 76
"Flamur Pisli Rron Te Känga" (Flamur Pisli Lives in Song), 95
food sustainability, 34
fossils, 28, 29, 30, 36
Franks, the (Europeans), 108
Freud, Sigmund, 132, 139

ganimet, 12
gathering up of children (*devshirme*), 135, 136

gecmişle yüzleşmek (confronting the past), 60, 68
Gell, Alfred, 16
gender dynamics, 92
genocide, 60, 66
gerçek anlatıcı (truth-teller), 59
Germany, 118. *See also* Nazis
Giannaris, Constantine, 91
Giordano, Christian, 111
Gjinaj, Ded, 96, 97*f*, 98, 99, 100
glaciers, 31
God's will, tools of, 109
Gökçen, Sabiha, 61
Gow, Peter, 134
graves, exhumation, 106
Great Depression, 17, 139
Great Famine of 1941-1943, 29, 37
Great Idea, 11
Greco-Turkish population exchange (1923), 75
Greco-Turkish War of 1919-1922, 2, 11, 13, 73
Greece, 12; Athens, 29; attachments to place, 74-77; bus hijacking, 88, 89, 90-92; civil wars, 31; Cold War, 74; common inhabiting, 80-83; crisis experience in central, 28-40; critical events, 118-120; democracy, 127; energizing objects, 33-36; Greek Civil War (*see* Greek Civil War [1946-1949]); life on the border, 71-84; meanings of monuments, 123-124; media events, 88 (*see also* media events); monuments, 120-121; multitemporalities, 124-126; post-civil war, 117-128; raising of monuments, 121-122; refugees, 73; remains of civil wars in the present, 77-80; tangible histories, 31-33; topographies of time, 36-38; topologies of crisis experience, 30-31
Greek Civil War (1946-1949), 36, 71, 73-74, 120, 125, 126, 127, 135
Greek Communist Party (KKE), 82
Greek War of Independence (1821-1829), 7
Green, Sarah, 3

Halbwachs, Maurice, 7, 8
hate, 64
Hellenism, 110

hermitages, 81
heroic song (*këngë kreshnike*), 94
Herzfeld, Michael, 3, 5, 12, 14, 47
hidden things (*krypteia*), 136, 137
hijacking, 88, 89. *See also* bus hijacking
Hirsch, Eric, 13
Hirschon, Renée, 10
historical consciousness, 112
historicism, 132, 141
historicizations, 112
history: autonomic, 138-139; Bosnia-Herzegovina, 43-55; post-Ottoman topological, 139-141; prayers as, 44-45; recollection of historical events, 30; relationship with landscape, 36; tangible histories (Greece), 31-33; temporalities of media events, 88-102; topological historicizing, 134-138
holy bridge (*ieran gefyran*), 111
holy site visitations (*zijaret*), 48
Holy Synod, 106
homeomorphism of events, 16
honor (*besa*), 92
Horden, Peregrine, 38
Hostage (*Omiros*), 91
Houston, Christopher, 8
Hrant Dink Foundation, 57
human temporalities, 119
human trafficking, 83
Humphrey, Caroline, 62
hüzün, 7, 8

identity, 10, 11, 48
ieran gefyran (holy bridge), 111
immediation, 94-96
indigenous historicization, 32
intermarriage, 80
International Monetary Fund, 33
Islam, 53. *See also* Muslims
Islamic Community of Bosnia-Herzegovina, 53
Istanbul, Turkey, 59

Judaism, 1, 14

kairos (time passing, weather, and era or epoch), 125-126
to kako (the evil), 118
Kapferer, Bruce, 12
Karakasidou, Anastasia, 12

Kemal, Mustafa, 106
Kemalism, 8
këngë kreshnike (heroic song), 94
"Kengë per Flamur Pislin" (Song for Flamur Pisli), 90
kidnapping (*paidomázoma*), 135, 136
Kilani, Mondher, 111
Kiousis, Thanasis, 121, 122, 125
klefts (thieves), 94, 101
Knight, Daniel, 12, 137, 138
Kontoglou, Photios, 113
Konuk, Kader, 61
Kopytoff, Igor, 6
Kosovo Albanian Muslims, 77
Koulouris, Yiorgos, 89
krypteia (hidden things), 136, 137
ksilosompes (stoves), 33
Kwon, Heonik, 76, 78

landlords of great estates (*tsiflikades*), 33, 35, 39
landscape, 36. *See also* topographies
landscapes, embedding martyrs in sacred, 51–53
Last, Murray, 76
Latour, Bruno, 17
Lefebvre, Henri, 72
leoforeiopeirateia (bus piracy), 93
Lesbos, Greece, 104–115; archives, traces and, 112–114; Asia Minor refugees in, 106–107, 108, 109; conflation of historical periods, 107–109; discovery of Agios Rafaïl (monastery), 105–106; exemplariness in the post-Ottoman world, 110–111; immanence of the past, 111–112; liberation of, 109; Ottoman occupation of, 107; search for local saints and commemorations, 109–110
Lévi-Strauss, Claude, 5, 8, 135, 137, 139
Lévy, Pierre, 89
Liakos, Antonis, 3
linearity, 51
literature, 11; memory, 45; on Southern Europe, 32
Loizos, Peter, 10, 133

Madımak Hotel (Sivas, Greece), 139, 140
Mannheim, Karl, 141
marriage, 80

martyrs, 43, 45, 46, 90, 111, 140; Bosnia-Herzegovina, 48–51; embedding in sacred landscapes, 51–53; neo-martyrs of Thermi, 110
Marx, Karl, 5
Massumi, Brian, 92
Mauss, Marcel, 44
Mazower, Mark, 3
Mazzarella, William, 95
media events: Albanian folk singer (*rapsod*), 96–99; bus hijacking, 88, 89, 90–92; manipulation of perceptions, 92–94; mediation, 94–96; migrant soundscapes/mobile listening, 100; temporality of, 88–102
mediation, 94–96
Meister, Robert, 63
memory, 11, 120; collective, 31–32, 39, 104, 105, 136; of identity, 10; Lesbos, Greece, 104–115; literature, 45; memories of war, 47–48; studies, 9, 60
Messogites, 117, 118, 125
Metaxas, Ioannis, 71
militarization of migration, 101
Millas, Iraklis, 11
millets, 1, 2, 6
Minos (King), 136
Mintz, Sidney, 6
mobile listening, 100
Möbius strip, 89
modernity, 32, 33
modernization (*eksynchronismos*), 94
monasteries (Agios Rafaïl), 104–115
monochromatic societies, 2
monocultural societies, 2
Montesquieu, Charles-Louis de Secondat, 4
monumentalization, 51
Monument Dedicated to Liberty, 127
monuments, 81, 117–128; Greece, 120–121; meanings of, 123–124; multi-temporalities, 124–126; raising of, 121–122; time, 122–123
mourning, carnal, 63, 65
multi-temporalities, 124–126
Munn, Nancy D., 119, 124, 127
Museum of Shame, 8
Muslim funeral (*dženaza*), 49
Muslims, 1, 5, 10, 43, 135; Albanian farmers, 77; Bosnia-Herzegovina,

44–45, 46, 47, 48, 49; Kosovo Albanian, 77; Rohingya, 15
myths, topological historicizing, 134–138

nationalism, 61–62, 102, 119
National Liberation Front (EAM), 121
nation-states, 1, 117–128; cultures of temporality, 2–9; Greece, 117–128; Ottoman half-lives, 9–13; post-Ottoman, 2, 3, 13–18; Turkey, 59
NATO, 77
Navaro-Yashin, Yael, 51
Naxos, Greece, 44, 112, 138, 139
Nazis, 118, 120, 121
neo-colonialism, 33
neo-martyrs of Thermi, 110
Neyzi, Leyla, 12
Nichanian, Marc, 67
non-governmental organizations (NGOs), 79, 82
Nora, Pierre, 14
Nor Zartonk, 57, 63

objective (B-series) time, 16
oikoumenê, 6, 12
Omiros (Hostage), 91
Ônibus 174 (Bus 174), 93
open fires (*tzakia*), 33, 34, 39
Orthodox Church, 104
Ottoman Empire, 1, 6, 7, 105, 106; fall of, 3; half-lives, 9–13; occupation of Lesbos, Greece, 107; population movements, 73; post-Ottoman, 2; Revolution against, 123
outdoor prayers (*dovište*), 43, 52
out-marriage, 80

Padilha, José, 93
paidomázoma (abduction or kidnapping), 135, 136
pallikaria (adolescents), 35
Pamuk, Orhan, 7
Panhellenic Socialist Movement (PASOK), 73
Paris Bar Association, 64
PASOK, 118
Persian Letters ([1721] 1973 [Montesquieu]), 4
Peru, 72
Pheraios, Righas (Velestinlis), 2

photovoltaics, 33, 34, 39
pilgrims (*putnici*), 49
Pindos Mountains (Greece), 36, 37
Pisli, Flamur, 88
place, attributes of, 78
pluralism, 79
poems, 98f, 99f
poetic value (*blerje poetik*), 98, 100
political value (*blerje politik*), 98, 100
Pontians, 74
populations, 2; Greco-Turkish population exchange (1923), 75; Ottoman Empire, 73
post-civil war Greece, 117–128; critical events, 118–120; meanings of monuments, 123–124; multi-temporalities, 124–126; raising of monuments, 121–122
post-Ottoman, 2, 4, 5, 6, 8, 9, 10, 13–18; temporal topology in, 131–142; topological history, 139–141
post-war Bosnia-Herzegovina, 43–55; embedding martyrs in sacred landscapes, 51–53; martyrs, 48–51; memories of war, 47–48; prayers as history, 44–45; war as critical events, 46–47
Povinelli, Elizabeth, 59, 60, 63, 65
Prayer for Martyrs (Šehidska dova), 52, 53
Prayer for Martyrs in Solun (Šehidska dova u Solunu), 51
prayers, Bosnia-Herzegovina, 43–55
Premilovac, Aida, 77
prosfighes (refugees), 3
public secrecy, 60

racism, 64
rain, prayers for, 52
Ralli, Vasiliki, 106
rape, 94
rapsod (Albanian folk singer), 96–99
Red tourism, 82
refugees (*prosfighes*), 3
religion, 1, 2; divisions, 2; persecution, 6. *See also* specific religions
Renan, Ernest, 13
Republic of Turkey, 59. *See also* Turkey
Resistance, 123
retsina wine, 117

Revolution (against the Ottoman Empire), 123
Ricoeur, Paul, 141, 142
Robbins, Joel, 132
Robinson, Jackie, 134, 135, 137
Rohingya Muslims, 15
Rombou-Levidi, Marcia, 83
Rousseau, Jean-Jacques, 5
ruined house, 78f

Sahlins, Marshall, 5
sainthood: Lesbos, Greece, 104–115; temporality of, 104–115
Saint Rafaïl, 105, 106, 107, 109
saints of Thermi, 109
Savage Mind, The (Lévi-Strauss), 137
Scott, David, 72
Šehidska dova (Prayer for Martyrs), 52, 53
Šehidska dova u Solunu (Prayer for Martyrs in Solun), 51
September 11, 2001, 93
Seremetakis, Nadia, 11, 38
Serres, Michel, 17, 30, 31, 36, 119
Simitis, Kostas, 101
Sivas, Greece, 139, 140
Sivas Massacre (1993), 139, 140
social time, 47
Song for Flamur Pisli ("Kengë per Flamur Pislin"), 90, 96, 97f
souls (*duše*), 45
space/place (*topos*), 15, 89
Spirit of the Laws, The ([1748] 1989 [Montesquieu]), 4
Srebrenica massacre (1995), 48, 49
Srebrenica-Potočari Memorial and Cemetery, 51
Sri Lanka, 12
Sterne, Laurence, 132, 133f
Stewart, Charles, 13, 44, 51, 107, 108, 112
Stewart, Kathleen, 51
stoves (*ksilosompes*), 33
subjective (A-series) time, 16
sultana, 75
survival (Dink, Hrant), 57–69
sustainability, food, 34
Sutton, David, 11
symbolism, 53

Taiwan, 76
Tataryan, Nora, 62
Taussig, Michael, 60, 138
Telloglou, Tasos, 92, 101
temporality: of culture, 120; cultures of, 2–9; Dink, Hrant, 61, 62; Greece, 118–120; human, 119; Lesbos, Greece, 104–115; of media events, 88–102; monuments, 117–128; multi-temporalities, 124–126; of sainthood, 104–115; topology in post-Ottoman world, 131–142
temporal linearity, 112
terrorist (*tromokratis*), 93
theory of *durée*, 17
Thermi, saints of, 109
thieves (*klefts*), 94, 101
time: Greece, 118–120; *kairos* (time passing, weather, and era or epoch), 125–126; monuments, 122–123; multi-temporalities, 124–126; reconfiguration of, 89; recovering the past, 133; relationship with landscape, 36; representation of, 131; social, 47; topographies of, 36–38. *See also* history
Todorova, Maria, 3
topographies (of time), 36–38
topological historicizing, 107, 134–138
topologies: of crisis experience (Greece), 30–31; temporal in post-Ottoman world, 131–142
topos (space/place), 15, 89
tragedy of 1944, 118, 120, 121
trauma, cultures of, 9
tristesse, 8
tristezza (bleakness), 80
Tristram Shandy (Sterne), 132, 133f
tromokratis (terrorist), 93
truth-teller (*gerçek anlatıcı*), 59
tsiflikades (landlords of great estates), 33, 35, 39
Turkey: Armenian community in, 58; democracy, 67; Dink, Hrant, 57–69; nationalism in, 61–62; nation-states, 59
Turkish Penal Code, 61
Turkish War of Independence (1919–1922), 106
tzakia (open fires), 33, 34, 39

ultra-modernity, 33
United Panhellenic Organization of Youth (EPON), 121, 123
Van Boeschoten, Riki, 136
vasilochoria (communities friendly to monarchy), 118
Vietnam, 76
violence, expressions of, 107–109
virtualization, events, 89, 92, 98
"Visual March to Prespa" art projects, 82
Vlachs, 74, 77, 79
Wagner, Sarah, 48, 49
Warnier, Jean-Pierre, 6
war on terrorism, 93
wars as critical events, 46–47
World War I, 73, 141
World War II, 14, 29, 30, 58, 73, 75
Yugoslavia, 71, 72
zijaret (holy site visitations), 48